# THE
# STORY OF
# SPAIN

MARK WILLIAMS

## ABOUT THE AUTHOR

Mark Williams is a freelance writer living near San Francisco, California. He received an M.A. in History from the University of California (Santa Barbara) in 1975 and did further studies at the University of Madrid. He was formerly Senior Contributor for *Lookout* magazine (1978-82) and Chief Editor of *Chevron USA/Odyssey* magazine (1983-87). Williams has written for *The International Herald Tribune, Washington Post, Los Angeles Times, El Pais* and many other newspapers and magazines. His book *Northern California: Off The Beaten Path* was published in 1989.

*To Eleonore*

## ACKNOWLEDGEMENTS

For their enlightened and enlightening guidance and influence during my graduate studies in history at the University of California (Santa Barbara), I would like to thank Professors Harold Kirker, Joachim Remak, and the late Philip Powell. For his assistance during my studies at the University of Madrid and later suggestions for this book, I thank Professor Richard Herr of the University of California (Berkeley). Fact-checking of the manuscript was done by two doctoral candidates in Spanish History at the University of California (Berkeley): Paloma Fernandez and Francisco Garcia Serrano, both Spaniards. Technical assistance was provided by Luis Carlos Lopez and Josee Lafortune; spiritual assistance by my wife, Eleonore Austerer, and dog, Chico. Finally, I must thank the one person without whom this book would never have been written: Ken Welsh. He gave me a piece of his mind and much more.

First Published by Lookout Publications, December 1990

Published by Mirador Publications, May 1992

1996 Edition published by Ediciones Santana, S.L.,
Apartado 422, 29640 Fuengirola (Málaga) Spain.

Printed by Gráficas San Pancracio, S.L., Pol. Ind. San Luis, C/. Orotava, 17 - Málaga
ISBN: 84-921229-2-7          D.L.: MA-183/1993

# CONTENTS

# THE SPANISH STAGE

The Iberian Peninsula is a bridge between two continents and two seas. The southern coast is only a few kilometres from North Africa. Throughout history, the threat of invasion was always present, and control of at least one side of the Mediterranean gateway became crucial.

With roughly 492,000 square kilometres, Spain occupies about 85% of the peninsula, the third largest European nation after Russia and France. (Its islands comprise another 15,000 sq. kms.) Its area is roughly twice that of the British Isles or the same size as California plus about one-third of Nevada.

The most prominent of Spain's many mountain ranges are the Pyrenees, which stretch in a largely unbroken natural barrier from the Mediterranean to the Bay of Biscay, one reason that Spain has seldom been invaded from the north (the average height is more than 1,500 metres).

Spain has been likened to a castle, its courtyard occupied by a lofty plateau called the *meseta* and its walls formed by mountain ranges, in turn surrounded by narrow strips of fertile coastal land. The Spanish plain is bounded on the northwest by the Cantabrian range, a mountain barrier that partially explains the existence of Galicia, Asturias, and the Basque region as geographical and ethnic entities. On the *meseta*'s north and east lie the Iberian mountains, which help define the regions of Navarra, Aragon, Catalonia (Cataluña), and Valencia. On the south, the Sierra Morena range separates the central tablelands from Andalucia.

The central plain itself consists of two plateaux separated by more mountains. Old Castilla and the Duero River lie to the north; the much larger region of La Mancha, together with Extremadura, spread southward.

Almost half Spain's soil is unproductive (only about 10% could be called rich) and mineral resources are nearly exhausted. Few rivers are navigable. Extremes in climate add to the harsh picture.

In terms of rainfall, the country can be split into "wet Spain" (taking in most of the far north from Catalonia to rainy Galicia, more like Ireland than the traditional picture of sunny Iberia) and "dry Spain," about three-fourths of the country which receives less than 50 centimetres of rain per year. Rainfall in La Mancha and Andalucia is extremely erratic, alternating between drought and torrential downpours.

Rugged terrain and nasty weather are often stressed to explain Spain's intense regionalism, poverty, and national traits. But Spain also has rich pasturelands in the north and carefully irrigated farms near Valencia which yield up to four harvests a year. The *vegas* of Andalucia grow every sort of fruit and vegetable. It's no wonder that many Arabs still long for their "vanished gardens of Córdoba."

## A WORD ABOUT NAMES

With place names the Spanish spelling has been used except in cases where confusion might arise. Thus Spain and the Canary Islands (not *España* and *Las Islas Canarias*), but Sevilla, Zaragoza, and Mallorca rather than the English variations.

Throughout the section dealing with antiquity and the early middle ages, the anglicized versions of the names of historical individuals are used (Theodosius instead of Teodosio and St. Isidore, not San Isidoro). Later, however, the Spanish spellings seem more appropriate — Pedro rather than Peter, Rodrigo instead of Roderick — unless dealing with historical figures who were not Spanish to begin with (Christopher Columbus rather than the Spanish Cristobal Colon).

Spaniards have *at least* two family names, those of the father *and* mother in that order. Normally, the first surname (rather than the second or both) is used; hence Francisco Franco Bahamonde is almost always just Francisco Franco. There are exceptions, especially if the father's name is a common one. Pablo Ruiz Picasso called himself Picasso and Federico Garcia Lorca is often referred to as Lorca, or as Garcia Lorca, but never as Garcia.

# INTRODUCTION

"**A**frica begins at the Pyrenees," wrote Alexandre Dumas in one of the most famous unintentional put-downs in history. Even though the author meant to praise Spain's romantically rustic, hence "African", qualities in the mid-19th century, the phrase stuck. And stung, especially coming from a Frenchman. It also touched a central theme of Spanish history: the peninsula's uncertain relationship with the rest of Europe.

Spaniards have historically looked beyond the Pyrenees with mixed emotions — admiring their neighbours, but fearing the loss of their own identity should the European influence gain the upper hand. Spain is a part of Europe both geographically and culturally. But it is a highly distinctive part, with the ability to confound even those foreigners who think they know it well. The Duke of Wellington remarked, "In Spain, two times two does not always equal four." More recently, noted British anthropologist Julian Pitt-Rivers added, "Every country and society is different, but Spain is a bit *more* different." It is this difference which makes the Story of Spain so intriguing.

During most of antiquity Iberia lay directly in the path of ancient civilizations, much more a part of the glories that were Phoenicia, Carthage, Greece and Rome than most of its northern neighbours. Later, the peninsula's evolution largely followed the rest of Europe until the year AD 711, when the Moors crossed the straits from North Africa and began several centuries of occupation. Moorish culture would reach dizzying heights and profoundly affect Spain's history. It can even be argued that for centuries civilization *ended* at the Pyrenees, that is, the "barbarians" lived to the north.

Equally important to Spain's "difference" was the Reconquest, which created a militant brand of Christianity to deal with the Moorish infidels. Spain began to go its own way, paying only grudging notice to such fundamental European developments as feudalism and the Renaissance. Under monarchs like Ferdinand and Isabella, Charles V, and Philip II, the newly united nation had other concerns, namely launching the greatest colonial venture in history — the Spanish Empire.

That first voyage of Columbus in the year 1492 marked the birth of a new world and a "new man." It also helped push a somewhat bewildered young nation to the pinnacle of power. In a few decades, Spain emerged from behind the Pyrenees to dominate the European stage for more than a century. It would conquer and colonize most of the Americas, bringing its distinctive language and culture to untold generations. Spanish genius would fully blossom during the breathtaking Golden Century with Cervantes, Velazquez and other cultural giants.

And yet within 150 years after 1492 Spain was already in an advanced state of decay. Political and economic greatness were long gone, and the last embers of the Golden Century were growing cool.

Spain's sudden rise and its equally rapid decline have puzzled historians ever since. Many, especially Spaniards, have concluded that the original achievements were more illusion than reality, though for others the period from Ferdinand and Isabella to Philip II represents an era to which they can forever aspire to return.

When faced with other major European movements — the Protestant Reformation, the Enlightenment, the French Revolution, Liberalism — Spain's unshakable role was to stand fast against all change. This posture inevitably pushed it ever further into a kind of intellectual, political, and economic backwater from which it could never seem to emerge. But the question persists: what makes a society so dynamic, and how does it lose this dynamism in such a seemingly rapid and humiliating fashion? This decline and the centuries of floundering that appeared to follow — right down to the Spanish Civil War — is the central enigma of Spain's modern history.

Most Spaniards would prefer to forget much of their violent modern past, but no people can ever really escape from their own history. The philosopher George Santayana, born in Avila, Spain, but raised in the United States (where he became an eminent Harvard scholar), once remarked that "Those who cannot remember the past are condemned to repeat it." If there is one place where history *does* repeat itself, it is Spain.

The Story of Spain is much more than a dry roll-call of battles and kings and prime ministers. It involves literary archetypes like Don Quixote and Don Juan, magnificent buildings such as the Alhambra, the Escorial, and Gaudi's Sagrada Familia, and timeless masterpieces of art — from the cave paintings at Altamira to El Greco, Velazquez, Goya, Picasso and Miró.

"Spain is different" (as the tourist posters used to proclaim) in ways that sometimes make one wonder if it really belongs to Europe in the same sense as France, Germany or Italy. Readers who follow the story of Spain will eventually come to realise that if Africa does not begin at the Pyrenees, Spain most certainly does.

# CHAPTER 1

# IN THE BEGINNING WAS IBERIA

I t began one day in the confused muddle we call pre-history, when the first eccentric innovator picked up a piece of charcoal from the cold ashes and scratched a few lines on the wall of a cave. With a little practice the rough outline of a bird, fish, or horse appeared. Then, as generations passed and aspiring artists perfected their primitive techniques, charcoal was replaced by crude mixtures of ochre, blood, minerals and animal fat. Certain styles developed and gained acceptance. Cave painting had been born, and with it Art.

In 1879, a Spanish marquis and his daughter were poking around in a recently discovered cave near Santillana del Mar (Santander). From deep inside the 275-metre-long cavern the little girl called out "Bulls! Bulls!" and her father went to investigate. The bulls were really bison, just two of about 150 animals painted on the walls and ceiling of what came to be called the "Sistine Chapel of pre-historic art."

The paintings were prehistoric but hardly primitive. Those fortunate enough to visit Altamira Cave are astounded that our remote ancestors, who lived here more than 600 generations ago, could create art that seems almost contemporary in style and technique. These are not childish doodles by grunting cavemen. The artists were thinkers and dreamers whose creations have somehow managed to survive for more than 15,000 years.

The Altamira paintings are vivid and realistic: bellowing bison stand proudly, wild boars cavort, horses gallop. In order to depict the swelling muscles of stampeding animals, artists used the irregular relief of the cave's rocky surface. The strokes are confident, the colours bold — reds, yellows, browns and shades of violet and black.

The artists employed flint tools to incise outlines on the rock face, then added colour using brushes made of twigs, feathers, tufts of hair or fur, and clumps of moss. Working with artificial light, they painted in awkward positions, often lying on their backs like Stone Age Michelangelos in places where the roof and floor were just a metre apart. Even more amazing than the technique are the sophistication in terms of perspective and the artists' ability to capture the animals' innate qualities.

Indeed, the discovery seemed so incredible that it met with widespread scepticism until similar paintings were later discovered in France. It was — and still is — hard to believe that people so distant from us in time could seem so near in spirit. The paintings span that seemingly infinite void that hides the dark and murky origins of life on the peninsula.

Preserved by some remarkable act of serendipity, they are a tiny but treasured piece of the story of Spain.

IN GEOLOGICAL TERMS the story began about half a million years ago, when water from the Atlantic punched its way through the primeval land bridge between Europe and Africa to form the narrow Straits of Gibraltar. This became the basic fact of all Spanish history. Despite the Pyrenees, the Iberian Peninsula was inextricably linked to Europe, the beginning of a long and stormy affair.

During much of Iberia's pre-history the climate was vastly different from today. The evidence is flimsy and difficult to interpret, but among the first indications of human habitation in Spain were the elephant hunters of Torralba (Soria) depicted at the National Archaeology Museum in Madrid. They lived during the Old Stone (Paleolithic) Age, when the inter-glacial climate resembled that of equatorial Africa. Along with quartzite hand-axes and other weapons, the bones of elephants, hippos, rhinos, giant bears and lions have been unearthed.

Other very early remains have been dubbed "the Gibraltar Woman," from the same period (ca. 50,000 BC) and race as her more famous cousin dug up in Germany about the same time: the Neanderthal man. These legendary low-brows, who fashioned the first spears and observed primitive funeral cults, probably came from beyond the Pyrenees; an African origin is unlikely because the Neanderthals did not have boats to cross the straits in large numbers. They were nomadic hunters who used fire and stone tools, but didn't have a clue about agriculture or raising livestock.

The Neanderthals were the first "Iberians" to feel the brunt of foreign invasion, when Cro-Magnon man began arriving around 40,000 BC. Thus, the debate over Spain's relationship with Europe begins early: Spanish historians hotly argue the origin of this new culture, that is, whether it sprang from Africa or north of the Pyrenees. The Cro-Magnons were precursors of modern man in physical appearance and could boast flint tools, rituals and art. Because theirs was a colder time, they tended to live in caves, and still used rough stone (rather than polished) implements, hunted mammoth, bison and reindeer, and had quaint customs like fashioning drinking cups from human skulls. Among the many caves that sheltered this race is the one at Nerja (Málaga).

The pinnacle of Old Stone Age life came with the Magdelanian culture, which stretched across southern France and the Cantabrian range in Iberia over a period of some ten thousand years. These are the cultural innovators who painted Altamira and hundreds of other caves in the region. The "capital" of Magdelanian Spain was the area around present-day Santander, but one outpost may have been at Benaojan near Ronda (Málaga), site of La Pileta Cave and its magnificent wall paintings. However, there is some debate about the origins of this marvel of troglodyte art, as the drawings depict a giant fish and an archer, rare subjects in the Magdelanian world.

Another major discovery of prehistoric art was the unearthing of several thousand stone plaques, mostly engravings of animals, at Parpallo Cave (Valencia). This astounding collection consists of sketches from some kind of training school for cave artists (possibly sorcerers as well) over a period of three thousand years.

Even more mysterious than these artists are the origins of the extinct Guanche culture of the Canary Islands, which still existed when the first Europeans arrived around AD 1400. Although some romantics believe the Guanches were survivors from the "Lost Continent" of Atlantis, archaeological evidence suggests that these tall, fair people arrived from North Africa during the Cro-Magnon era. The Guanches left hundreds of caves (300 in one mountain alone) and an alphabet which has not been deciphered.

The end of the last Ice Age (about 8,000 BC in Iberia), ushered in a long transitional period before the arrival of Neolithic (New Stone Age) cultures from the eastern Mediterranean five millennia later. With the gradual warming, the nomadic life of the hunters began to melt away too, as reindeer, vital to their survival, migrated north. One theory holds that with the climatic changes, Magdelanians departed en masse, leaving behind isolated pockets of stay-at-home types. Hence the possible origin of the Basques, who speak a language unrelated to any other.

Evidence suggests that new races entered the peninsula during these 50-odd centuries, probably from North Africa. They have been called Iberians, proto-Berbers, or even refugees from Atlantis for lack of more concrete evidence. Whoever they were, they brought their own form of art: the "rock-shelter" paintings which have survived along Spain's eastern coast. These are quite distinct from earlier cave drawings and resemble African and even Anatolian (Turkish) art. They were done out-of-doors for all to see and depicted group hunting and dancing scenes that seem extroverted compared with the brooding introspection of Altamira. On one hand, rock-shelter painting showed progress, using human forms to tell stories. Animals are different species from those in cave art: cattle, deer, mountain goats, wild asses, and boars. Civilization was changing. On the other hand, the new art took a distinct dip from earlier standards; the images are smaller, often just red or black stick men. They are fascinating nonetheless. Even though done outdoors, the paintings have survived due to the seepage of water with high calcium content onto them, just as the calcium hydrate in mortar preserves a fresco. We shall never know if the artists planned it that way.

Neolithic is the name given to a host of remarkable changes that marked the dawn of civilization in Mesopotamia and Egypt about the year 5,000 BC. With the arrival of these "reforms" —cultivation of wheat, use of the plow, livestock raising, use of polished stone implements, basket and pottery making, permanent villages and fortifications, communal burial rites, boat building, weaving of cloth, even rudimentary work with copper — one can speak of *civilized* man.


IN CONTRAST TO the painfully slow development of the Old Stone Age, when it took man 100,000 years to figure out how to use stone chips for tools, the innovations of the new era arrived at breakneck speed — within the span of three millennia, the blink of an eye in prehistoric time. The shortage of excavated finds means a lot of guesswork, but it appears that the "new age" reached Iberia by 3,000 BC and spread slowly during many centuries.

Most likely the new culture came from the eastern Mediterranean area via the Danube Valley, or from Egypt along the north African coast. The impact of being drawn into this world was as dramatic for the peninsula as the arrival of Spaniards would be to America thousands of years later.

This new influence explains the rise of what is called the Culture of Almeria, a neolithic society in south-eastern Spain dating from about 2,500 BC. Hotly debated theories abound regarding the roots of this culture, which is considered one of the ethnic cornerstones of the Spanish people. One school traces them to the Hammites, descendants of the biblical Ham; another says that the newcomers were migrants seeking refuge from the choking aridity then transforming much of north Africa into a desert.

A second phase at Almeria is called the culture of Los Millares, and the faint ruins of its capital now stand on a bare, eroded hill which 4,000 years ago yielded rich harvests. This emerging bronze culture revolved around local copper deposits. Again, theories of its origins proliferate: the Aegean area, perhaps Crete, is mentioned most often.

One intriguing chapter of Iberian pre-history, emanating from the Almeria beachhead, was the "era of megaliths." These striking stone burial chambers, often called dolmens, are found throughout Europe, but appear in abundance on the peninsula. The origins of the megalith building culture are obscure, but probably go back once again to the eastern Mediterranean. According to the Bible, "In those times the earth was inhabited by giants" (Genesis 6, 4). Similarly cryptic references also appear in ancient Scandinavian and Germanic lore. The Great Barrow Grave of Newgrange in Ireland dates from about the same time, and legend has it that missionaries of the megalith came from the south to build it. Stonehenge, dated about a thousand years later, may also have felt the influence of this culture.

With the spread of these great prehistoric stone cathedrals, Iberia achieved its first "golden age" of architecture. The best examples of megalithic dolmens are found near Antequera north of Málaga. Entering the Menga Chamber for the first time is a humbling experience; about 30 cyclopean size boulders (weighing up to 130,000 kilos each) were somehow carried from the nearby mountains to build a table-like tomb 25 metres long and 4 metres high. The massive roof is supported by a row of gigantic stone pillars. Modern French architect Le Corbusier was so impressed by this stunning architectural feat that he signed the guest book "to my predecessors."

One thing is certain: even the ancients had their version of "The Two Spains." Throughout most of the peninsula's lengthy history, nearly every advanced culture has developed on or flocked to the "periphery," the hospitable eastern coast and Andalucia. Both the *meseta* and the rainy north were shunned by civilized men and reserved for barbarians. Hence, the central plateau was little touched by the megalith builders.

At the dawn of the second millennium BC the Millares culture of Almeria was already in decline and may have gone down in a blaze of strife and anarchy. The times were changing: megalithic practices were dying out in favour of individual burials in cists. More importantly, true bronze technology (mixing copper and tin to the correct proportions) began to appear on the peninsula, with ore-rich Almeria once again taking the lead.

The Bronze Age — in which metal replaced stone, wood, and bone for tools and weapons — lasted until the introduction of iron many centuries later. Metal workers made everything from bronze jewelry to shields (the same level of technology Spaniards encountered in Mexico 3,500 years later). The centre of this new way of life was El Argar near Almeria, from which it spread north and west over the next few centuries. Many historians like to call this Bronze Age people the first "Iberians" (archaeologists use the term in a stricter sense). In any case, settlers from Argar colonized Menorca and built huge cone-shaped stone piles called *talayots* that were part defensive tower, part sepulchre.

By 1500 BC the cultural centre of gravity was shifting from the Almeria area to the valley of the Guadalquivir River, which was a smaller version of Mesopotamia in its role in the rise of an advanced civilization. Here agriculture thrived. The nearby Sierra Morena mountains held important deposits of copper and silver. These became the linchpins of the fabulous lost civilization of Tartessos, the most intriguing riddle in ancient Iberian history.

History, said Bacon, is like the planks of a shipwreck: more of the past is lost than has been saved. So it is with Tartessos, forgotten until an intrepid German archaeologist named Schulten rekindled interest in the 1920s by publishing a book on the subject. Using scraps of evidence and vague clues, he pieced together a flawed mosaic of the past. A major find appeared during routine dredging off a pier of the Tharsis Copper Company at the mouth of the Rio Tinto, near Huelva. An ancient wreck yielded more than 400 bronze weapons, plus needles, buttons, and other artefacts. Caches of jewelry were also found throughout Andalucia, adding to the mystery. Professor Schulten spent the rest of his life in a futile search for the famed Tartessian capital, which he believed lay somewhere between Cádiz and Huelva. But he died without producing a shred of proof for his theories.

Evidence of Tartessos' existence has remained more literary than archaeological, references such as "the boundless silver rooted springs of the Tartessus River" (Strabo). Perhaps it was Scheria, the land at the end of the world described by Homer in *The Odyssey*, which was a wealthy sea power boasting a capital with a solid-bronze palace. In Greek mythology, the tenth task assigned to Hercules was to travel to a land in the west and capture the magnificent oxen of Geryon, a three-headed king. Someone by the same name appears in Tartessian mythology, as reported by Greek historian Hesiod. He was the dynasty's founder and a kind of early cattle baron.

Then there is the biblical reference about Jonah, who, before being swallowed by the whale, was travelling by ship to a place called Tarshish: "And from Tarshish came ships bringing gold, and silver, ivory, ape, and peacocks." Were Tarshish and Tartessos the same place? The reference suggests a well-developed empire, whose ships may have reached Britain and the African coast in search of tin.

Despite all the allusions, we know few facts about Tartessos. The most fanciful notion is, once again, that the kingdom was a colony of refugees from Atlantis. It is curious that Plato, our main source on Atlantis, dated the destruction of the continent at around 1500 BC, just about the time Tartessos began its rise, and that he placed the "lost civilization" somewhere near the Pillars of Hercules, the Straits of Gibraltar of antiquity.

Today most historians believe Tartessian civilization was indigenous rather than springing from a sudden invasion. The origin of Tartessos might stretch back to Los Millares, and may even be connected to the dolmens of Antequera and elsewhere. This would make Tartessians the peninsula's first fully developed indigenous culture and the legitimate historical ancestor of all later Iberians.

Greek historians said the kingdom encompassed all of southern Iberia, and included some 200 towns and villages. (Spanish place names with Tartessian origins end in -ippo, -uba, -igi, -ucci, and -urgi.) Later, the geographer Strabo described an extensive network of canals near the mouth of the river we call the Guadalquivir. He added that the Tartessians claimed to have books six thousand years old and laws written in verse. Unfortunately, these writings vanished long ago, except for a few undeciphered inscriptions.

The chief task for researchers is to find the location of the sumptuous capital, if indeed one existed. Greeks used the name Tartessos for the river, then for the territory, but never for a city. Schulten and others placed it at the mouth of the Guadalquivir, perhaps buried under tons of silt deposited over centuries. (Most of the Las Marismas swamps were formed over the past 3,000 years.) A more likely site is the mouth of the Rio Tinto, which has run red since antiquity from copper deposits in the interior. Yet despite the many puzzle pieces Tartessos continues to elude us.

THE NAME "IBERIAN" can be used to describe the people and culture of Spain at the dawn of history. However, a narrower definition is applied specifically to cultures of the southern and eastern peninsula, which stretched along the seaboard as far as the Rhone in southern France. (Place names with Iberian roots often carry the endings -ili, -ilti, -ilu, -iltu, and -urris.) These Iberians included a confusing medley of tribes. In Catalonia alone lived the Cerretani, Andosini, Arenosi, Ausetani, Indicetes, Laietani, and Cvossetani.

Iberians were a dark people with elongated skulls who lived in easily- defended hilltop settlements. Using various sources, we can piece together a common character sketch of the typical Iberian: he was stoical, quarrelsome, devoted to bulls and horses, suspicious of strangers, superstitious in religion and respectful of elders. Above all, he was individualistic and disliked organization; in short, much like Spaniards throughout history.

Some historians thought they could detect links between the Iberian language and that of the enigmatic Basques, and even proposed that this race is a surviving pocket of the first Iberians. Iberians spoke at least two languages that, like Basque, were not Indo-European or related to Celtic. There is also a curious correlation between some words:

| Iberian | Basque |
|---------|--------|
| *egiar* | *egin* (to do) |
| *salir* | *zillar* (silver) |
| *saltu* | *saldi* (horse) |
| *nescato* | *neskato* (young girl) |

Nevertheless, attempts to use modern Basque lexicons to translate 2,300- year-old Iberian texts have failed, and the link has been dismissed by most scholars. But questions about both races persist, and the Basques, who remain very much on the modern scene, defy ethnic or linguistic classification.

One theory holds that they are survivors of a stone age culture like the Magdelanians and are totally unrelated to the coastal Iberians, to the Berbers (as some have suggested), or to any other modern race. Other linguists claim vague similarities between Basque and Finnish, Hungarian, Turkish, and even some American Indian tongues. Some romantics have even claimed Basque was the language spoken by Adam and Eve in the Garden of Eden!

In any case, the Basque language is exceptionally difficult and complex. (It's said that the devil, as a punishment for some outrageous offence, was condemned by God to learn Basque.) It was once spoken in most of the western and central Pyrenees and parts of the Cantabrian range. Words of Basque origin in Spanish are few: *izquierda* (left), *barro* (mud), and *perro* (dog), for example.

After the year 1000 BC, however, the Basques were already surrounded by Celtic speakers. The Celts in turn present their own historical puzzle. This fair, round-headed middle European race began moving into the peninsula about 900 BC and were long considered, along with the Iberians, as a key component of the Spanish race. Today some sceptics doubt they were even in Spain. Yet the reliable Greek historian Herodotus referred specifically to Celts on the peninsula by the fifth century BC, if not earlier. The problem seems to lie in distinguishing Celtic from purely indigenous remnants that pre-dated the invasions. The Celtic practice of burning the dead has made investigation almost futile because archaeologists rely heavily on burial sites for evidence. One of the few existing remnants of Celtic culture are the sculpted stone bulls, *los toros de Guisando* in Avila province.

Nevertheless, a few basic facts are generally accepted. Celtic penetration across the Pyrenees flowed and ebbed during several centuries and spread over about two-thirds of the peninsula. Although nothing like an empire ever existed, the Celts did occupy the entire *meseta* and most of the north and west. (Place names with a Celtic connection often end in -briga.) The Celts brought iron metallurgy (and the short broad sword) with them at about the same time the Phoenicians were spreading it along the coast. They also introduced the custom of wearing trousers and preferred beer (*cerveza* is a Celtic word) and lard over the wine and olive oil of the Iberians. One strange practice involved placing the infirm alongside roads and paths in case anyone passing might have suffered the same illness and be able to help.

The Celtic racial influence has been diluted almost beyond recognition over the centuries, although Spaniards claim that a definite blonde or red-haired type, lyrical and melancholic, comes from Galicia in the northwest. It is curious too that both Galician and Irish legends support the idea that Eire's first people came from Iberia. In Galicia, tradition holds that King Breogan and his sons sailed north and encountered an island. One son severed his own right hand and dramatically threw it ashore so that he should be remembered as the first person to touch the unknown land.

ABOUT THE SAME TIME Celts were entering Iberia from the north, Phoenician traders were gaining a toehold in the south. They were the first colonizers from an identifiable civilization: Phoenicia was a commercially oriented empire of Semitic peoples based in what is today Lebanon and northern Israel. Phoenicians were dark, with wide foreheads, high cheekbones, and hooked noses. Their most important legacy is the alphabet we use (in slightly modified form) today. Though never a great military power, Phoenicia grew strong as a trading partner to mightier empires and virtually controlled Mediterranean commerce by 1000 BC. Expansion was chiefly triggered by the need to find raw materials, chiefly metals, for the manufacture of luxury goods for the neighbouring (and often threatening) Assyrians and Babylonians.

According to legend, one Phoenician king was following an oracle when he ordered an expedition from Tyre to found a city near the Pillars of Hercules. The old cliché about the ancients believing the Pillars marked the end of the world, the beginning of a "sea of darkness," is only partly true. In fact, the Phoenicians went far beyond the Pillars in search of tin and other wealth, north and south along Atlantic shores as far as Britain and western Africa. Even so, the voyage across the Mediterranean was breathtaking in its audacity, an adventure comparable to Homer's *Odyssey*.

Phoenician sailors called the peninsula *i-schephan-im*. According to two schools of feuding scholars, this could be translated as either "remote" or "filled with rabbits." The name was later altered to *Spania* and to *Hispania* during centuries of Roman rule. Still later, it became España.

The founding of Gadir by the Phoenicians around the year 1100 BC would make today's city of Cádiz the oldest in Europe. The chronology comes from a Roman historian writing much later, who dated the founding 80 years after the fall of Troy. But archaeological evidence and the first literary references suggest a later date. In either case, Gadir was still very old, older in fact than Rome. The name means "fortress" in Phoenician, and the town occupied the strongest part of a small archipelago near the mouth of the Guadalete River. (Today the islands are linked by landfill, and the existence of modern Cádiz prevents excavation of the site.)

Other colonies sprouted along the entire southern coast: at Malaca (Málaga), Sexi (Almuñecar), and Abdera (Adra), where both the climate and the natives were hospitable. The Phoenicians were seeking copper and silver, both abundant in Andalucia, and hoped to exchange manufactured goods in return. However, they underestimated hostility from nearby Tartessos, which monopolized this mineral wealth. A naval battle to decide the issue ended in the burning of the Tartessian fleet. Henceforth, the Phoenicians not only exploited the mines, but also took over their rival's old Atlantic trading routes.

Fishing was second to mining in economic importance (tunny fish appear on Phoenician coins). Vast schools of enormous blue-fin tuna migrating through the Straits of Gibraltar on spawning runs to the Black Sea were caught, salted, and shipped throughout the known world.

Gadir became a thriving seaport that served a substantial merchant fleet, and the streets teemed with Phoenicians, Tartessians, Greeks, and Celts. The city's most important religious temple was devoted to Moloch, the fire-god to whom children were sacrificed. It sat on the same spot today occupied by the Cadiz cathedral. Another temple of note, boasting a pair of solid bronze columns, was dedicated to Melkart, the protective god of the city and trade. It was famous throughout the ancient world (it was once visited by Julius Caesar), but was razed by the Moors who conquered the peninsula centuries later. Today it lies covered with sand and water somewhere near a place called Sancti Petri.

Phoenician towns followed a pattern, with sheltered anchorage, fresh water, arable land, and an elevated site for defence. Almuñecar (Sexi) is a perfect example of the ideal site, atop an isolated promontory jutting into the sea. The cemetery here has yielded outstanding Phoenician artefacts, including alabaster jars bearing the names of Egyptian pharoahs and decorated ostrich eggs filled with red ochre, which was used as a cosmetic.

With the coming of the Phoenicians, Iberians came into direct contact with an advanced Mediterranean civilization. They readily adopted many new ways to form a fairly uniform society by the fifth century, which made it easier for later colonizers to take over. Tribes of the interior (like the later Castilians) fought the "opening up" of Iberia for several more centuries. They lived in flea-infested squalour and brushed their teeth with urine, while the coastal Iberians became part of a larger Mediterranean culture — building towns, mining silver, working iron and bronze, and drinking wine.

The Iberian language took on written form by adopting the Phoenician alphabet (the origin of our own). Imported gods crept into the local pantheon. Carvings and figurines reveal an acquired taste for the sumptuous burials favoured by the Phoenicians. The tomb of Pozo Moro in Albacete province has proved very rich, yielding sculpture of the god Reshef, a giant marine monster, a boar fighting monsters, and ancient — but no less interesting — erotica. This tomb has been reconstructed at the National Archaeological Museum in Madrid.

When Phoenicia was defeated by Assyria and again by Babylonia, the stage was set for the rise of one of its colonies — Carthage. And led by the city of Phocaea Greeks too took advantage of Phoenicia's decline to set up trading posts in Spain.

SINCE TIME IMMEMORIAL Greeks had been fascinated by kingdoms to the west. In mythology, Hercules reached the limits of the Mediterranean and raised two great columns called the Pillars of Hercules, the twin mountains of Gibraltar and Mt. Acho in Ceuta. (As an interesting footnote, the story goes on to say that the hero engraved an S-shaped legend around the pillars which read "Do not go beyond here." The image evolved into the widely used dollar sign.) Hercules then proceeded on his quest for the golden apples of the Hesperides and the cattle of Geryon in the mysterious land beyond.

It was the Greeks who gave us the name "Iberia", possibly taken from an indigenous word for "river." They also used *Hesperia*, meaning "land of the setting sun."

According to Herodotus, the first Greek in Iberia was the adventurer Kolaios of Samos, who was blown off course and landed at Tartessos during the reign of Arganthonius. His reception was a warm one, and he returned to Greece with a cargo of 1,500 kilos of silver from the king, whose name itself meant "he of the silver land." It is more likely that the voyage of Kolaios, about 2,300 kilometres each way, was actually planned with the fabulous Tartessian silver mines as the objective.

Phocaean traders followed, reaching Iberia around 600 BC, and founded the colonies of Rhode and Emporion ("market place") on the north-eastern coast. The Greek presence was limited mainly to present-day Catalonia and did not penetrate the interior; they wanted trade, not conquest. Many places suggested as colonies were just small trading posts or landmarks; these include Mainake (Velez-Málaga), Hemeroskopeion (Denia), Alonis (Benidorm), and Akra-Leuke (Alicante).

The Greeks are credited with developing the olive and vine cultures on the peninsula. Besides metals, they traded for products such as esparto grass, which was used by Xerxes for the famous rope bridge across the Hellespont (the Dardanelles) during the wars with Persia. Perhaps the most notable Greek legacy is the classical influence on Iberian sculpture, including the famous Dama de Elche. Her elegant serenity reflects classical models, but the elaborate attire is clearly native (the head-dress almost seems to be a high comb and *mantilla).* This superb statue of carved sandstone was accidentally unearthed in 1897 near the palm grove at Elche (Alicante). Like its "sister," the Dama de Baza, it had a funerary role, with a cavity in the back for ashes and bones.

Greek commercial expansion was cut short by the heir to Phoenicia's hege-mony, its upstart North African colony of Carthage. Founded about the same time as Rome, Carthage (located near present-day Tunis) was one of the last Phoenician colonies. The Carthaginians were a strange breed, hard-nosed businessmen who preferred to leave their fighting to foreign mercenaries like Numidian horsemen, Libyan archers, and the dreaded Balearic slingers. Not that they shunned violence; the citizens of Carthage were practicing human sacrifice as late as the fifth century, when Athens gave us Plato and Aristotle.

The battle of Alalia off Corsica (535 BC) left the Greek fleet devastated and made Carthage master of the western Mediterranean. Archaeologists find that the abundant supplies of Greek bronze and pottery work in southern Iberia abruptly ceased about this time. Nevertheless, Alalia did not mean the end of the Greeks or Emporion, which held out as an independent city for another two centuries.

The world was changing from the days of free trade and a rabbit in every pot. With Carthage in control of the Straits of Gibraltar, a curtain of secrecy slammed down on the lands beyond. One later writer could only affirm that "Beyond the Pillars of Hercules no wise man can tread, and no fool either... beyond lies darkness."

About the same time, the Phoenician colony at Gadir called on their Car-thaginian cousins to help put down some Tartessian sabre-rattling. Their capital was taken with the help of a new technological marvel, the battering ram, and "disappeared, as if sunk into the sea." Thereafter, Carthaginian soldiers were paid in Tartessian silver. From this point Carthage was firmly in control of the entire southern coast, and under these secretive conquerors even the memory of Tartessos soon began to fade. Within decades, historians were confusing it with Gadir and other mysterious points beyond the Pillars.

Even though Carthage ruled most of the Mediterranean coast(from the Algar-ve to Valencia) for more than two centuries, historians know remarkably little of the era. It was an empire of businessmen which sought trade above all else; most Iberian tribes lived under a form of protectorate and outright conquest came only toward the end. Gadir remained the chief city at first and served as port of departure for daring sailors like Hanno, who explored the west African coast around 480 BC.

Iberia's most important Carthaginian, or Punic, site lies on the island of Ibiza, where about 4,000 tombs were arranged staircase fashion up a hillside. Although much was lost to grave robbers (Spanish peasants believed everything old involved Moors and treasure), some fascinating items survived: death masks, mass-produced phallic figurines of men grabbing their own testicles, and beautifully painted ostrich egg shells which were symbols of immortality.The Balearics lay right in the shipping lanes and more Punic artefacts have turned up on Mallorca, including a massive bronze bull's head weighing 33 kilos.

In 237 BC Carthage began the serious conquest of Iberia. This change of strategy sprang from the ashes of defeat at the hands of Rome in the First Punic War, fought for the control of Sicily. (The name "punic" derives from the Roman word for Carthaginian, *Poeni*). Carthage was left humiliated and bankrupt. Looking for virgin lands, veteran general Hamilcar Barca (of the Barcid family) and his nine-year-old son Hannibal disembarked at Gadir and began the systematic subjugation of the south. Here his mostly Libyan troops defeated an army of 50,000 Turdetanos, a tribe that traced its ancestry to Tartessos.

By this time Celt-Iberians had a reputation as fierce warriors, but "well-dressed" ones who wore gold collars, amulets, horned helmets, and sandals into battle. Resistance increased as the Carthaginians moved inland, and Hamilcar himself drowned in a river while fleeing from a successful Iberian counter-attack. His son-in-law Hasdrubal and son Hannibal, still a boy, managed to escape. Hasdrubal Barca took a softer approach and tried to win over the Iberians. Tradition credits him with founding Barca (Barcelona) and a capital at Cartago Nova (Cartagena), where he built a palace. A prosperous town grew up there, based on silver mining, and all went well until Hasdrubal was assassinated by an Iberian slave seeking revenge for the crucifixion of a native leader.

With this a man of true destiny entered the scene. Power passed to Hannibal Barca, considered one of history's greatest military geniuses. Only twenty-five at the time, Hannibal carried the conquest onto the *meseta* as far as present day Salamanca. And from the growing concern over his success sprang the Carthaginians' greatest contribution to Iberia: they brought the Romans.

## SIGHTS & SITES

### Pre-Historic
*Avila province:* Los Toros de Guisando, *stone figures believed to be Celtic.*
*Antequera (Málaga): Menga and Viera chambers and Romeral dolmen; El Torcal (16 kms. south) was the possible source of giant stones.*
*Benaojan (Málaga): La Pileta Cave has excellent cave art.*
*Canary Islands: Canaries Museum in Las Palmas de Gran Canaria features Guanche ethnography; at Cuatro Puertas on Gran Canaria is a mountain honeycombed with burial caves; Los Verdes Cave on Lanzarote, at the foot of Corona Volcano, has underground galleries where Guanches took refuge from pirates.*
*Menorca (Balearic Islands): More than 200 megalithic monuments called talayots; sites include Trepuco near airport and Els Tudons near Ciudadela.*
*Nerja (Málaga): Nerja Cave chronicles many epochs of prehistory.*
*Puente Viesgo (Cantabria): El Castillo Cave, with the very first Iberian images — outlines of human hands — which pre-date Altamira.*
*Ribadesella (Asturias): Tito Bustillo Cave is another site for good cave art.*

*Santillana del Mar* *(Santander): Altamira Cave, the "Sistine Chapel of pre-historic art."*

## Pre-Roman Colonial Period

*Alicante:* *Castle of Santa Barbara, original site of Carthaginian fortress overlooking town and harbour.*

*Ampurias* *(Gerona): Ruins of Emporion, largest Greek settlement in Iberia.*

*Elche* *(Alicante): Palm Grove where the* Dama de Elche *was found, originally planted by Phoenicians; museum at Alcudia contains early Iberian pieces.*

*Ibiza* *(Balearic Islands): Large Punic necropolis at Puig des Molins has about 2,000 tombs; Archaeology Museum features mostly ceramics.*

## General Museums

*Barcelona Archaeological Museum* *is especially good on megalithic civilization; also Greek and Roman collections from Ampurias and a scale model of Emporion.*

*National Archaeological Museum in Madrid* *spans entire ancient period and contains outstanding displays, including the* Dama de Elche.

# CHAPTER 2

# THE ROMANS WERE HERE

Segovia's magnificent aqueduct captures the spirit of Spain's Roman heritage. Standing proud and mighty on the Plaza del Azoguejo, it is an aesthetic and engineering triumph, and an inspiring sight that has awed observers for the past 2,000 years.

Sometime during the first century after Christ, white granite boulders weighing several tons each were carted down from the nearby Guadarrama Mountains. They were cut and chiseled into building blocks so perfect that no mortar was needed to join them; each stone fit like a piece in a giant three-dimensional mosaic. The Segovia aqueduct is about 800 metres long with 118 tiered stone arches providing its strength and simple beauty.

It is an example of the Romans' genius for civil engineering, but Segovia's aqueduct did not serve solely to transport water. Just as today we stand in awe before it, so too did the semi-barbaric Celt-Iberians under the Roman rule. It is curious that no other remnants survive here — no theatre, forum, or arena as in most Roman towns. The reason is simple: Segovia was a military post to keep conquered tribes at bay, and the aqueduct served to intimidate these rebellious rustics with the glories of Roman civilization.

Rome... the name itself resounds like the deep ring of a bronze bell or the clang of an iron sword against a heavy shield. Romans destroyed their foes mercilessly and violence became the national sport, but they also brought peace and culture to the Mediterranean world. Romans built roads, bridges, and aqueducts; towns and commerce flourished, and law prevailed over the whims of the few. Even today, Roman ruins in the most desolate corners of North Africa are the only sign that civilization has passed that way.

Rome ruled the Iberian peninsula, which they called Hispania, for more than six centuries (218 BC to AD 409). During this decisive period, the country was changed to such a degree as to make previous history seem irrelevant. Romans brought the language that forms the base of all peninsular tongues (except Basque), an advanced legal system, and architectural and engineering principles still used today. Some have argued that under Rome Spain enjoyed political and cultural unity for the first *and last* time.

From Hispania Rome received much in return. Vast mineral and agricultural wealth financed imperial projects. Here were born three emperors and some of the great names in Latin literature. Hispania was the pride of the empire, the most Roman of all its provinces. But reaching such an exalted status required two centuries of bloody struggle.


BEFORE HANNIBAL DISEMBARKED with his father at Gadir, he had sworn an oath of eternal hatred for Rome, and he lived his life with the dream of its destruction. When he finally took charge 16 years later, Hannibal was fighting lean, with an incredible tolerance for physical suffering. And he enjoyed the fanatical loyalty of his men.

Hannibal's successes on the peninsula caused alarms to go off all over Rome. An earlier treaty between the two powers had divided the peninsula into two zones — everything north of the Ebro River fell under Roman control, while lands to the south belonged to Carthage. There was one exception, a Greek/Iberian town on the east coast named Saguntum which looked to Rome for special protection. Hannibal saw in Saguntum a chance to provoke his sworn enemies. After a bitter, eight-month siege, the town fell and Rome was forced to respond. Iberia was suddenly thrust into centre stage of the greatest military encounter of ancient history: the Second Punic War (218-201 BC).

In this struggle between the titans of antiquity the stakes were high and the fighting particularly savage. Carthage was larger and wealthier, but Rome superior in manpower and enthusiasm.

Two Roman legions (about 5,000 men each) landed at Emporion, but Hannibal had already left the peninsula with an army of 50,000 foot soldiers, 9,000 cavalry, and 37 elephants. The most famous trek in military history would take them across the Alps and into Italy. There, at Cannae, a Roman army was annihilated and 80 members of the senate perished. Many of the dead were found with their faces buried in the earth, preferring to choke to death rather than be captured alive.

Then, in one of history's most debated military decisions, Hannibal decided to rest his army for the winter rather than pressing on to complete his conquest. After the lull, he never managed to finish off his enemy.

Meanwhile in Hispania, Rome had opened a second front. Roman legions pinned down and defeated an army under Hannibal's brother, Hasdrubal, who was thus unable to reinforce his countrymen in Italy. (When he finally did arrive, Hasdrubal's force was badly beaten, Hasdrubal killed, and his severed head thrown into his brother's camp.)

A member of an illustrious Roman family arrived in Hispania to assume command, the dashing Publius Cornelius Scipio. The new general captured Cartagena in a surprise attack, then followed up with a series of victories which climaxed with the fall of Gadir. Scipio went on to defeat Hannibal and end the war at Zama in North Africa.

To celebrate the Iberian victory, Scipio decided to settle wounded and retired soldiers at a spot he called Italica, whose ruins lie near present- day Sevilla. It became Rome's first colony in southern Spain.

The war's cost to Rome was frightening, but that was only the beginning of the bloodshed; it would take two centuries and more than 150,000 lives to subdue the peninsula.

Over the past several centuries intermixing between Celt and Iberian, especially in the Ebro basin, had created the Celtiberians, a hearty race that Romans called *robur hispanae* (Spanish hearts of oak) feared for its courage and tenacity. Not that the blending was complete; one Roman historian noted that Iberian soldiers wore purple linens while Celts preferred sheepskin and black woollens. Celts were mostly pastoral by nature, lived in the interior, drank a fermented wheat beer, and cooked with lard. Iberians resided along the coast as farmers, fishermen or merchants, ate more fish than meat, and preferred wine mixed with honey.

The Romans were baffled by these Celtiberians: they were a tough and wiry race with strong features, unkempt hair, and a "harsh" way of speaking. Their system of justice was likewise severe — criminals were thrown off cliffs — and they were wildly superstitious, reading the entrails of slain enemies to predict the future. Celtiberians were heroic and loyal, loved liberty but lacked discipline, and could endure terrible hardships. They carried the leaves of poisonous plants into battle, and would swallow them rather than be captured alive. Even today, the Spanish refer to a stubborn person as "very Iberian."

To collective-minded Romans, "hispanic" individualism was disconcerting. Strabo noted that tribal pride prevented the Celtiberians from uniting into a defensive confederation, and added that they never learned to hold their shields together (Roman style) in battle. Though they fought bravely, it was always "every man for himself." This lack of cohesion cut both ways, however. Because Celtiberians never united, they could not be decisively defeated. War thus became a never-ending affair that brought neither submission nor peace.

Savage guerilla tactics, made so effective by the rugged terrain, proved so exasperating that legionnaires dreaded service to the point of mutiny. In battle, Celtiberian warriors would charge shouting war cries, shaking their long locks, and leaping around as if dancing to confuse and intimidate the well-disciplined legionnaires.

These *hispani*, as Romans called natives, enjoyed superior numbers and, surprisingly, better weapons. The Celts in particular had fearsome cavalry and a short iron sword that the Romans later adopted. Iberians used an infamous sabre which "cut off arms at the root of the shoulder, severed heads from bodies with a chopping blow, exposed entrails, and caused horrible wounds," according to one observer. The *hispani* may never have learned to hold their shields together, but they did something no other colony did — they held out for 200 years against mighty Rome. Gaul, in contrast, succumbed to Caesar in a mere ten years.

After the Punic War and with the arrival of a complex foreign culture, Iberians were forced to undergo profound changes. Areas along the coast, long-exposed to colonial powers, readily accepted the Roman presence, but there was strong resistance in the interior. The Lusitanians, a fierce tribe living in what are today Portugal and Extremadura, led revolts in the west.

In 150 BC a massacre of 8,000 unarmed Lusitanians sparked an eight-year revolt led by Viriathus, a shepherd who had escaped the slaughter. This charismatic figure, claimed by both Spain and Portugal as their first national hero, abandoned his flocks for a life of banditry and brilliant soldiering. He soon outwitted the Roman army in the west and at one time controlled most of central Spain. In the end, only treachery could defeat Viriathus: the Romans bribed three of his aides to murder him in his tent. At a spectacular funeral, his corpse was burned on a elevated pyre, while warriors danced in a frenzy around it.

The death of Viriathus smothered the Lusitanian revolt but, about the same time, several tribes on the *meseta* rose up. The Celtiberian War lasted twenty years and broke the back of two Roman armies before another Scipio, the grandson of Hannibal's nemesis, arrived to crush the revolt. The town of Numantia (near present-day Soria) emerged as the immortal Spanish symbol of resistance as her six thousand souls faced the cream of the Roman army.

Ringed by barren peaks, Numantia sits above the Duero River on a dry, stony plateau of Old Castilla. Here, it was said, the wind was so strong it could knock down a legionnaire carrying a heavy pack. Although this was perfect guerilla country, the Numantians chose to make a stand in their heavily walled town. Repeated attacks were thrown back, and a force of 20,000 Romans surrendered in disgrace. The outraged Roman senate was forced to send its finest general and an army of 60,000 men to starve out a wretched Celtiberian village.

Scipio the Younger was an interesting type: intelligent, cultured, a patron of the arts, and the person credited with introducing the Greek custom of shaving to the bearded Romans. Yet in war he was a ruthless commander who gave no quarter.

Upon arriving at Numantia, the general launched a get-tough campaign on the demoralized legionnaires which included forbidding hot baths and making them eat breakfast standing up. Then he established a seamless blockade around Numantia, hoping to starve the defenders into submission, and after nine months the Numantians sued for peace. But when Scipio insisted on unconditional surrender, the Numantians dug in for the final defence. Finally, in the ultimate gesture of Iberian defiance, the last survivors got drunk on beer, set fire to their town, and perished in the flames rather than surrender. (Cervantes later immortalized the events in his play *The Siege of Numantia*.)

For his efforts the conquering general became known as Scipio Numantinus, but Rome had paid a harrowing price. And the job was still not finished, for in the wild Cantabrian mountains hardened defenders would resist the invaders for another century.

THE PROCESS CALLED Romanization began about 200 BC and continued for six centuries. Roads, bridges and other buildings were the first visible sign of the new order. Romans were ancient history's greatest builders, and eventually 34 different major roads covering 21,000 kilometres linked the far-flung corners of Hispania. Among the earliest were the Via Herculea, a coastal road from the Pyrenees to Gades (Cádiz), and the Via Augusta running through the heart of the country.

The peninsula was divided into two provinces — Hispania Citerior and Hispania Ulterior — with Cartago Nova (Cartagena) and Corduba (Córdoba) the respective capitals. Above all, Hispania's precious metals enticed Rome, just as the mines of Mexico and Peru would attract Spaniards centuries later. At Cartagena alone, forty thousand slaves worked the silver mines, and at Rio Tinto existing works were greatly expanded.

The other economic pillar was agriculture: olive oil, wheat, and wine. The Romans introduced both irrigation and the *latifundia*, huge land grants to men of power. The salting of fish became an important industry in the south; even more so was the production of *garum*, a kind of fish paste that Romans craved around cocktail time.

Towns and cities became key components of the Roman way. Urban life lured *hispani* with pleasures and privileges, and later with the ultimate prize — citizenship. Little by little the new towns exerted influence on the countryside, and cities such as Italica and Mérida represented the triumph of urban civilization in a wild and hostile environment. The first area urbanized was Baetica, a province named for the Baetis River (Guadalquivir) that corresponded roughly to Andalucia. Roman writers made note of the "clusters of small dwellings of whitened adobe" there, Iberian forerunners of the whitewashed *pueblos* of today. Urban life also flourished along the eastern seaboard, where towns had long existed.

Rome's ultimate legacies were its language and laws, which filtered down to replace the local practices. Latin was crucial in cementing Roman control, and the vulgar language spoken by soldiers — quite different from literary Latin — began to evolve, ever so slowly, into the various Romance tongues spoken on the peninsula.

You can see first-hand the meaning of Roman law in the Charter of Urso, on display in Madrid's National Archaeological Museum. Inscribed on these bronze tablets are the fundamentals of citizenship and law-and-order, just two of the rewards Rome promised in return for submission. There are provisions for due process under the law and guarantees of public works, along with clauses forbidding burials within the city walls and other such practical matters.

Local religious customs and burial practices were deeply rooted and gave way only over centuries. Romans tolerated traditional gods (numbering in the hundreds) except in extreme cases, such as a cult of human sacrifice they stamped out at Gades. Gradually, Roman gods — Jupiter, Juno, Minerva, Mars — replaced local ones with similar identities. The old Phoenician god Melkart, for example, became Hercules. Roman burial customs could be quite elaborate; at Carmona (near Sevilla) a huge necropolis of 900 tombs contains some large enough to include banqueting rooms and seats for slave butlers.

ROMAN IBERIA

GALIA

LEGIO (LEON)    POMPAEIO (PAMPLONA)
ARTURICA (ASTORGA)                        EMPORION (AMPURIAS)
                    CAESARAUGUSTA (ZARAGOZA)
                                    TARRACO (TARRAGONA)
            TARRACONENSIS

LUSITANIA                    SAGUNTUM

    EMERITA (MERIDA)

        BAETICA
    ITALICA    CORDUBA        CARTAGO NOVA (CARTAGENA)
            ASTIGI (ECIJA)
    HISPALIS (SEVILLA)

    GADES (CADIZ)
            MALAGA

Roman society was highly structured, but life for the average person was probably not all that bad. The conquered became tributes more often than slaves, and later the *hispani* were the first people outside Italy to enjoy Roman citizenship.

At the bottom of the social scale were slaves, essential to an economy based on large-scale mining and agriculture. Above them came free peasants and urban artisans, who sold their goods and services in the open market. Next came full citizens, often from the professional classes, and finally the elite members of the "orders," the gentry and aristocracy. The *equites*, for example, had enough money to own and equip a horse, while foot-soldiers came from the poorer classes.

In Hispania, the fall of Numantia ushered in 50 years of peace, but the province would soon find itself riding a whirlwind. Concern over social inequalities led

The paintings discovered in 1879 at Altamira cave, near Santillana in the north of Spain, are spectacular examples of Magdelanian art (above). Left, La Menga Dolmen near Antequera, north of Málaga. Dating from ca. 2000 BC, La Menga was constructed with some 30 boulders weighing up to 130,000 kilos each. (PHOTOGRAPHY BY AGE FOTOSTOCK, BARCELONA)

The Romans built the Segovia aqueduct (above) both for practical reasons and to impress the newly-conquered natives of Iberia. The Romans ruled the Iberian peninsula, which they called Hispania, for more than six centuries, and reminders of their presence still abound. Right, the theatre at Mérida, which at one time was the ninth largest city in the Empire. (PHOTOGRAPHY BY AGE FOTOSTOCK, BARCELONA)

to a century of civil war that brought down the Roman Republic. The first upheaval involved a struggle between the aristocratic supporters of Sulla and the so-called popular party of Marius. Neither leader was a likable character: Lucius Cornelius Sulla was a moody patrician who could order an execution as easily as read a poem; Gaius Marius was the son of a farmer and passionately hated aristocrats. He was a grim figure, a hard, ruthless fighter who became involved in several vicious slaughters.

One of Marius's biggest supporters, and therefore on the patrician hit list, was Quintus Sertorius. After Sulla's victory he was exiled to Hispania, where he organized a small army to lead a rebellion against patrician-controlled Rome. The western colony soon became a hotbed of popularist support, and many *hispani* gladly joined in the fracas. Sertorius was a swashbuckling character puzzling to historians, who can't agree if he was a Republican hero or an ambitious traitor who wanted to set up his own kingdom. At first defeated, he fled to Mauretania (Morocco) and helped locals battle the king of Tingis (Tangier), then led an expedition to the Canary Islands. A year later, he returned to Hispania at the head of a new rebellion.

Fighting for Sulla's faction was Gnaeus Pompeius, the future Pompey the Great, then only 23. Pompey was a brilliant cavalry officer, but had to appeal to Rome for aid nonetheless. (During this period he founded the town of Pamplona.) Finally, when strategy alone would not suffice, he bribed some enemy traitors to murder Sertorius in his sleep and the rebellion petered out. Pompey returned to Rome, in typically "pompous" fashion, to boast that he had conquered 876 Hispanic towns.

The next round of civil conflict involved Pompey and Julius Caesar. Caesar had built his military reputation in Hispania and Gaul and was described as a man "furious for war." The poet Lucan recounted that the morning after one particularly bloody battle, Caesar ordered breakfast served amid a field of corpses so that he could contemplate their faces. Sulla once dismissed the future dictator by saying "he wears his girdle too loosely" — a sign of effeminacy to Romans. But Caesar was handsome and a notorious womanizer, deemed "one of the great fornicators of antiquity."

When Caesar crossed the Rubicon River and entered Italy (49 BC) to unleash a civil war, he had six loyal legions in Hispania while Pompey could count seven. (Armies in the provinces tended to grow independent of Rome and were faithful to their commanders.) Eventually Caesar met forces loyal to Pompey at Llerda (Lérida), and fought what Napoleon claimed was the Roman's most brilliant battle.

One final engagement occurred at Munda, a site which has never been pinned down conclusively but lies somewhere between Córdoba and Osuna. Here, Caesar's army met 30,000 men led by the sons of Pompey and, after so many victories, himself nearly tasted defeat. With his forces falling back and appearing to panic, Caesar desperately grabbed sword and shield and rushed into the maelstrom shouting, "Are you going to let your general be delivered up to the enemy?" Inspired legionnaires lunged forward and carried the day. Caesar remarked, "On other occasions I fought for victory; today I fought for my life." It was his last battle.

After Munda, Caesar was joined by his 18-year-old grand-nephew, Gaius Octavius (Octavian), and the pair travelled together by carriage throughout Hispania for several months (Mark Antony claimed they were lovers). At last Caesar returned to Rome to meet his day of reckoning, and Octavian, of course, went on to become Rome's first emperor. But that, as they say, is another story.

LONG AFTER THE FALL of Numantia, mountain-dwelling tribes from the "wild Cantabrian land" still would not bow to the Romans. Nevertheless, in 38 BC. Hispania was officially declared a part of Rome and a general tax introduced. (In Castilla, for the next fourteen centuries, until AD 1383, years were counted from this date.)

The Cantabrians and Basques were not impressed by the Roman declaration. They believed liberty was worth more than Latin. To Rome's embarrassment, another round of revolts broke out. It lasted a decade. Fighting was savage and the rebels so unbelievably stubborn that several legions mutinied rather than return to the front. The Cantabrians always seemed to have the last word: they sang and shouted victory slogans while being crucified, and mothers killed their own children rather than let them be taken captive. It is interesting that Cantabria-Asturias was the very region that stood alone against the Moors seven centuries later. And though defeated, the neighbouring Basques were never Romanized.

Finally Octavian — by then known as Augustus — intervened personally, but was forced to remain several years before achieving final victory. During the campaign he contracted a serious illness and lived for a time at the future provincial capital of Tarraco (Tarragona). Today, you can wander through some of Spain's best-preserved Roman ruins there and see remains of the tower where he stayed and a temple built in his honour. (In Tarraco was born the infamous — for Christians, at least — Pontius Pilate.)

Augustus Caesar was not an imposing figure: he limped, was frequently ill, and wore thick-soled shoes to disguise his shortness. And yet by the time of his death Rome had set its course towards imperial grandeur and was enjoying the first years of the Pax Romana, two centuries of unparalleled peace and prosperity. Hispania too entered the longest period of calm in its entire history, during which the last traces of Iberians and Celts ceased to exist as identifiable races.

By the time of Augustus, Baetica (Andalucia) was considered the "most Roman" area outside Italy, with all the trappings of civilization, including the best postal system the world would see until the invention of the railroad. Bridges, aqueducts, baths, theatres and arenas sprang up everywhere. Under Rome, urban life developed a lasting vigour; each of the hundreds of towns had its own charter and enjoyed a good deal of local autonomy. Under Augustus the inhabitants of fifty Hispanic towns had Roman citizenship, a privilege not lightly granted.

Among the most important *civitas* were Emerita Augusta (Mérida), Corduba (Córdoba), Tarraco (Tarragona), Caesar-Augusta (Zaragoza),Emporion (Ampu–

rias), Cartago Nova (Cartagena) and Gades (Cádiz). Gades had a reputation as a wealthy and wicked town. Apart from 500 millionaires it boasted provocative dancers called *puellae gaditanae*. These "girls from wanton Gades with endless prurience swinging lascivious loins in practiced writhings" (as one writer put it) were in great demand at parties given by wealthy merchants. There are even references to hand-clapping and castanet clicking (the *testarum crepitus*) and to a peculiar form of singing described as "deep and emotional." Upon these descriptions Cádiz bases its claim as birthplace of flamenco music.

Hispania's greatest city was Emerita Augusta (Mérida), the capital of Lusi–tania province (roughly Portugal and Extremadura). During the Pax Romana, Mérida ranked ninth in size in the entire empire, ahead of cities such as Athens, and boasted a 25,000-seat *circus maximus* (only traces remain) for chariot races. One famous charioteer named Diocles retired here after 1,462 victories. Contrary to popular, Hollywood-induced mythology, Romans never used chariots in warfare, only for sport.

The theatre survives as the most impressive reminder of Mérida's former glories. One inscription here tells us that each spectator was allotted about 56 centimetres of bench space, and from this we know the capacity was 5,500. Sitting today in this architectural gem, it's hard to believe the theatre lay buried under rubble for 16 centuries before being excavated. Other important ruins include a 14,000-seat arena (amphitheatre) for gladiatorial events which could also be flooded for simulated naval encounters; a bridge over the Guadiana River with 64 arches; and the Los Milagros aqueduct, with its three levels of elegant arches.

Mérida lay in the heart of a huge cereal-producing region, just one piece in the mosaic of Hispania's thriving economy during these prosperous centuries. Especially productive was the highly cultivated river valley in the heart of Baetica, a source of wine and olive oil. Other Hispanic exports included knives and swords from Toletum (Toledo), and minerals such as lead, iron, copper, silver and gold. Spain, later the great world colonizer, lived through centuries as a colony itself, and its wealth ended up in Roman coffers.

One of the most significant events in Spain's entire history is the disappearance of its forests.Ancient Iberia, even the now treeless *meseta*, was thickly wooded over almost half its surface with oaks, junipers, and evergreens. During the Roman conquest, Strabo mentions how giant tree trunks were used as battering rams against Iberian fortifications. The long process of deforestation started about this time, as trees were cut down both for use as fuel and for timber to feed the insatiable appetite of Roman mining. Later, other activities contributed to the consequent erosion of the topsoil. We know that the entire Ebro delta, about 300 square kilometres, has been formed by eroded deposits over the past 1,600 years.

Major gold mines lay in the north-west, especially at Las Médulas de Caruseco, where the Romans left pyramids of slag 50 metres high. Asturcia (Astorga) became a kind of early-day gold rush town, swarming with both free and slave workers. At many mines the shafts were so cramped that miners had to work on their hands and knees, putting ore into esparto baskets hanging around their necks. Slave labour was vital to the empire, and slaves formed a sizable part of Hispania's population of about seven million. Slaves had an average life expectancy of about thirty years, while free workers could expect to live to the ripe age of forty.

AT FIRST, PEOPLE of mixed Roman and Iberian blood were so unusual it meant a special status. There was even a colony founded at Carteia, near Algeciras, for the offspring of legionnaires and local women. The distinctions gradually vanished, as Roman and *hispani* became one people.

The one Roman institution that changed least over the centuries was the family. The father demanded and received absolute and unquestioning obedience from his wife and children, and family unity formed the bedrock of Hispanic society, just as it does today. The emperor in turn regarded his subjects as children, and the state granted privileges and protection only to the well-behaved. Rulers supplied "bread and circuses" to keep the masses content, and the system worked remarkably well.

Hispano-Romans considered worship as an excuse for communal gaiety, and enjoyed great processions and games in honour of the gods. There were so many holidays, in fact, that critics charged they were seriously interfering with normal affairs. The festive calendar opened in March, with the re-dedication of the vestal flame and the clanging of sacred shields at the temple of Mars. The same month also witnessed the festival of Liberalia, a time of unrestrained merriment. April was crowded with activities, climaxing in a festival to honour the goddess Flora, during which both men and women donned flower-adorned garb. December was another month of wild, wine-filled festivities.

The infamous Roman feasts *did* occur in much the way we are told, with course after course of rich food served to reclining guests. Often a bath and massage came after the first round of courses to stimulate the appetite. (However, reports of "vomitoriums", where guests would induce vomiting in order to make room for more food, were undoubtedly invented by Christians to prove Roman decadence.) The elaborate Roman baths were mini-cities dedicated to leisure and pleasure. Besides baths and steam rooms, there were gardens, shops, restaurants, reading rooms, art galleries, swimming pools, rooms for wrestling or gambling and, of course, prostitutes of both sexes.

Gladiatorial contests were the most popular diversion. Under the emperor Domitian, women battled dwarfs to the death and spectators thrilled at seeing people being torn apart by wild animals. The games followed an established ritual; according to accepted custom, the loser of an encounter was always stabbed in the throat, and even the way he presented his neck for the thrust was taught at gladiatorial school. Later, an attendant used a hot poker to make sure the gladiator was dead. However, contrary to legend, the crowd did not point thumbs down to demand the loser's execution; scholars say thumbs down meant "throw down your sword," which saved the defeated from death.

Legitimate theatre provided less brutal entertainment, but had suffered a decline in status since the Greeks. Playwrights and actors were no longer held in high regard; indeed, an acting company was known as a *grex*, the same word used for a flock of sheep. Performances were given in vulgar Latin, the common language which was quite unlike the literary Latin of Cicero or Virgil.

One Spanish-born master of the language was Seneca the Elder, a famed instructor of rhetoric. His son, Lucius Seneca, was born in Corduba, a centre of Roman intellectual life. The young Seneca moved to Rome, where he served as Nero's private tutor and a kind of imperial ghostwriter, composing speeches for the emperor. But no man could survive so close to Nero, and in the end trumped-up charges of treason led to an order that Seneca slash his own wrists and bleed to death, aristocratic style.

Seneca the Younger was a brilliant philosopher and writer who expounded the ideas of Stoicism, by which an individual sought to transcend the restraints of pain and pleasure, happiness and woe, in order to free the spirit. He was known for his pithy remarks, such as: "Spain was Christian perhaps before Christ." His views about such matters as slavery were remarkably liberal, and it has been suggested that he was secretly a Christian himself.

Other writers born in Hispania during the first century helped create Spain's "Silver Age" of literature. Seneca's nephew Lucan was an erudite historian who wrote an epic poem about the war between Caesar and Pompey which seemed to defend the Republic. This got him into hot water with Nero, and he suffered the same fate as his uncle.

The poet Martial was born near Caesar Augusta (Zaragoza), but left Hispania for sophisticated Rome. He is remembered for his satiric epigrams about the licentious life of Roman high society. They range from sweet to scathing, such as:

> It is very strange, as it seems to me,
> that you and your wife should not agree,
> since each is as vile as vile can be.

Martial returned to his native land to retire in peace, and his later poems reflect the tranquility of country life during the idyllic days of the Pax Romana. He penned an adage for all ages: "Live today, for tomorrow will be too late."

DURING THE FIRST century came an event of monumental significance: the arrival of Christianity to Iberia. Popular legend says that Saint James the Elder (Santiago), believed to be the half-brother of Christ, brought Christianity to the peninsula around AD 40. Reaching Zaragoza, he built a temple to the holy virgin, who had appeared to him above a marble pillar. The *virgen de pilar* became the inspiration for naming countless Spanish girls "Pilar."

According to tradition, James spent seven years spreading the faith, then returned to Palestine, where he was beheaded during a wave of persecutions. Later, his remains were supposedly carried back by his followers to Campus Stellae in the far north-west of Hispania, today called Santiago de Compostela. Although no historical evidence confirms any of this, the story forms an important chapter in Spain's national heritage. It is more likely that St. Paul visited

Hispania, but most historians think that Christianity really arrived, ironically, via North Africa.

Whichever way the faith came, its seeds fell on fertile soil, thirsty for mystical ideals so lacking in Roman religion.

It would be a mistake to think that Christianity spread quickly; the process took two centuries, with urban workers first to convert. The country folk were slower to give up the old ways. The very word "pagan" derives from Latin and means "peasant" that is, one who lives in a *pagus* (village). As late as the seventh century, many country districts remained stubbornly pagan. The eternally hard-headed Basques were the last to convert.

Tales of martyrdom have been exaggerated; at first the new church was too insignificant to receive much official attention. But some notable Iberian exceptions include St. Vincent, who taunted his tormentors as they stretched him on the rack, and St. Engracia, who had her breasts ripped off and her liver cut out and fed to birds. St. Eulalia was only 13 when she arrived at Mérida eager for martyrdom. She burst into the governor's chambers and shouted "The old gods are worthless and the emperor himself is nothing." For her efforts the young girl had her body torn apart with hot pincers. According to legend she continued to sing out triumphantly and her spirit, in the form of a white dove, flew out of her mouth and up to heaven.

For circus-loving crowds, Christian martyrs were a new sort of athlete, "running on hot coals as if on roses, plunging into fires as if into streams of cool water, and garlanding themselves with tortures as if they were spring flowers," in the words of St. John Chrysostom.

The official Roman religion provided no doctrine or moral code, no promise of an afterlife, and no mystical aspects. Thus, it is not surprising that Christianity found converts in Rome and her provinces. But for centuries it had to compete with other religions from the east. Mithraism from Persia was the strongest rival. Mithras was a divine figure representing the sun and was always pictured as a young man stabbing a bull; initiation rites involved the sacrificial killing of a bull. Women were excluded from the religion, which became immensely popular with soldiers. Temples to Mithras sprouted throughout the empire.

The spot on which Mérida's bullring stands today was once a temple to Mithras. Here, legionnaires were anointed with the still steaming blood of slaughtered bulls, which they believed made them invincible in battle. (You can draw your own conclusions about the origins of bullfighting.)

Another eastern cult eagerly adopted by Hispano-Romans revolved around Bacchus, god of wine. The rites often degenerated into drunken orgies. Equally sensational was the cult of Cybele, the great mother-goddess. A complex pageantry swirled around her, such as processions of the faithful accompanied by drums, flutes and cymbals. There were scenes of self-flagellation and, on the "day of blood", novice priests performed their own castration. The finale was a literal bloodbath, when devotees sat in holes and were showered with blood from a slaughtered bull lying on the grating above.

Christianity and its rivals borrowed liberally from one another. The priests of Cybele celebrated the vernal equinox to compete with Easter, and the bull sacrifice took on aspects of the slaughter of the Christian lamb. The followers of Mithras celebrated December 25 as marking the sun's rebirth and the beginning of the end to winter.

Even today, it seems at times that Spaniards never really gave up their pagan heritage, but have welded old rituals to their own version of Christianity. Thus, we have dazzling Easter processions of virgin queens and hooded penitents whipping themselves, and wild, wine-sodden parties mobbed by hysterical devotees, such as the procession of the virgin at El Rocio near Huelva. Many saint's-day celebrations end with a *corrida* , when six bulls are slaughtered in an elaborate ritual that the word "bullfight" does not adequately describe.

ROMANIZATION WAS NOT a one-way affair, and before long Hispania began to influence Rome itself. Trajan (Marcus Ulpius Traianus), born in Italica, became the first Roman emperor from the provinces. Under Trajan Rome reached its greatest extent, an area about the same as the United States with a population of over 100 million and 300,000 kilometres of roads. Every centimetre of the Mediterranean shore belonged to Rome.

Trajan became emperor in AD 99 and ruled for 18 years. He was broad-shouldered and had an intelligent look, brows furrowed as if he was deep in thought. Trajan was known as an artist and lover of the arts, and he oversaw magnificent public works and monuments. But, as a soldier, Trajan believed Rome was getting soft for the lack of good enemies, and he vowed to revive military virtues. He personally led expeditions of conquest and was the first (and last) emperor to navigate the Persian Gulf.

On his deathbed Trajan adopted Hadrian, another Hispano-Roman, as his son and heir. Also from Italica, Hadrian was married to Sabina, the emperor's niece. He was fair-skinned, curly haired, and wore a beard — the first emperor to do so. His moderate temperament and feeble health made him very different from the energetic Trajan. It was said that Hadrian's curious accent, typical of southern Spain at the time, caused laughter in the senate. While other emperors might have lopped off a few heads, the proud Hadrian studied Latin intensively instead and became a great orator.

In Hadrian's time, Roman conquest had ceased and defence was largely unnecessary. Notable exceptions, of course, were the construction of Hadrian's Wall in Britain and the brutal suppression of a revolt in Palestine, which marked the end of the Jewish state for almost two millennia. Jews were scattered throughout the Roman world. Thousands of families settled in Hispania.

Hadrian encouraged the arts and public building and even dallied in architecture himself. This was truly Rome's Golden Age in Hispania, climaxing with such stunning achievements as the Alcantara bridge over the Tajo River, in the high country near Cáceres, and a 24-kilometre-long aqueduct serving Tarraco.

The Romans built to impress, and they succeeded. Their builders were successful, thanks to the versatility and strength of the arch and the fact that their mortar did not buckle under stress. They used a particularly effective blend of sandy earth called *pozzolana* and lime (with a dash of pork fat and the milk of figs) to create a quicklime unsurpassed until the 19th century. With these twin strengths they could build major structures like the amphitheatre at Italica, which seated 30,000 spectators.

Just as Mérida is a town of the Augustan age, so Italica is of the Hadrianic. It lay next to an important port until the Baetis River changed its course and trade moved to nearby Hispalis, site of modern Sevilla. (Hispalis-Sevilla was much closer to the Atlantic in Roman times, before the Guadalquivir delta was formed.) Italica was transformed by its native son into a showcase of Roman architecture, and its ruins reflect the city as Hadrian rebuilt it around the year 125. In its heyday Italica boasted wide streets, rows of mansions (one with 40 rooms), public baths, and the fourth largest amphitheatre in the Roman world. You can still peer down into the arena (the name "arena" comes from the Latin word for "sand," which was used to soak up the blood that flowed so profusely there). Below it are the chambers where Christians and other prisoners huddled in fear before being tossed to the lions.

Italica's arena reminds us of the dark side of the Pax Romana, when power and cruelty became perversely equated, and the axe and rods (the *fasces* resurrected in our time by Italian fascists) were the symbols of authority. Those not in lock-step with the Roman way might be flogged, crucified, burned or buried alive, hurled from a cliff, drowned in a sack, fed to wild beasts, or worse.

Although thousands of Christians perished in Spanish arenas, the Romans could not kill the new religion; it was a force to be reckoned with by the end of the second century. Finally legalized by Constantine, himself a convert, it later became the empire's official religion. Christianity had come a long way since the crucifixion of a humble carpenter's son three centuries earlier.

The year 248 marked the 1000th anniversary of Rome's founding; it also marked the beginning of Roman decline. Chinks in the imperial armour were beginning to appear, signs that the Pax Romana, like all things, must have an end as well as a beginning. To shore up the crumbling empire, Constantine later moved his capital east to the Bosphorus and the ancient city of Byzantium (present-day Istanbul), far from Hispania.

Archaeologists tell us that Spanish towns were already building massive walls against attackers by the third century. The Roman walls in Barcelona's old quarter, for instance, were built to repel waves of Franks and Alemanni raiding in Hispania toward the end of the century, long before the main barbarian invasions came. And not all of Hispania's trouble came from the outside: there were peasant revolts and demands for regional autonomy; the provincial administration had become hopelessly corrupt; and the slave system, hence the entire economy, was breaking down under the influence of Christianity.

Christianity eventually became the unifying principle of the empire and finally a force of repression. Once it was established as the official religion, Christians began to root out heresies with a passion. Most serious was Arianism, which denied the concept of the Trinity. Bishop Hosius from Córdoba led the battle against it and was one of the fathers of the Nicene Creed (325), the cornerstone of Roman Catholicism. (It's little known that at age 99 he himself accepted Arianism.)

A uniquely Spanish heresy was expounded by Priscillian, the bishop of Avila. He claimed that the world had been created by the devil and was ruled by him, and that life was a punishment for sinful souls. Its founder was decapitated, but his heresy survived for three centuries. Priscillianism allowed dancing in the church ritual, a practice that survives in the "dance of the Seises" held during Corpus Christi at the Sevilla Cathedral.

At the end of the Roman era another Spanish-born emperor, Flavius Theodosius, banned all forms of paganism, outlawing the olympic games, squelching heresy, burning temples, and behaving in a quite un-Christian manner. By then, Rome's power was just a memory. On his deathbed in 395, Theodosius divided the once-invincible empire into two sections ruled by his two sons, one in Constantinople, the other in Rome. Just 14 years later, Hispania would fall to rampaging barbarians from the north, who slammed shut the book on six centuries of Roman rule.

The eastern incarnation of the empire survived as Byzantium until a generation before Columbus, who arrived on the scene to unwittingly launch the successor to the glory that was Rome — the Spanish Empire. Indeed, Rome's two most important legacies — language and religion — form the core of *hispanidad* (Spanish civilization and culture) which pervades most of *Latin* America down to this day.

## SIGHTS & SITES

**Alcántara** (*Cáceres*) *Arched bridge 194 mts. long and 70 high (highest in Roman world) over Tajo river.*

**Ampurias** (*Gerona*): *Costa Brava's major historical attraction with ruins of old houses; traces of plaza and amphitheatre.*

**Baelo-Bolonia** (*Cádiz*): *Near Tarifa, remnants of large fish salting enterprise; temples dedicated to Juno, Jupiter, and Minerva.*

**Barcelona:** *Archaeological Museum has many artifacts from Roman Ampurias; defensive wall in the Barrio Gótico is partially Roman.*

**Carmona** (*Sevilla*): *Main attraction is a huge necropolis of 800 tombs, some just delicate urns filled with ashes.*

**Itálica** (*Sevilla*): *Excellent museum; ruins of one of the largest arenas outside Rome; network of streets.*

**Mallorca** (*Balearic Islands*): *Ruins of theatre at Alcudia near Cabo Formentor; artifacts from Pollentia at Bellver Castle in Palma.*

**Mérida** (*Badajoz*): *Temples, theatre, two aqueducts, arches, Guadiana bridge, museum of Roman art.*

**Sagunto** (*Valencia*): *Site of ancient Saguntum features variety of ruins.*

**Salamanca:** *Called Salamantica by Romans; well-preserved bridge over the Tormes River.*

**Segovia***: The world-famous aqueduct is an inspiring sight.*

**Sevilla:** *Archaeological Museum with pieces from Italica, including Mercury with winged sandals and a bust of emperor Trajan.*

**Soria***: Museum of Numantia dedicated to famous last stand.*

**Tarragona** *: Ruins of walls and amphitheatre; museum includes superb mosaic Head of Medusa; outside town are triumphal Arch of Bera, the Tower of the Escipiones (a two-tiered aqueduct), and the Mausoleum of Centcelles.*

CHAPTER 3

# MEDIEVAL SPAIN

T he view of Toledo from the far bank of the Tajo River stirs images of savage sieges and heroic defenders. A deep gorge nearly encircles the granite rock on which the city stands, and the sheer cliffs dropping to the river make other defences redundant on three sides. It is not surprising that the Visigoths chose this imposing site, an important Celtiberian and Roman stronghold, as their capital.

What *is* surprising, however, is the almost total absence of Visigothic remnants in Toledo and in Spain generally. A rough-hewn country church, a few pieces of jewelry or a regal crown sitting in a seldom-visited museum, an obscure law code... these are the legacies of *three centuries* of Gothic Spain.

In Toledo, guides will point to the spot where King Roderick deflowered the lovely daughter of a count whose vengeance would bring the Moors to Spain. But the place and the story itself are highly suspect. The Visigoths (or West Goths) seem destined to inhabit a murky region sandwiched between the Romans and Moors, the Spanish version of the Dark Ages.

There is something oddly fascinating about this Germanic race so ill-at-ease in Latin Spain and their peculiar kings with strange names — Witteric, Wamba, Wittiza, Chindasuinth.

Of 34 Visigoth kings only 15 died of natural causes. Atawulf, the first in a dismal line of succession, was killed at the urging of Sigeric, who reigned for just one week before he in turn fell at the hands of Walia. The path to the throne bounced from elective to hereditary and back again, but the issue often became moot as regicide came like clockwork. Between the years 531 and 555 alone, four successive kings were murdered. Among them was one notoriously amorous monarch, who was enjoying dinner when the lights suddenly were extinguished and a dozen sword thrusts from outraged husbands and fathers ended his life.

Despite the chaos and confusion, the Visigoths for a time boasted the largest and strongest kingdom in western Europe. The shaky unity they finally achieved was Spain's first attempt to become a unified nation. Yet Gothic accomplishments in Spain proved inconsequential: the large- scale herding of animals, the horseshoe arch, a few dozen surviving words are their legacy. Among the Germanic words that entered both English and Spanish: *werra* (war/*guerra*), *raubon* (to rob/ *robar*), *helm* (helmet/*yelmo*), and *harpa* (harp/*arpa*).

The Goths' apparent lack of significance is misleading, however. Ortega y Gasset, one of Spain's foremost modern thinkers, went so far as to blame most of his country's later political ills on them. They were barbarians, he said, but even worse they were *weak* barbarians, who never achieved any stability and never introduced the feudal institutions found in the rest of Europe. Spain was being "different" for the first time.

THE GOTHIC CHAPTER opens in 409 with the first arrival of the legendary blond barbarians from the north, trying to grab slices of the splintering Roman empire. The Suevi (Swabians) from the upper Danube and the infamous Vandals from the Vistula River area swarmed across the Pyrenees. According to one story, these tribes were invited by a Roman general making a personal bid for power, but, as barbarians will do, they soon got out of hand. Within a short time they had overrun the peninsula with virtually no opposition, not even in Cantabria, which had held off Rome for two centuries. The Suevi headed for Galicia and the Vandals landed in the south. In fact, the name Andalucia could derive from the Berber for "land of the Vandals".

Rome itself was sacked in 410 by another barbarian horde of Teutonic persuasion, the Visigoths. These flaxen-haired warriors dressed in skins had moved down slowly from the Baltic region (perhaps Gotland) and settled in Transylvania and the Danube basin. From there they began to nibble away at the crumbling empire. Under Alaric, they violated Rome itself, the first time in eight centuries that a hostile army entered the eternal city.

The emperor was spared, however, and soon allied his tottering dominions with these Goths, the most "civilized" of all the barbarians. Rome's last- ditch defensive plan involved pitting one tribe against another, and the Goths under Atawulf were signed on to rid Hispania of other invaders. In return, they would receive lands in southern France and become senior partners in a Roman confederation. The plan seemed to work: after scattering Rome's enemies in short order, they returned north of the Pyrenees and formed a Gothic nation with its capital at Toulouse.

While the defeated Vandals were busy licking their wounds, an invitation arrived from yet another rebellious Roman general asking them to fight for him in North Africa. After crossing the sea in Roman ships, about 80,000 Vandals settled in what are today Morocco and Algeria. Meanwhile, the Suevi set up a kingdom in the north-west of Iberia which would survive for another 180 years.

Goths continued to trickle slowly into the peninsula, but the floodgates really opened when the last remnants of the empire at Rome fell in 476. Gothic King Euric and his son Alaric suddenly found themselves ruling over the largest political unit in western Europe, stretching from the Loire River to the Pillars of Hercules. When shortly after the upstart Franks pushed the Goths out of Gaul, Hispania became their new power base. But although they were in the majority at court, Goths numbered about 200,000 — mostly in the rural interior — compared with several million Hispano-Romans. Like oil and water, they would not mix. During most of the period, the two races lived separately, both legally and socially.

Nevertheless, Gothic laws did not try to subjugate the *hispani* other than with an onerous tax system. Indeed, these most Romanized of barbarians seemed awed and intimidated by the legacies of their predecessors. Euric's law was written in Latin and drafted by Roman lawyers; Goths used Roman coins; even their gravestones were inscribed in Latin. They lived in Roman cities because there were no Gothic ones. The *hispani* kept their own governors and town councils.

A major difference between the two peoples was religion. The Goths had adopted the Arian view of Christianity (which denied the Trinity) and came to think of it as their own, while Hispanics practiced the "Roman religion." Feelings ran high, and when one king failed to convert his new bride, a Frankish princess, he ordered that cow dung be poured over her on her way to church. While Catholics and Arians feuded, pagan practices survived in the countryside. Priests fought in vain to stamp out the dances and bawdy songs of pagan crowds on saint's days, and many " Christians" still considered Thursday to be Jupiter's Day and refused to work.

Hispano-Romans looked with disdain on their overlords. To these urbane people the Goths, with their long locks and gaudy jewelry, seemed illiterate, primitive, and warlike, country bumpkins with unusual customs and harsh laws. For example, tampering with public documents brought 200 lashes, a shaved head, and amputation of the right thumb; conviction of homosexuality meant castration while rape was punished less severely — with public circumcision. Another curious legal custom was the "ordeal of hot water," by which those accused of theft were questioned while being submerged in boiling water. Confessions were fast and frequent.

Capital punishment fell on "magicians, makers of spells, anyone invoking storms to damage the grape harvest or demons to make men mad, and on those who inquire into the future or offer sacrifices by night." Such laws did not go down well among free-spirited city dwellers along the coast, who looked to Rome and Byzantium, certainly not Toledo, as models of civilization.

This spirit of independence did not bode well for Gothic hopes of controlling the peninsula, and by the middle of the 6th century Byzantine armies were threatening to retake Spain for the empire based in Constantinople. In an effort to restore lands of the old Roman Empire, Justinian led a series of successful forays against the Vandals of North Africa, climaxing with the conquest of *Septum* (Ceuta) in a key position on the Straits of Gibraltar.

A few years later Byzantines landed in southern Spain, where they allied with a myriad of factions — anyone opposing the current king, Catholics, and the bulk of coastal residents who traditionally resented the Goths. The invaders established important posts at Málaga and Cartagena to serve as bridgeheads for the reconquest of Spain.

This "second coming" did materialize, and they succeeded in taking over most of the south and the eastern coast plus the Balearic Islands in a new Byzantine province called *Spania*. This little-known occupation lasted about 75 years and brought Greek and near-eastern culture to Spain. Many priests went to Constantinople to study Greek, once again the literary language of the educated. Indeed, there was more cultural contact between Spain and the imperial capital than with France, which was wallowing in medieval squalor at the time. Yet little remains of the Byzantine period, other than some scattered artwork and the ruins of a few churches.

Gothic control of the peninsula was also compromised by the sizable Suevian kingdom in the north-west, which was like a tick on the back of the government in Toledo. Then there were the Basques, who were never conquered and at one point even invaded the Gothic domain, sweeping down the Ebro Valley to the Mediterranean before retiring.

The Suevi were finally conquered during the reign of king Leovigild, considered the greatest of all Visigothic rulers despite his rabid persecution of Catholics (including his own martyr son, St. Hermenegild). Among other things, he established a truly regal court at Toledo, annulled the ban on marriage between Goths and Hispano-Romans (it had been a capital crime), and crushed a rebellion in Cantabria.

Leovigild tried to make the monarchy hereditary (rather than elective) by passing the crown to his son Reccared, who turned out to be a crucial figure in his own right. With great flourish he converted to Catholicism, burned all Arian books he could find, and united the kingdom under one religion. This concept of national unity stemming from religious unity later became fundamental to Spanish political thought. Toledo became the religious (as well as political) capital of Spain, an honour it retains to this day, and a crucial alliance formed between the monarchy and the church against the nobility. The clergy thereafter wielded substantial political power and were given control of education to boot.

The trend toward unification spilled over into the cultural arena as well, as the border between Gothic and Hispanic styles and customs became less rigidly defined. The Goths felt threatened and insisted on keeping both their language and their distance from the natives, but inevitably fell under the power of the superior Roman-Latin culture. Although archaeological evidence is slim, it appears they adopted Roman and Byzantine styles with gusto, as seen in artefacts such as the treasure of Guarrazar or the magnificent crown of Reccesuinth.

The Goths had their own smiths and potters, but could not boast architects, sculptors, or painters. It is ironic that the word "gothic" came to describe the splendid architectural style seen in churches built hundreds of years later, a style unknown to the Goths. The word itself came to mean "barbaric and uncouth," and Renaissance architects, enamoured with the classical style, sneered at the late-medieval cathedrals as crude and ugly, in other words "gothic." The name stuck.

The cultural intermingling is seen in St. Isidore (560-636), the era's leading intellectual figure. He is known for a history of the Goths as well as theological writings, but his father was governor of Cartagena and may well have been Byzantine, not Gothic. Isidore expounded the glories of Roman civilization and universalism as preserved through Christianity and compiled a renowned encyclopedia that could be found in nearly every European monastery. Unfortunately, he also wrote the first anti-Jewish treatise in the West, and one of his pupils, King Sisebut, decreed that Jews must accept conversion or leave — another common refrain throughout Spanish history. Those who refused to convert moved to North Africa, and at the time of the Moorish invasion a hundred years later their descendants had not forgotten what the Goths had done.

After decades of skirmishes the Byzantines were finally pushed out in 624, and at long last Goths ruled the *entire* peninsula with the exception of the Basque lands. The peninsula had one ruler, something that did not occur again until the reign of Felipe (Philip) II a thousand years later. The Goths replaced the old Roman system of provincial government with their own. But these advances were only straws in the wind; the seventh century witnessed a progressive collapse of the social order which would climax in the crucial year of 711, when the Moors changed Spain forever.

In essence, very few people felt any allegiance to the crown. The monarchy faced chronic revolts by generals and bishops, popular local uprisings, and economic disruption and chaos. In addition, massive numbers of escaped slaves were roaming the kingdom. (The Catholic Church was the largest slave-holder.) When the monarchy attributed its troubles to a "Jewish conspiracy," savage anti-semitic riots broke out, leading to hundreds of deaths. To make matters worse, a *real* invasion plot hatched between Jews and Moors was discovered; tales of conspiracy had fulfilled themselves and repression was turned up a notch.

TO UNDERSTAND THE TIMES, it must be remembered that throughout history Spaniards have lived in fear of invasions and piracy from North Africa. The Goths were no exception and had very good reasons for concern. In 675, the Moors made a half-hearted attempt to invade the peninsula, but were turned back before they could disembark.

Who were these Moors who would rewrite Spanish history so profoundly? The word derives from the Latin *mauri*, a name for the Berber tribes living in Roman *Mauretania* (roughly modern Algeria and Morocco). Although the name "Moors" has no real ethnographic meaning, it can be used to refer to all Muslims, Berber or Arab, who conquered the Iberian peninsula. If nothing else, these Moors were religious fanatics. Islam had swept across North Africa and within a generation of Mohammed's death it had reached the far west at Tingis (Tangier). Here the Arab vanguard encountered Byzantine colonies and native Berbers, that mysterious race which resisted from their mountain strongholds until Arab general Musa finally triumphed.

In response to the failed Moorish invasion of 675, Gothic King Wamba made the mistake of calling up priests for military service. His reign came to an abrupt end when the clergy joined a band of hostile nobles led by Ervigius. Wamba was drugged and while unconscious the rebels dressed him like a monk and shaved his head. When the king awoke he was so embarrassed he did not even dispute the naked power grab, and Ervigius became king. The final crisis of Gothic Spain erupted a few years later, when King Witiza tried to pass on the throne to his son Achila. The nobles elected their own man, Roderick by name, and thrust the peninsula into a civil war that ended with Roderick seated on the throne.

That same year (710) Musa sent 400 Moors under Tarif to reconnoiter the soft Iberian underbelly. They landed at the spot closest to Africa, today site of Tarifa. The Moors returned with both information and booty, including "women of rare beauty." But Musa still had doubts about a full-scale invasion that involved crossing the sea. Arab commanders felt far more comfortable in the desert, "an ocean where no oar is dipped," according to the Koran.

From the very beginning Moorish Spain is cloaked in myths and legends, a kind of rosy romantic haze akin to "A Thousand and One Nights." Thus we hear the story of lovely Florinda, a patrician girl at the royal court whose feminine charms nearly drove Roderick to madness. The stricken king would hide in the bushes while Florinda bathed in the Tajo, and one day he was finally overcome with desire and took the beautiful maiden right on the river bank.

Florinda's father was Count Julian, the Byzantine governor of Septum (Ceuta) on the African side of the strait. Julian came to fetch his daughter, and as they left the king, unaware that his crime was known, asked Julian to send him a certain breed of African hawk. The count promised to send hawks such as the king never dreamed of. According to the story, Julian then approached the Moors with an invasion plan. There may be some truth to this yarn, but the real count, whose name was probably Olian Olban, may merely have made a pragmatic deal with Musa to save his own skin. Some evidence also points to supporters of the ousted Prince Achila as the culprits in inviting the Moors into Spain. They believed that after deposing Roderick and taking some booty, the invaders would leave.

Whatever the truth, Musa ordered Tariq ibn-Ziyad (the prefix *ibn* means "son of"), governor of Tangier, to mount another reconnaissance mission. This time about 10,000 men made the trip. The Moors were still not thinking of staying; only later did they realize that no riper plum awaited plucking than Gothic Spain.

"You must know how the Grecian maidens, as handsome as houris, their necks glittering with innumerable pearls and jewels, their bodies clothed with tunics of costly silks and sprinkled with gold, are awaiting your arrival, reclining on soft couches in the sumptuous palaces of crowned lords and princes..." So spoke the Arab Tariq to his mostly Berber troops on the eve of their departure for Spain.

In April of 711 they landed at ancient Calpe, the limestone mass they called *jabal-tariq* (Tariq's rock), or Gibraltar. The attack caught Roderick off guard, but he rushed from the far north with an army of questionable loyalty to do battle with the Moors. In July, the two forces met somewhere near the Guadalete River in south-western Andalucia in a confused encounter in which followers of Achila, including the bishop of Sevilla, fought alongside the Moors.

Roderick's army was annihilated after a large number of his troops changed sides in mid-battle, and the king himself vanished. As the dust cleared, all that could be found was his white charger with its gilded saddle adorned with rubies and emeralds, his golden mantle embroidered with pearls, and one silver boot. According to another legend, Roderick escaped and was rescued by an old hermit. The dying king gave his last confession and was absolved on the condition that he lie entombed with a serpent until his soul departed. Roderick agreed and was last heard uttering faintly, "Now he is gnawing, gnawing me in the part where I most sinned."

Thus commenced the Moorish chapter of Spanish history, several centuries during which most of the peninsula experienced a significantly different development from the rest of Europe. It was a traumatic period in which a new religion, language, and culture were stamped on the land. This culture became so imbedded in the Hispanic mentality that it ceased to be alien; in fact, many natives willingly became Muslims. Spain was being "different" again.

Two centuries after the conquest, Al-Andalus (as the Moors called Spain) was Europe's cultural capital, glittering in a medieval sky with few stars. But the Moors also destroyed the burgeoning, albeit feeble, Gothic unity and left a legacy of separatism and strife that poisoned Spain for centuries. If it was the best of times in some cultural areas, the worst has too easily been forgotten.

After his victory, Tariq gave orders that a group of prisoners be cut to pieces and their flesh boiled in cauldrons. The rest of the captured Goths were released and told to spread the word of Moorish methods. The tactic worked, and token resistance melted away. Tariq spent the winter of 711 in Toledo, the old Visigoth capital.

Perhaps a bit jealous of his underling's remarkable success, Musa himself led another wave across the straits the following summer, mostly Arabs this time. The Goths made their last desperate stand at Mérida, and remnants of their broken army fled to Asturias, where they joined tough local defenders to form the nucleus of the Christian Reconquest. But that was yet to come. In just a few years the Moors swept over most of the peninsula and into southern France, only to be stopped by the Franks under Charles Martel at the battle of Poitiers (732). But Hispania now belonged to the caliph at Damascus, capital of the Muslim world.

The Moors' easy conquest has puzzled historians, especially Spaniards suckled on stories of Viriathus and Numantia. The answer seems to lie in the basic weakness of the Visigoth state and the lingering hostility among Hispano-Romans toward their Germanic rulers. "Old Spaniards" naively believed that the Moors would fill their sacks with loot and be gone. Oppressed classes such as Jews and serfs had reason to celebrate the Goths' demise and to welcome the invaders. Jews in particular aided the Moors, and memories of this collaboration (Count Julian himself was suspected of being Jewish) cropped up throughout the Reconquest.

The Moors' Al-Andalus encompassed all the peninsula except for the extreme north-west. As this territory shrank over the centuries the name was retained, and the last area of Moorish occupation became Andalucia. The word's origin is not clear, but Berbers called this the "land of the Vandals,"*Tamurt Wandalus.* Al-Andalus is possibly a corruption.

According to Muslim legend, when Allah was creating the earth and dealing out good and bad, each place was given five wishes. The land of Al-Andalus asked for a clear sky, a beautiful sea full of fishes, ripe fruit and fair women. All these were granted, but a fifth wish — for good government — was refused because that would have created paradise on earth.

The first Moorish descriptions reveal astonishment and admiration for the new land: the luxury of its kings, the wealth and monuments (chiefly Roman) of its cities, especially Sevilla. General Musa travelled to Damascus with an entourage of captured Spanish women and told the caliph tales of thirty thousand captured virgins and phenomenal wealth such as Solomon's Table, made of solid gold and studded with hundreds of rubies. He also remarked that the most striking thing about the Goths was the "effeminacy of the princes." (Three decades later, St. Boniface blamed the Goths' quick fall on their "moral degeneracy and homosexual practices.") Musa arrived at the wrong time, however, and became immersed in a power struggle following the caliph's death. He was arrested by the new caliph and spent his last days in a filthy Arab prison dreaming of Al-Andalus.

Back in Spain, his son had taken the vanquished king Roderick's widow as his wife (as was Muslim custom) and named himself governor of the conquered lands. But he too was swept away by events and decapitated in Sevilla; his head was sent to Damascus to remind others of the pitfalls of ambition. Indeed, from the very outset the Moors became entangled in seemingly endless internal squabbles between rival Arab tribes and between the elitist Arab leaders and their Berber henchmen, who were treated as inferiors. The two leading Arab factions, the Yemenites and Kaishites, crushed a Berber revolt, then turned on each other in an orgy of massacres and assassinations.

This civil strife helps explain why the Moors did not conquer the entire peninsula in those first years. If they had done so, the Reconquest might never have developed and Spain would be a Muslim nation today. Instead, a shadowy figure named Pelayo led a band of Asturian mountaineers and Gothic survivors to the first Christian victory.

It was a *crucial* turning point in Spanish history.

Moorish historians relate how, after years of fighting, only thirty men remained of Pelayo's army, living like wild beasts on honey in the mountains. Finally the weary Moors retired, saying "What harm can thirty savage asses do to us?" But from the cave of Covadonga (where a shrine stands today), Pelayo organized resistance that culminated with the battle of Covadonga in about 720.

According to Christian reports, 400,000 Muslims were miraculously killed when all the weapons they hurled flew back at them. In fact, Pelayo defeated a small marauding band in a skirmish. Nonetheless, the seeds of the Reconquest were planted at Covadonga. The "savage ass" named Pelayo also helped create a great dynasty when his daughter married a local chieftain named Alfonso, founder of the kingdom of Asturias. Alfonso I reigned 18 years and won back extensive territory; by his death (757) the Christians occupied about one-quarter of the peninsula. To honour this role as cradle of the nation, the heir to the Spanish throne is called Prince of Asturias, the equivalent of Britain's Prince of Wales.

The small fortress-kingdom with its back to the coast welcomed refugees from the south and assumed the role of defender of Christian civilization. Between the Moors and Christians lay wide strips of uninhabited land called *marcas* ("marches").

It is far from the truth to imagine Moorish Spain as ruled and inhabited by Arabs. Although many Arabs, mostly Syrians, occupied high positions, the bulk of the Muslims were Berbers. Later, converted Christians called *muwallads*, together with the offspring of the first waves of invaders, formed the nucleus of Moorish Spain. (The invaders brought no women, hence the second generation of Moors was already half Hispanic.)

Another misconception about Moorish Spain is that the Muslims vigorously tried to convert Christians and other "infidels," by sword point if need be. Many, possibly the majority of Hispanics, converted by choice and slowly adopted Arabic as their language. Moreover, Muslims allowed both Christians and Jews, as "people of the Book," to practice their religions if they submitted to Moorish rule. Every non-Muslim had to pay a special tax — one good reason for tolerance. This attitude lasted until the arrival of fanatical sects from North Africa three centuries later. Forced conversions, pogroms, and deportations are largely the legacy of Christian Spain, not Moorish.

AFTER THE FIRST forty volatile years following 711, Al-Andalus cried out for order and unity. It arrived in the person of Abd-er-Rahman, called "the Wanderer," who would transform this mere province of Damascus into an independent state that would become the cultural light of Europe. This Syrian prince and future emir was one of those rare individuals who crop up every few generations. He was tall, fair-haired (almost red-headed) and considered handsome although he had only one eye.

When he was 19, the Umaiyad dynasty to which he belonged was overthrown and massacred by the Abbasids, descendants of the Prophet's cousin. Abd-er-Rahman escaped miraculously and made his way across North Africa, driven by a sense of destiny based on a prophesy that Al-Andalus would be conquered by one who had (as he did) two curls of hair falling across his forehead. His mother had been a Berber slave in the caliph's harem, and he settled with her tribe upon reaching Morocco. Then, after encouragement from a pro-Umaiyad faction across the strait, he landed at Almuñecar south of Granada in August of 755 and rallied his supporters. Within a year he had crushed the opposition and was proclaimed Emir (commander) of Al-Andalus.

Abd-er-Rahman I ruled for 32 years. To protect his power he created an army of 40,000 Berbers and slaves from southern Europe. Threats from insurgents were soon smothered; the leaders' severed heads were filled with salt and myrrh, packed in boxes, covered with the Abbasid flag, and sent to Damascus. When they arrived, the caliph supposedly exclaimed, "Allah be praised, that the sea divides us from this devil."

In the year 777, the caliph bribed Frankish king Charlemagne into invading Spain, and an army led by his nephew Roland unsuccessfully attacked Zaragoza. Deprived of plunder, the Franks sacked Pamplona as they retreated through Roncesvalles Pass in the Pyrenees.

> "High are the hills, valleys dark and deep,
>   Grisly the rocks, and wondrous grim the steeps."

The pass is so described in the famous French epic poem *The Song of Roland*, which chronicles an attack on the retreating Franks. But contrary to the poem's version of history, the attack came not from the Moors, but from Basques outraged over the sacking of Pamplona. Roland and his men did not die for their faith, but from sheer greed. Moreover, the entire episode clearly shows that the struggle between two religions often played second fiddle to questions of power and money. After all, Charlemagne's army was fighting the Spanish Moors on behalf of the caliph of Damascus, not Christianity.

The caliph and his cavalry were too far away, however, and the dynasty started by Abd-er-Rahman would last almost three centuries. Many brutal rulers followed, but there were good ones too. The emir's son was a virtual saint, who dressed in simple clothes and personally visited the poor and infirm. Unfortunately, during the emirate's entire history (756-929) scarcely a generation passed without a major revolt or external attack.

Under Hakam I an uprising on the outskirts of Córdoba led to fierce repression which included the crucifixion of 300 rebels along the banks of the Guadalquivir. (The site is still called "the field of truth.") Those not killed were expelled, creating the nucleus of the Andalusian Quarter of Fez, Morocco, which still exists. Hakam also ordered the infamous Day of the Foss at Toledo. All local leaders suspected of disloyalty were tricked into entering the governor's castle, where they were beheaded one by one and their bodies thrown into a trench.

Hakam told his son: "Like the tailor who uses his needle to sew together pieces of cloth, so I used my sword to unite my divided provinces, for I have taken care that no rebel will disturb your slumbers." The son, Abd-er-Rahman II, was so nauseated by the blood-letting that he developed a nervous tic which caused him to blink his eyes constantly.

There were also threats from abroad. In 844, Norsemen (Vikings) suddenly appeared in "long ships" and started attacking ports along Iberia's Atlantic coast. From Galicia and Lisbon they crept south to the Guadalquivir, then up-river to Sevilla, where they went on a week-long binge of murder and pillage. Shortly after, the blonde intruders were defeated and limped back to sea with less than half their ships.

Reports of such battles are the stuff that remains as history, not the years or decades of peace between them. But clanging sabres are only part of the story. By the reign of Abd-er-Rahman II (822-852), the emirate was well established and the country prosperous. Al-Andalus was among the richest Mediterranean states, with flourishing farms, commerce, and culture. The emir himself was living proof of fecundity, having fathered 45 sons and 42 daughters, if we can believe Moorish chroniclers. His prized possession was the famous jeweled belt called *al-thu'ban* (the snake), which enjoyed a fascinating history down through the middle ages. Among its later owners were El Cid and Queen Isabel, who finally broke it up to help pay for the conquest of Granada.

Abd-er-Rahman II patronized philosophers and artists like Ziryab, a gifted musician and maker of royal tastes in ninth- century Córdoba. Ziryab introduced Persian music to the court, and some scholars believe that its piercing falsetto singing accompanied by arabesques played on a lute may have been a key component in the birth of flamenco. (Centuries later, Gypsies introduced its more formal elements.)

As everywhere in the Arab world, eunuchs played a vital role in regal affairs and often rose to high government posts; one reason was that castrated males at court and in the harem were considered safe and trustworthy. Castration was prohibited by the Koran, but Moors got around the rules by buying the "finished product" from Jews and Christians. Eunuchs came from throughout Europe via the south of France, where they were castrated. Others lost their manhood after arriving, especially at Lucena (south of Córdoba), where there was a virtual castration factory. It was a delicate operation often resulting in death; thus the price of a eunuch was four times that of an ordinary slave.

Harems were large and well-stocked with beautiful women of mind-dazzling variety. Moorish rulers favoured fair women from the north, especially Galician blondes, and the Galician version of the emerging Romance language was spoken widely at court. During periods of Moorish dominance, rulers of the small Christian kingdoms would often pay an annual tribute of young virgins, even their own daughters, for the harem. This continual inter-breeding of Christian and Moor produced a race of leaders in which Arab blood became insignificant. Even so, rulers were proud of their Arab ancestry and would dye their hair black in an attempt to look the part.

Although usually mere chattel, harem women could experience remarkable social mobility if they numbered among the "favourites." The same held true for eunuchs, who stood ready to serve the royal pleasure. Moorish men generally had relations with both sexes, but sodomy was regarded as more "spiritual."

The emir resided at Córdoba, the undisputed capital of Moorish Spain. Although we must be sceptical of claims made by Arab historians, the city may well have been the most civilized in Europe at the time, when most towns were squalid medieval mazes. Córdoba attained its lofty status in the 10th century, when its patios, gardens, fountains, and palaces bedazzled visitors from abroad. Its population reached several hundred thousand, according to Moorish chroniclers, and the city boasted hundreds of mosques and public baths, libraries, paved and lighted streets, and indoor plumbing — including the original WCs, literally closets containing a channel of running water.

The Great Mosque, arguably the Moors' greatest legacy, was built on the site of St. Vincent's Church, itself sitting atop the foundations of a Roman temple. When the Moors arrived, they had used half the church themselves and allowed Christians to remain in the other half. Then the emir actually *purchased* the Christian section, so he could tear down the structure to start a new mosque. So much for the myth of Muslim intolerance.

The Great Mosque was embellished over two centuries and became the second most important place of worship, after Mecca, in the Muslim world. Architects blended a number of Mediterranean styles, and used materials left from Roman and Byzantine buildings. The structural challenge presented by the huge roof was solved with about 800 pillars and rows of double arches, inspired by Roman aqueducts. Surfaced with alternating red and white stone, these candy-striped marvels seem to intertwine like branches in an endless forest of jasper pillars.

The mosque interior is the best place in Spain to get a feel for the vanished world of the Spanish Moors, when the muezzin's eerie call brought the faithful to prayer. This lingering mood is remarkable, given the fact that Christians retaking Córdoba centuries later bricked up most of the entrances, closed off the central courtyard, and built their own church right in the middle of the mosque. It was an architectural outrage, but probably saved Córdoba's Great Mosque from being razed.

For the Moors cleanliness was next to godliness; there were hundreds of public baths in Córdoba. An interesting social history of Spain could be written using soap and water as the central metaphor. The Goths (not known for their personal hygiene) closed or destroyed most of the old Roman baths, but under the Moors they returned as an important social phenomenon. Despite Christian charges of vile immorality hidden by wafts of steam, the baths were generally used for their intended purpose.

Later, Christian soldiers began to associate their own dirtiness with goodness, and bathing took on heathen or heretical connotations. For Spanish monks, physical dirt became the test of moral purity and faith, and they wore the same unwashed clothes for years and even used the phrase *olor de santidad* (odour of sanctity) to describe Christian godliness. One Moorish saying summed it up: "Christians were sprinkled with water at birth and thus relieved from washing for the rest of their lives."

In addition to its public buildings, Córdoba soon acquired fame for its leather and metalwork, silk weaving, and other skilled trades. The Moors also introduced fine glasswork to the peninsula, as well as the beautiful glazed tiles called *azulejos* still popular today. Incidentally, the flower-filled patios opening onto the street, so typical of Córdoba, became popular much later. Moorish houses had no windows or external adornment, keeping their inner charms veiled, like Muslim women, from public view.

While the Christian kingdoms remained pastoral and backward, Al-Andalus had thriving urban centres with lively souks crammed along tortuous streets, a panorama not unlike that of contemporary Morocco. In fact, the best way to picture what Spain would be like today without the Reconquest is to visit the medinas of Tetuan, Chechaouen, and Fez, historic refuges of Andalusian Muslims. Here, descendants of the Spanish Moors still huddle in tiny cubicles working metal, wool, leather, and wood. For centuries Spanish society was divided into three castes based on religion: Muslim, Christian, and Jew. There was a fair amount of toleration, and each caste had its accepted economic and social roles. Tailors, barbers, muleteers, masons, architects and shoemakers were usually Moors, while Jews invariably became the physicians, pharmacists, interpreters and money changers.

A babel of languages rose up from Moorish markets: Berber, Arabic, Hebrew, and Romance, which was the ever-evolving form of vulgarized Latin. But language per se was less important than social/religious orientation; there were many devout Muslims who could not speak Arabic and Christians who could. Those who remained Christians in belief but Muslim in culture and language were called *Mozarabs* ("almost Arabs"). They developed a distinctive culture that included architecture (such as the church of San Miguel de Escalada near Leon) and the Mozarabic rite for the mass.

Jews were much less prone to conversion or intermarriage than Christians and lived in close-knit communities centred around the markets. They were the greatest beneficiaries of Moorish rule, enjoying their most significant cultural flowering since being driven from Palestine by the Romans centuries before.

The emergence of three distinct castes based on religion had a profound effect on Spanish history. For one thing, feudalism and its hierarchy of rights and duties did not develop as in the rest of Europe. This in turn meant the lack of a strong class of leaders, the "elite" of society. Also, the concept of social position based on religious faith became a fundamental component of Spanish thinking down to modern times. (It was Franco who observed, "In Spain you are Catholic or you are nothing.")

Even after control appeared stable, periodic revolts plagued the Moors. The most famous involved Umar ibn-Hafsun, a *muwallad* of Gothic ancestry who ruled a rebel kingdom at Bobastro in the Málaga mountains for four decades. Today a few scattered stones remain of his impregnable fortress perched over a gorge of the Guadalhorce River, near El Chorro. The revolt continued under Umar's sons until squashed by Abd-er-Rahman III, who had the rebel's ten-year-old corpse exhumed and crucified beside his sons' in front of the Córdoba Mosque.

Abd-er-Rahman III had succeeded his grandfather, Emir Abdullah, whose death in 912 brought the curtain down on a disastrous reign in which none of his 11 sons survived: all were either beheaded or poisoned, victims of palace intrigue or their father's own suspicions. Abd-er-Rahman, short, stocky, was more European than Arab, his grandmother and mother having come from Navarra. His eyes were blue and his hair so light he dyed it black out of embarrassment, yet he spoke Romance with friends and family.

The young emir had a strong will and a violent temper. One time after a defeat, he became so outraged that he had dozens of officers crucified for cowardice. His reign was one of almost constant warfare, with annual raiding expeditions in the north. And yet it was under his long reign that Moorish Spain reached its zenith of power and cultural achievement. Seventeen years after becoming emir, he proclaimed himself caliph of an independent state encompassing both Al-Andalus and the Moghreb (western North Africa). The title comes from the Arabic *khalifa*, meaning "representative of the Prophet," and it carried with it absolute authority in religious as well as civil and military matters. The break with Damascus was complete.

## IBERIA IN 910

OVIEDO

KINGDOM OF NAVARRA

LEON

PAMPLONA

KINGDOM OF LEON

AUTONOMOUS MOORISH STATES

ZARAGOZA

COUNTY OF BARCELONA

BARCELONA

AL-ANDALUS

TOLEDO

VALENCIA

MERIDA

UMAYYAD EMIRATE

CORDOBA

GRANADA

SEVILLA

MALAGA

☐ CHRISTIAN STATES
▨ ISLAMIC STATES

Abd-er-Rahman III became Europe's most powerful and respected ruler, but the Christian kingdoms were growing ever stronger, and Moroccan Berbers were distant and questionable allies. The caliph relied on eunuchs and other slaves from eastern Europe, nicknamed "the silent" because they could speak neither Arabic nor Romance. The army itself was mostly Berber and not entirely reliable. Thus, the caliphs became increasingly cut off from the people they ruled, retreating into the refined and sensual world of the court.

Abd-er-Rahman III began the incredible palace of Medina Azahara outside

Córdoba and expanded and embellished the Great Mosque to its current dimensions. These were the crowning glories of Moorish architecture during the first centuries; the Alhambra came much later. Córdoba became Europe's leading city, a cultural beacon amid medieval backwardness. Even so, the figures given by Moorish historians — a million residents, 3,000 mosques, and 300 public baths — appear to be wild exaggerations. There is no evidence suggesting a city larger than about 100,000 residents, and the claim that the caliph's library contained 400,000 volumes is laughable.

There is also reason to question the Moors' heralded accomplishments in such fields as agriculture. For example, rather than introducing irrigation they merely adopted and improved earlier Roman works which had made Hispania the breadbasket of the empire. Nevertheless, under the caliphate new crops were introduced: the orange, lemon, peach, apricot, fig and pomegranate, as well as saffron, sugar cane, cotton, silk, and rice... in short, many of Spain's staple products today. The Moors also brought Arabian horses, which developed into the famed Andalusian breed.

Moorish goods were prized throughout Europe and the East: Cordoban leather, fruit and wine from Málaga, arms and damascene work from Toledo, Valencia's glazed pottery, silk from Granada. From the mines at Río Tinto came copper, and those at Almaden yielded most of the mercury for medieval Europe. Peninsular commerce was controlled by Al-Andalus, its currency used in the primitive Christian economies. The north was culturally impoverished as well. While the Moors produced a ten-volume history of the caliphate, the kingdom of Leon could only muster a pitiful 15 pages to record the reign of Alfonso V.

ALTHOUGH STANDING in awe of the vibrant civilization to the south, Christians were starting to assert themselves. The kaleidoscopic swirl of Christian kingdoms — forever merging, separating, and merging again — make Spain's medieval history the most complex in Europe. From this confusing labyrinth emerge an endless cavalcade of kings who occasionally achieve immortality through odd names like Sancho the Fat or Wilfred the Hairy. But distinctive patterns were starting to form.

Before the Moors people were either Goths or Hispano-Romans. The concept of being "Spanish," with a God-given destiny to retake the peninsula, took root very slowly. Even the word *español* (meaning Spaniard or Spanish) was imported from Provence much later. (A major Castilian dictionary did not include the word until 1967.) Residents of the north thought of themselves as Christians who belonged to a certain village or geographical area, or possibly to a small kingdom.

Asturias, with its capital at Oviedo, was the first of these. Later, the Asturians moved out from their mountain strongholds to found a new capital at Leon. The kings of Asturias-Leon assumed the title of *imperator*, harkening back to the fleeting days of Visigothic unity. Among the kings was Sancho the Fat, who was repudiated by his barons for being too obese to ride a horse. The pathetic monarch waddled off to Córdoba where he received treatment from the caliph's physician, then returned home to oust his rival, Ordoño the Bad.

At the peninsula's north-eastern corner was the Spanish March (*Marca Hispanica*), a Frankish buffer state founded by Charlemagne after the failure of his Zaragoza expedition. Wilfred "The Hairy" began an independent line of counts, but the region — with Barcelona as its capital — remained in Frankish hands for two centuries. It enjoyed limited autonomy and special privileges, the start of a tradition that lives to this day in Catalonia.

The area between Asturias-Leon and the Spanish March gave birth to the kingdoms of Castilla and Navarra. In 951 Castilla, whose name derives from the abundant castles along its frontier, became independent. According to legend, count Fernan Gonzalez appeared one day before the king of Leon with a beautiful horse and a hawk. The king insisted on buying them and promised to double the price for every day that payment was not forthcoming. After many years the money had still not been paid, and the sum was so large that he granted Castilla's independence as payment. The Basque heartland in the crook of the Bay of Biscay remained untouched after the Moors found "a people like beasts," and decided not to invade. The mountainous part of this region developed into the kingdom of Navarra in the early 10th century.

These early kingdoms were governed almost as family properties in which marital alliances were often the crux. Indeed, the history of the times reads like a lurid record of family feuds, lust, and bloodshed, with the Cordoban caliph often acting as arbiter between warring Christians. Compared with family ties, religion played only a minor role in political alignments. Toda, the queen mother of Navarra, for example, was Fernan Gonzalez's mother-in-law, Abd-er-Rahman's great aunt, and Sancho the Fat's grandmother.

Nevertheless, the Moorish-Christian frontier was often mobilized or in a state of war. To match the Koran-inspired fanaticism, Christians found their own inspiration in the cult of St. James (Santiago). The site of his supposed burial was neglected until the ninth century, when a local hermit saw a bright star shining above an oak tree and heard strange celestial music. When the local bishop investigated, he found three graves and an altar and proclaimed a miracle. (One of the corpses was decapitated, as James had been.)

Next, just before a major battle, Ramiro I of Galicia announced that the saint had appeared to him in a dream — mounted on a white charger and carrying a banner emblazoned with a red cross. And yes, he promised Christian victory. The next day Christian soldiers attacked while shouting "Santiago!" and the Moors fled. The simple disciple of Christ had become "the Moor slayer" and patron of the Reconquest. (Santiago remains Spain's patron today.)

The first pilgrims to the shrine of Santiago at Compostela began arriving in the ninth century. This trickle would later become a torrent, but before that happened Christian Spain would receive a nearly mortal blow that came close to stopping the Reconquest in its tracks. The resurgence of northern Spain had not gone unnoticed in Córdoba. In the middle of the tenth century a young man from a noble Arab family, named Muhammed ibn-abi-Amir (later called Al-Mansur, "the Victorious") appeared on the scene. He was charming and ruthless in equal doses — a deadly combination — and before long had insinuated himself at court.

One day the caliph Hakam asked suspiciously, "By what skills does this clever young man attract all my women and win their hearts?" He had reason to worry; Mansur soon became lover of his favourite, the Basque Aurora. Hakam's successor was the young and hopelessly weak Hisham II, and before long Mansur became caliph in all but name. Mansur played the part of the pious believer and once copied the entire Koran by hand, but reports of his cruelty persisted. For example, he once had an astrologer's tongue cut out when he foretold defeat. Upon hearing that his son was part of a gang of plotters, Mansur had him whipped to death while he dined; another son was decapitated. Indeed, cutting off heads was one of Mansur's favourite diversions, and he once made a giant pyramid of the ghastly trophies and rode round it in glee. He then had them salted, boxed, and sent around the caliphate to frighten his enemies.

Mansur was not the kind of enemy the resurgent Christians needed: he led 57 expeditions into their territory in about 20 years. Finally the worst happened. In the year 997, Mansur and his army captured Santiago de Compostela and destroyed its shrine. Only the tomb of the saint was spared, when an old monk refusing to flee impressed Mansur with his bravery. To add insult to injury, the basilica's doors and bells were carried by captives to Córdoba and used to embellish the mosque. News of Mansur's campaign struck like a thunderclap across Christian Spain. In one daring swoop, centuries of painstaking advance seemed shattered beyond repair.

## SIGHTS & SITES

### Visigothic and early Christian:

*Celanova* (Orense): *26 kms. south of town lies Santa Comba de Bande, a small Visigoth church in the shape of a Greek cross.*

*Covadonga* (Asturias): *Grand setting surrounded by Picos de Europa; shrine commemorates spot where Pelayo held off Moors; tombs of Pelayo and Alfonso I.*

*Leon*: *Parts of medieval town date from 10th century, when king of Asturias founded new capital.*

*Madrid*: *At National Archaeological Museum see crowns of Visigoth kings, Romanesque tombs and capitals.*

*Oviedo* (Asturias): *Cathedral contains holy relics from fall of Visigoths at Toledo.*

*Palencia*: *14 kms. from town is Baños De Cerrato, site of San Juan Bautista church, the oldest in Spain (661).*

*Roncesvalles* (Navarra): *Spot where Basques massacred rearguard of Charlemagne's army, described in* The Song of Roland.

*San Miguel de Escalada* (Leon): *28 kms. from Leon is a Mozarabic church built by monks expelled from Córdoba.*

*Tarrasa* (Barcelona): *Three churches on Roman-Visigoth site of Egara.*

**Toledo**: *Church of San Roman contains Visigothic Museum with bronze jewelry and votive crowns; more remains at Santa Cruz Museum include carved tombstone.*

## Early Moorish:
**Almeria**: *Alcazaba fortress dates to 8th century; badly damaged by earthquake, but walls still extant; extensive gardens and museum.*
**Córdoba**: *The Mosque with its forest of candy- striped pillars; Medina Azahara palace lies 6 kms. from town.*

# CHAPTER 4

# MOROS Y CRISTIANOS

A few kilometres west of Córdoba lie the ruins of Medina Azahara, "the City of the Flower," named to honour Abd-er-Rahman's favourite wife. This royal residence ranked among the most sumptuous in history. Shimmering white against the dark hills of the Sierra Morena, it was described by an Arab poet as "a concubine in the arms of a black eunuch." But, like the caliphate itself, Medina Azahara's glories were short-lived. Rampaging Berbers destroyed the palatial city in 1010, and it lay buried and forgotten for nine centuries.

Strolling around today, it requires a vivid imagination to summon up images of former magnificence. Built during the reign of Abd-er-Rahman III, the project consumed about a third of the royal budget and employed ten thousand workmen. Only the finest materials were used: ivory, carved cedar, ebony, onyx, and alabaster, mosaic tiles and marble columns. The caliph's rooms alone numbered 400; among them was one with walls sheathed in gold and a pearl the size of a dove's egg hanging from the ceiling. Thousands lived in or just outside the palace: servants, pages, musicians, and four thousand Slavonian eunuchs. Women in the harem numbered some 6,300 — enough for any man. Despite these amenities, Al Mansur preferred his own residence, and Medina Azahara fell into disrepair. During the crisis in the years following Al Mansur's sudden death (1002), rebellious Berber mercenaries fired by religious zeal pulled down the palace, and even used hammers to smash large pieces into smaller bits. Today laid out neatly on the floor are tens of thousands of stone and plaster pieces awaiting re-assembly in the world's biggest jigsaw puzzle. You can still see black burn marks where the intense heat of the Berber bonfires seared the marble floor.

THE FIRES OF ANARCHY and destruction consumed more than a palace. During the first three decades of the new millennium, Moorish Spain slipped from the pinnacle of wealth, culture, and military power — capped by Mansur's victorious march on Santiago — into a mire of bloody strife. Wrote the poet, "Weep for the splendour of Córdoba, for disaster has overtaken her, then bid her goodbye, and let her go in peace since depart she must."

The effete caliph Hisham II, who normally wore a veil and makeup, did not produce an heir. Instead, he named Mansur's son Sanchuelo, a drinking and debauching mate, to succeed to the throne. Revolt followed revolt and by 1031, the year the caliphate ceased to exist, six more caliphs had followed. With their failure, Al-Andalus fractured into about 20 *taifas*, or "party kingdoms," as geographical and racial particularism (essentially, Berbers battling Arabs) triumphed over unified rule. The Moors remained formidable, however, controlling about two-thirds of the peninsula.

The most powerful *taifa* kingdoms were Sevilla and Granada, followed by Córdoba, Almeria, Zaragoza, Badajoz, and Toledo. But religion alone did not define the political map. As a matter of course the party kingdoms often fought and betrayed one another, even if it meant allying with Christians.

One infamous Sevillan ruler was Motadid, who boasted a harem of 800 girls and used human skulls for flowerpots around his palace. For amusement, he kept the heads of defeated rivals in leather cases, taking them out occasionally to admire. (Motadid's son, on the other hand, had his virtues: when one wife longed for the sight of snow, he planted thousands of almond trees on a nearby slope, so that each winter she could enjoy a white sea of blossoms. Such were the Moors.)

As often happens in times of political decline, the decades following the caliphate's collapse witnessed a brief cultural flowering. Each king tried to surpass his neighbours in the number and quality of books in his library or poets under his patronage. It became a point of royal honour to write in the most refined manner on the finest parchment, using rhymed verses and intricate metaphors to score literary points.

The earthly temptations of Andalucia were hard to resist, and Moorish poets wrote of wine and women (or boys), dancing and song. The ceaseless search for poetic extravagance could lead to abominably bad verse. One bard wrote: "Such was my kissing, such my sucking of his mouth, that he was almost made toothless." Pleasure seeking became an end in itself, and the Moors' love of wine often degenerated into drunken orgies. These former sons of the desert began to lose their warrior virtues and employ mercenaries (even Christians) to do their fighting.

For centuries Moorish raiding parties had swept into Christian lands, cutting down trees, burning crops, sacking towns and lopping off a few heads before returning south across a wide "no man's land." There was no serious effort to conquer or hold land beyond natural barriers such as the Duero and Ebro rivers. Nor did the Moors lust for unconquered parts of "Spain" because no such place existed.

The frontier between Christian and Moor was far from being a well-defined, hermetically sealed border. It ebbed and flowed like the tide, depending on shady alliances and who was stronger or more able to pay bribes. You can trace some outposts of this centuries-long struggle in frontier towns with the words *de la frontera* tacked on, such as Arcos de la Frontera.

While Al-Andalus was falling from omnipotence to impotence, the northern kingdoms underwent the opposite experience. As Christian-held territory expanded, kings encouraged resettlement by granting municipal rights called *fueros*. Local liberties led in turn to popular representation in *cortes* (parliaments) a hundred years before anything similar happened in England (1163 in Aragon and 1188 in Leon compared with 1295 in England). These early rights and institutions offered more liberty than the feudal servitude found in most of Europe, but the *fueros* would come back to haunt Spain time and again throughout history.

The Moorish-Christian frontier was like an early-day version of the Wild West and attracted adventurous types from the peninsula and beyond, especially after the pope called for a crusade. Slowly Christians gained the spirit that created *La Reconquista* (the Reconquest), the most distinctive factor in medieval Spanish history. War was a fact of life, though armies of the day were tiny by modern standards and would often agree in advance on the time and place of a battle.

Christian progress was slow for several reasons. The central *meseta*'s rugged topography and harsh climate and the threat of Moorish reprisals discouraged settlers. In addition, every time a Christian king died he divided his domains among his sons, which led to the splintering of power built up over years of struggle. The Moors' tribute system was eagerly adopted by Christians and resulted in a northward flow of gold. Unlike developing areas of Italy or Flanders, where wealth sprang from industry and commerce, in Christian Spain it came from war or the threat of war. Compounding the problem, money was used to buy land or more weapons, not spent on economic development.

The kingdom of Leon championed the Reconquest until the blows struck by Al Mansur. Navarra then moved to the fore under Sancho III "the Great" (1005-1035). He married the sister of the Castilian ruler and, in the confusion following the murder of his brother-in-law, gained control of Castilla and placed his son Fernando in charge. Fernando (Ferdinand) I in turn occupied Leon and assumed the title "emperor of the Spains." Castilla had truly become a kingdom in its own right — and one destined for greatness.

Meanwhile other peninsular powers were forming; in the lands that became Aragon a strong tradition of limited monarchy developed. To the east, the future region of Catalonia had remained largely unoccupied by the Moors and in the 11th century Ramon Berenguer I, count of Barcelona, became the first ruler of a completely independent entity.

Fernando I of Castilla (Sancho's son) became a leading figure in the Reconquest, capturing territory from Valencia to Portugal. But when he died, this emerging Christian power was again partitioned among his own sons, and outright war soon erupted between Alfonso in Leon and Sancho in Castilla. At the time Sancho was served by a young knight who became one of the most exalted figures in Spanish history — Rodrigo Diaz de Vivar, better known as *El Cid Campeador*. (The name Cid comes from the Arabic *seyyid*, or lord, while *campeador* is from the Latin *campi ductor*, leader in the field.)

The amazing Cid achieved lasting fame through the first great epic poem of Spanish literature, *El Cantar del Mio Cid* (1140), as well as in countless biographies and a film epic starring Charlton Heston. Historians have long struggled to separate legend from fact, and some believe the Cid may be a composite of at least two individuals. In the epic he is a grave but majestic figure who can subdue lions at a glance and wears his beard in a net to prevent the dishonour of having it tweaked, a mortal insult at the time. (The Cid once yanked out a handful of a defeated rival's beard to further humiliate him.) From historical accounts we know that he was exiled by Alfonso VI and fought in the service of the Moors. Indeed, El Cid embodies the confusion of loyalties between Christian and Moor at the time.

Nonetheless, Christian Spain adopted El Cid as a national hero, and historians now feel that the epic might be close to the truth. Rodrigo was born in Vivar, a backward village a few kilometres from Burgos. He learnt the soldier's profession early and rose rapidly in the service of Sancho. In an event that became the stuff of legend, the Cid's lord was murdered by a treacherous aide one dark (and probably stormy) night, and his brother fell under suspicion. Rodrigo personally made Alfonso swear an oath that he had no part in the crime. In a famous ceremony at Burgos, the Cid repeated three times, "If you are lying, please God that a traitor and a vassal kills you..."

This did not endear him to Alfonso — ruler of a reunited Castilla and Leon — and following a quarrel a few years later, the king sent the Cid into exile. He proceeded to fight in the service of the potentate of Zaragoza, a Moorish city in vassalage to Alfonso, then slipped briefly from the scene.

Alfonso himself became a major military figure. His armies penetrated deep into Andalucia and even reached Gibraltar, where he rode into the Mediterranean and exclaimed: "Here is the uttermost limit of Spain. I have touched it." In addition, Alfonso is remembered for replacing the centuries-old Mozarabic rite for the Mass with the Latin rite of the Roman church. Today, the only place in the world to see a Mozarabic Mass is a tiny chapel in Toledo's cathedral, where it has survived in an odd time-warp of the kind found only in Spain.

In 1085, Alfonso's army recaptured Toledo in the first crucial victory of the Reconquest. It was a huge strategic step as well as a boost to morale, bringing Christians to the old Visigoth capital and into the heart of the *meseta*, the part later called New Castilla.

Shock waves flashed through Al-Andalus at the news of Toledo's fall. A Moorish poet wrote: "Take to your horses, men of Andalucia! To remain is pure folly.

*Above, the Alhambra Palace in Granada, a later example of Moorish architecture. Following pages, the Great Mosque of Córdoba. (PHOTO THIS PAGE BY AGE FOTO-STOCK, BARCELONA; FOLLOWING PAGES BY JEAN-DOMINIQUE DALLET)*

*Medieval carving adorns the Pórtico de la Gloria in Santiago de Compostela, the spiritual centre of Christian Spain. (PHOTO BY AGE FOTOSTOCK, BARCELONA)*

Garments begin by fraying at the edges, but our kingdom has ripped down the centre." Yet Christian elation was premature; the Moors were not going to roll over just yet. The kingdom of Sevilla, heretofore a Christian vassal, issued calls for help to Muslim Africa.

THE ALMORAVIDS WERE dark-skinned nomads from the Sahara — ancestors of the modern Tauregs — who had converted to Islam and swept north to conquer Morocco. Yusuf ibn-Tashufin founded Marrakesh and governed lands stretching from Senegal to Algeria. This warlike sect, whose name means "vowed to God," consisted of religious fanatics sworn to root out anyone who slipped from Muslim orthodoxy.

Alarmed by Alfonso's victories, Mutamid of Sevilla petitioned Yusuf for help, remarking "If I have to choose, I would rather tend camels for the Almoravids than pasture swine under the Christians." His words were prophetic; as so many before and after, the invaders would decide to stay. The party was over for the "party kings."

An Almoravid army landed at Algeciras and marched to meet Alfonso near Badajoz. The Christians were used to fighting man-to-man style, by which a collection of individual triumphs brought overall victory. In the invaders they faced a compact force of infantry supported by lines of archers, which moved to the command of thunderous drums. Muslim victory was assured when Yusuf called in his Negro guard, equipped with rapiers and shields of hippo hide. After the battle carts laden with severed heads rumbled off for display. Alfonso himself barely escaped. Panic reigned throughout Christian Spain, which feared that the infidel was once again on the march. In Galicia, one group even tried to gain protection by transferring its sovereignty to William the Conqueror, who had completed his conquest of England twenty years before.

After this crushing defeat, Alfonso was forced to turn again to the Cid. The enigmatic hero had meanwhile gained control of Valencia, and despite his nominal loyalty to the king, set himself up as an independent ruler. The Muslims supposedly stood in awe of the Cid, who seemed to be fulfilling an old prophecy: "If a Roderick it was who lost Spain (a reference to the last Visigoth king), another Roderick (Rodrigo) will restore it."

Unfortunately, the Cid died suddenly in 1099. According to one story, his corpse was clad in armour, lashed to his charger, and led out in front of the Christian army, causing a panicked retreat by the Moors. In reality, his followers gamely held Valencia another three years, then surrendered. During the next few years, the Almoravids controlled most of southern Iberia from their capital at Marrakesh.

Almoravid Spain was very different from the tolerant society of the caliphate and *taifas*. Driven by strict religious fundamentalism, they began to persecute Christians and Jews as hopelessly corrupt. Wrote one chronicler: "Muslim women must be forbidden to defile themselves by entering a Christian church, since the priests are libertines, fornicators and sodomites." The persecuted fled north.

The Muslim revival in fact helped consolidate the main Christian kingdoms and goad them into joint action. Alfonso I of Aragon, "El Batallador" (the Fighter), led the counter-attack by retaking Zaragoza (1118), thus providing the young kingdom with its historic capital. When he died without an heir his brother Ramiro, living quietly as a monk, was lured out of his cell long enough to sire a daughter, the infanta Petronilla. She in turn was married off to Count Ramon Berenguer IV of the Catalan ruling family, thereby uniting Aragon and Catalonia. Ramiro returned to his monastery, unaware that his brief escapade had created a union of monumental consequence for Spanish history.

The "Kingdom of Aragon" was a misnomer because real power lay in Catalonia and its capital city of Barcelona. During the 12th and 13th centuries, this kingdom prospered as a wealthy trading power. "Not a fish dared show itself in the Mediterranean without having the bars of Aragon on its tail," wrote one historian.

Meanwhile, another major peninsular force was born in the west — the kingdom of Portugal. Alfonso VI had two daughters: one married Raymond of Burgundy and their son reigned as Alfonso VII of Castilla. (The House of Burgundy ruled Castilla from 1126 until 1369.) The younger daughter married

*Henry* of Burgundy and the couple ended up with the county of Portugal as part of the dowry. Their son founded an independent Portugal in 1139, and independent it remained, with the exception of one 80-year period centuries later.

Among these Christian kingdoms, Castilla would overshadow its neighbours because it was larger, more populous, and was to become standard-bearer of the Reconquest. Wrote one historian: "Castilla was born to war and suckled on war, and it was in war that she forged her warrior temperament, her will to command, and her ambition to achieve a great destiny." During the crucial centuries when the Spanish identity and character were formed, the "land of castles" was the centre of gravity.

Castilla's role as linchpin of a new nation spread far beyond mere military leadership. The Romance language of Castilian (known to the world as Spanish) originated in the north as a backwater dialect, but would emerge as the dominant peninsular tongue, despite the ongoing presence of Catalan, Basque, Galician, and Portuguese. (Scholars date Castilian as a distinct language with the publication of the Cid epic.) And, as every Englishman knows, language is a potent weapon to have on your side.

Although Christian resentment against the Muslim intruders had smouldered since 711, the idealized concept of a "holy war" to eliminate them took hold in this period. The Moors were henceforth considered usurpers of Spanish soil and enemies of the Catholic faith. Castilians in particular began to look upon themselves as God's chosen race. Their soldiers fought for all Christendom, not just for their own kingdom.

Fundamental to Reconquest mythology was the legend of *Santiago El Matamoros*, St. James the Moor Slayer, and his shrine at Compostela. In the decades following Mansur's destruction of the old church, the faithful began to rebuild. The magnificent Romanesque cathedral of today was embellished over centuries, including the incredible *pórtico de la gloria* by Master Mateo, perhaps the finest example of medieval carving in existence.

Christian pilgrims once again flocked to Santiago de Compostela along a famous route sprinkled with Benedictine monasteries. The faithful carried cockleshells — part of their penance involved swallowing a raw scallop — and camped out along the way or enjoyed the hospitality of monks. The Road to Compostela became the greatest pilgrimage of the middle ages and the site began to rival Jerusalem and Rome. There was even the occasional anti-pope from Compostela, usually a local bishop who had decided that St. James ranked above St. Peter in the hierarchy of saints.

Another Christian icon was the Holy Grail, a gold-and-sardonyx chalice reputedly used by Jesus at the Last Supper. According to legend, it was brought to Spain in the 4th century and later became the proudest possession of the Aragonese monarchy. (The cup can be seen in Valencia's cathedral.)

But religion was just one of many motives driving the war wagons of the Reconquest; gold and glory spurred on many a knight-errant. The fusion of faith and warfare is best seen in the armies of monastic knights, the famous orders of Calatrava, Alcantara, and Santiago, the romantic heroes of song and story.

The knights of St. James (Santiago), for example, wore white mantles emblazoned with a red cross, swore perpetual war on the infidel, and devoted themselves to the service of "God and the ladies."

For these Christian warriors, victory in battle meant more than the remission of sins. Nobles and the more successful knights received huge land grants in the conquered territories, which survived as the hated *latifundios*. Many of Spain's noble families trace their lineage to the Reconquest and the lands granted to their ancestors. At the top of the pyramid were the *grandes* and beneath them the lesser-nobility or *hidalgos*, an arrangement corresponding roughly to English barons and knights. (The word *hidalgo* comes from *hijo de algo*, son of some substance.) *Hidalgos* lived by a strict code that glorified land ownership and discouraged business activities and manual labour.

When warfare waned, the rank-and-file tended vast herds of sheep and cattle. Spain became the original home of the cattle ranch, an institution later taken to the Americas, especially Argentina and Mexico. The mounted Spanish *vaqueros* were direct ancestors of the immortal cowboys of the American West, and just like the cowboy, these Castilian herdsmen were the vanguard of an expanding society. For gentlemen, raising livestock was considered superior to digging the earth, and large sections of Castilla and Andalucia let farm go to pasture. After the introduction of the merino breed of sheep a bit later, demand soared for Spanish wool, the mainstay of the economy for centuries — wool that was exported to the burgeoning factories of *other* countries.

After the conquest of Toledo, the problem arose of how to incorporate two alien, and in many ways superior, cultures. It came to be accepted that the proper order of society consisted of Christian herders, warriors and priests, Muslim cultivators and artisans, and Jewish technicians and traders. The extreme form of this attitude held that *all* physical work was for Muslims and Jews (and later for Indians or Blacks), while the proper Christian job was to rule.

WHILE CHRISTIAN SPAIN continued to evolve, the Moors chafed under the yoke of their Almoravid rulers and began to rebel. What really sealed the fate of the Almoravids, however, was the rise of another fanatical sect in Morocco, the Almohades. Around the year 1126 the son of a mosque lamplighter from the Atlas Mountains claimed inspiration from Allah and took the title of mahdi. Berber followers rallied to calls for a holy war to stamp out Almoravid "heresy."

Coming from the Atlas and Moroccan plains, the Almohades (which means "unitarians") were natural enemies of the desert-dwelling Almoravids. First they conquered Marrakesh. Next, encouraged by reports of local sympathy, Almohad armies invaded Iberia, and before long Al-Andalus was again united under one Muslim reign.

The Almohades were as intolerant as they were bellicose. Abd al-Mumin ordered all churches and synagogues razed, and Christians and Jews swarmed across the northern frontier. Friction with the north stepped up a notch, culminating in a stunning Christian defeat at Alarcos (between Toledo and Córdoba) in 1195. The flower of young Spanish knights fell, and the Castilian king himself narrowly escaped capture.

Despite their fanaticism, the Almohades ushered in a period of great cultural achievement for Moorish Spain, the brightest era between the caliphate and the glories of Granada centuries later. Interest revived in philosophy, medicine, mathematics, and literature, and the proto-sciences of astrology and alchemy. Architecture flourished with construction of the soaring minaret of the Seville mosque, today called La Giralda. This splendid tower, built with a wide ramp inside so that the sultan could ride his horse to the top, is one of a nearly identical trio by the same architect; the others are the Koutoubia of Marrakesh and Rabat's Hassan Tower. Another Almohad remnant in Sevilla is the Tower of Gold, once covered with gilded tiles.

Arab poetry too enjoyed a renascence of sorts during the 12th century. Every ruler worth his salt composed verse, and even scientific works were embellished with the appropriate lyrical flourish. Yet much of the poetry is tired and jejune. Princes are always lions or suns; women are gazelles or doves; the lightening in the rainstorm is like "the fire of the poet's love amidst his tears." This poetry was crafted for recital and song, and its lyric forms inspired the first ballads of European troubadours and, quite possibly, the soul-stirring adagios of *cante jondo* flamenco. At the end of each stanza of a recitation, Moors cried out *wa-allah* (Oh God!), just as today the flamenco singer's refrain is greeted with shouts of "Olé!"

The philosopher Averroes, born at Córdoba in 1126, is often cited as the pinnacle of Moorish learning and influence. He translated into Arabic the works of Aristotle, which had been virtually forgotten in the West, and when his commentary was in turn put into Latin, it caused an intellectual upheaval among Christian theologians such as St. Thomas Aquinas. (One theory holds that Averroes was really a Mozarab, that is, a Christian.) Another son of Córdoba was the Jew Maimonides (1135-1204), who left Al-Andalus under cloudy circumstances and spent his life wandering the Mediterranean world. He was a renowned doctor who served as personal physician to the sultan of Cairo, and he wrote many medical treatises, including one on human sexuality. Maimonides' chief fame rests with his philosophical works, such as *Guide to the Perplexed*, a summary of medieval religious thought.

THOUGH DURING MUCH of the early Reconquest Christian rulers were more concerned with fighting each other than the Moors, after the debacle at Alarcos they decided to cooperate, especially when the pope called for a new crusade against the Almohades. In June of 1212 — a year as famous in Spain as 1066 is in England — soldiers from throughout Spain and Europe gathered at Toledo, then marched south for the Sierra Morena.

Here they were aided by a mysterious shepherd who led the army through a pass marked by a cow's skull. (The young man was dubbed *cabeza de vaca*, and his descendants later gained fame in the Americas.) The Moors could have easily ambushed the Christian forces in the mountain passes, but they made a huge tactical error by awaiting them on the rolling plains of Las Navas de

Tolosa. Here the Almohad forces were annihilated — 60,000 killed compared to only 50 Christian deaths, according to chroniclers. After the battle hundreds of thousands of Moors fled to North Africa, and the defeated Moorish commander drank himself to death.

Such reports are suspect, but the battle did mark the beginning of the end for Muslim Spain; the 13th century was to bring many more Christian victories. Portugal was the first to follow up, expelling the Moors in 1249. Aragon retook Valencia and the Balearic Islands. But again it was Castilla which gained the most after Las Navas, adding the lion's share of Andalucia to its rule. Fernando (Ferdinand) III, later proclaimed a saint for his martial skills, captured Córdoba and re-consecrated the Great Mosque as a cathedral. With poetic justice, he sent captured Muslims to Santiago with the same bells Al-Mansur made Christians lug to Córdoba two centuries earlier.

The writing was on the wall and the ruler of Granada, one Mohammed-ibn-Alhamar, saw it clearly. Turban in hand, he approached Fernando and proposed an alliance. The price for cooperation in the conquest of Muslim Sevilla was Granada's independence as a Castilian vassal. Fernando was startled by Mohammed's grovelling performance, but agreed and took Sevilla with his help. Upon returning to Granada and shouts of victory, the embarrassed Moor uttered ironically, "There is no victor but Allah." The words were inscribed a thousand times throughout the Alhambra palace.

When Fernando died four years later, a hundred knights from Granada carried torches at his wake. With his passing the Reconquest seemed to die as well, though his son led a handful of mop-up victories. But Mohammed's deal endured; for another two centuries the kingdom of Granada remained a Castilian vassal and the Moors' final bastion.

AT SOME POINT one must sum up the Moors' legacy in Spain. Even a cursory look at the dates reveals that "the Arabs" did *not*, as is commonly stated, rule Spain for 800 years. In actual fact, the mostly Berber-Hispanic (not Arab) Muslims inhabited two-thirds of the peninsula for 375 years, about half of it for another 160 years, and the tiny kingdom of Granada — present-day Málaga, Almeria, and Granada provinces — for a final 244 years.

Along with the faulty chronology comes a whirlwind of praise for the earthly paradise the Moors supposedly created, the rose-tinted version found in Washington Irving's *Tales of the Alhambra*. For many romantics Al-Andalus will always be the epitome of chivalry and culture. In truth, the Moors did have a profound effect on the peninsula — for good and bad — which persists to this day.

During their heyday they led Europe in many endeavours, such as alchemy (the forerunner of chemistry) and medicine. Surgeons at Córdoba dissected corpses and were familiar with anesthesia. Doctors even used music for the treatment of mental disorders. The Moors introduced an advanced system of specialized hospitals for lepers (lepers were burned in France), the insane, and wounded soldiers. Muslim scholarship also excelled in astronomy, botany and geography. Al-Idrisi, who ranks as the greatest medieval geographer, insisted that the earth was round; it's said that Columbus later got most of his ideas from Arabic translations of classical works. The Moors brought Arabic numerals, replacing the clumsy Roman system, as well as algebra and other forms of higher mathematics.

The word algebra itself is Arabic in origin, as are thousands of others in modern Spanish. Among them are *alcázar* (castle), *arroz* (rice), *aduana* (customs), *alcalde* (mayor), *naranja* (orange), *azucar* (sugar) and *limon* (lemon). Spanish-English cognates from the same Arabic source include alcohol, alchemy, alkali, camphor, elixir, syrup, talc, nadir, zenith, almanac, zero, coffee, jasmine, saffron and sesame.

Following Roman examples, agriculture and irrigation were Moorish strengths, seen in the splendidly cultivated *vegas* of Andalucia and Valencia. The Moors are also credited with bringing the technology for the manufacture of paper and gunpowder to Europe. They can also claim many things thought of as typically Spanish, such as the guitar (developed from their lute), certain aspects of flamenco music, the tiled patio with its gurgling fountain, and even *gazpacho*, a cold soup of raw vegetables for poor field workers.

Moorish art was a fusion of east and west, using materials and techniques from the Romans, Goths and Byzantines. When they conquered Spain, the Moors were an uncultured, nomadic people, but they came to be imitators and transmitters of more developed civilizations. To this they added their own light, unmistakable touch whose ultimate expression is the Alhambra. Moorish Spain survives most visibly in its buildings. In them we see those typical touches — the horseshoe arch, superb carving in wood and plaster, imaginative use of textiles and tiles. The Moors definitely had a weakness for florid detail, and it lives on in Spanish *artesania*.

But there is the other side to the Moorish story. For every building they put up, they tore down another with equal fervour. When the Almoravids took Segovia, for example, they destroyed 36 arches of the magnificent Roman aqueduct. No better metaphor is needed for the triumph of barbarism over civilization.

The Moors profoundly changed the course of Spanish history. In 711, the peninsula was at least as developed as the rest of Europe and might have become a powerful, unified state. Instead, Iberia's destiny was to bear the brunt of the Muslim invasions and deflect its national energies at a critical time. The old Roman-Gothic quest for unity was overturned by the Muslim fondness for anarchy, disunity, and separatism. The struggle between these two polar tendencies has haunted Spanish history ever since.

The Moors' obsession with warfare and bloodshed, their lust for booty and gold, their fondness for torture and cutting off heads — all these spilled over into Christian Spain. Their constant raiding, cutting down trees and burning vegetation made a desert of La Mancha and other areas, which even today are desolate and under-populated.

Many Muslim attitudes crept into Spanish thought. Among them was the treatment of women, whom the Moors jealously veiled and guarded; for centuries Spaniards kept women firmly behind the *rejas*, the iron grating on the windows. Christian kings readily adopted the Arab custom of taking foreign concubines; Alfonso VI for example had five wives, including the daughter of Motamid, ruler of Seville.

Finally, there was the Reconquest itself. If the holy crusade brought *fueros*, it also meant an economy based on tribute, plunder, and sheep-herding, all-powerful military orders, and a strong, aggressive aristocracy and church. This fusion of religious and military ideals became the driving force of society, and Christianity was equated with the good and the right. Even today, Spaniards often regard political issues as moral questions on which there is no possibility of concession or compromise. In a constant state of alert, Spaniards developed a siege mentality that degenerated into an almost paranoid fear of foreign doctrines and influences.

The Moorish occupation was a mixed blessing for Spain. And yet a tiny slice of romantic Al-Andalus lives on. Anyone doubting this lingering presence need only hear the singing of a *saeta* during a Holy Week procession. This triste, piercing song is a spiritual soul-mate to the hymns of praise to the Prophet sung during Islamic festivals. And the cries of "Olé!" and "Ojalá!" (from *aj-allah*, or "God willing") are clear echoes of Muslim calls to Allah.

ONE OF THE MANY paradoxes of medieval Spain became evident after the virtual fall of Andalucia around 1250. While Islam was the great enemy for Christians, it was also the source of a culture in many ways superior to their own. Typical of this cultural confusion is the tomb of Fernando III in Sevilla's Cathedral. Here, a massive silver casket sits beneath an altar flanked by perpetually burning candles; three times a year it is opened and the saint-king's eerily preserved body exposed to public view. But the most significant detail is that his epitaph is written in four languages: Latin, Castilian, Hebrew... and Arabic.

The fall of the Almohades after Las Navas de Tolosa did not, as might be imagined, unleash a reign of intolerance and reprisals against Moors. In fact, Spain seemed to return for a few remarkable decades to an open, tri-cultural society. Every town had its prosperous Jewish quarter (*juderia*). In Toledo, the Church of Santa Maria La Blanca was used for worship by all three religions: Muslims on Fridays, Jews on Saturdays, and Christians on Sundays.

Fernando was succeeded by one of the bright lights among Spain's monarchs — his son Alfonso X "The Learned." This scholar-king oversaw an epoch of enlightened tolerance for Jews and Moors (he called himself King of Three Religions), but also recognized the unifying cultural role of Christian Castilla. Alfonso was fertile in mind and body; he fathered eight children with his wife and at least four others on the sly, wrote bawdy love poems, and denounced his enemies in rhyme. He authored a history of Spain and a treatise on chess complete with diagrams. He also edited one of Spain's literary treasures, the *Cántigas de Santa Maria*. This compilation of music, poetry, and about 1,300 illustrations opens a fascinating window on medieval life.

Alfonso helped build the bridge between medieval Europe and antiquity. Arab and Hebrew scholarship had survived the Reconquest in Toledo, and the king realized the possibilities by expanding the existing school of translators. Persian literature, Greek philosophy, Arabic medicine, and other wisdom were cast into Latin here. By 1251, Aristotle was being taught at the university of Paris, a profound step in the history of philosophy. Another work that arrived via Toledo was the *Canon of Ibn Sina*, Europe's standard medical textbook for the next five centuries.

Most significantly, Alfonso had many translations made from the original into Castilian, not Latin, which was an astonishing departure from scholarly norms. It was another major step toward the evolution of the "Castilian mystique." Castilian swallowed up both the Leonese and Aragonese dialects early on, though Galician continued as both a spoken and literary language. Even the stubborn Basques adopted Castilian as their written language until modern times.

The growing prominence of Castilian led to an emerging national literature. Among the earliest forms were epics about the Reconquest, medieval legends comparable with the Arthurian stories of England. They often revealed much about the formation of national traits; in *Las Mocedades del Cid* Guillen de Castro writes:

> "Always endeavour to attain
> what is honourable and important;
> but if you have made a mistake
> defend it and don't correct it."

Another classic was *The Book of Good Love* (1335) by Juan Ruiz (the Archpriest of Hita), a surprisingly ribald gem comparable to *The Canterbury Tales*.

The then backwater island of Mallorca produced an outstanding mind in Ramon Llull (1235-1315), who wrote in Arabic and Latin as well as Catalan. In an age when a man could still know all there was to know, Llull was a poet, philosopher, and mystic (he saw visions of Christ), and he wrote on every conceivable subject. Tragically, he was stoned to death by Muslim fanatics while visiting Tunis.

The two centuries following the reign of Alfonso X witnessed an architectural flowering. With the passing of the solid but stodgy Romanesque came the lofty, refined Gothic style, the splendid cathedrals of Toledo, Burgos, and Leon — all soaring spires, stained-glass windows, and flying buttresses. When Sevillans met to plan their cathedral they remarked, "Let us put up a building so immense that the rest of the world will think us mad." Such was the spirit of the age.

The decline of the Moorish kingdoms left many areas of Spain — especially in Aragon, Valencia, and Andalucia — with Muslim majorities. These *mudejars* (from the Arabic "permitted to remain") presented no real threat, because they were largely glad to be rid of their Moroccan overlords. They created an innovative architectural style known as *mudejar*, based on traditional Moorish skills at working in plaster and wood, fabric and tile. Bare walls of no great consequence were transformed into works of art. The horseshoe arch, florid detail, and other Moorish motifs were adapted to Christian and secular buildings, such as Toledo's Church of Cristo de la Vega. Two authentic *mudejar* masterpieces are the *alcazares* (castles) of Coca (Segovia) and Sevilla.

*Mudejar* remained in vogue until the Renaissance style took over late in the 15th century, at a time when anything Muslim was considered inferior. But its themes and techniques survived and later turned up in buildings both in Spain and Spanish America.

THROUGHOUT CASTILLA'S HISTORY the pendulum seems to swing between short creative outpourings and succeeding stages of profound malaise, unrest and the inability to achieve a stable society. Such was the case in the years following the glorious era of Alfonso the Learned. Political struggle bubbled over between the monarchy and aristocracy, whose power was virtually unchecked by the kind of strong middle class found in Catalonia.

Castilla's dark days began when the nobility forced Alfonso to abdicate to his son Sancho. When they turned on the young heir like a pack of wolves, only the queen, Maria de Molina, held the kingdom together. Sancho died prematurely some years later, and she stepped in again to save the throne for her infant grandson. In a rough and wild age dominated by men, this exemplary woman managed to defeat the crown's enemies and was later immortalized in a play by Tirso de Molina called *La Prudencia en la Mujer*.

As if there were not enough problems, the Almohades had been replaced in Morocco by another belligerent dynasty, the Marinids. Encouraged by the chaos in Castilla, they captured Gibraltar, Algeciras and Tarifa with the treacherous aid of the king's own brother, Juan. The siege of Tarifa witnessed one of the more famous incidents in Spanish history, the defence of its castle by Perez de Guzman. When he refused to surrender, the attackers threatened to murder his son, but Guzman, henceforth known as "*El Bueno*," replied in true Iberian fashion. He threw out his knife and shouted, "Here is the weapon to do it, but I will never surrender." (No one is sure what happened to the son.)

The Marinids were crushed at the battle of Rio Salado (1340), in which artillery was used for the first time in Europe. Four years later Alfonso XI, with the help of Chaucer's "knight," recaptured Algeciras. (The Marinids somehow managed to hold Gibraltar until 1462.)

While Castilla watched the Straits of Gibraltar, Aragon had set sail on a very different course by turning outward to the Mediterranean in the manner of the prosperous Italian republics of Genoa and Venice. This was the era of Catalonia's famous maritime code, *Llibre del Consulat de Mar*. With Catalonia ever leading, Aragon managed to annex Sardinia and Sicily into its loose-knit empire, and they would remain in Spanish hands for centuries. In the early 1300s the feared Catalan army (the *almogavars*) was sent from Sicily to battle the Ottoman Turks. Somehow along the way they established a duchy in Athens, and Catalan became the official language for sixty years! The great figure of Aragon's medieval empire was King Pedro (Peter) IV "The Ceremonious." During the century Barcelona was Spain's greatest city and the largest shipbuilder in the Mediterranean, and Catalan sailors ranged freely from the Black Sea to the coast of Senegal.

To match its economic power, Aragon's commercial class enjoyed a good deal of political independence. The rights of the ruled were protected through a strong parliament and by a unique individual called the *justicia*, a kind of watchdog of the king. Compared with Castilla and its vast estates, the nobility was economically weak, but together with the middle class they were a feisty lot. Parliament's oath of allegiance to the king read: "We who are as good as you swear to you who are no better than we, to accept you as our king and sovereign lord, provided you accept all our liberties and laws; but if not, not." This was delivered by the seated *justicia* while he crowned the kneeling king. Later Spanish rulers, from Felipe II to Franco, would have to deal with this kind of spirit.

One bizarre figure from this period was Pedro de Luna, cardinal of Aragon, who was elected as Pope Benedict XIII during the Great Schism that wracked Christianity at century's end. Pontificating from Avignon in France, he refused to abdicate even after being branded an anti-pope in 1409, and he withdrew to the stronghold of Peñiscola near Alicante. Here he waited for a call to return that never came.

While Aragon was creating a Mediterranean empire, Castilla had wet its own commercial feet by developing the ports of Cartagena and Sevilla. Merchants from Genoa made inroads into this virgin market and controlled Castilian commerce for two centuries. (Hence, it was entirely appropriate that Columbus came from Genoa.) But by the end of the middle ages, Castilians had developed a "sheepherder's mentality"; commerce and industry were "things of the Jews and Moors."

The history of wool can even be taken as a capsule history of the entire economy. Thanks to the powerful *Mesta*, an organization of wealthy livestock owners, the rights of herders took precedence and agriculture suffered accordingly. (There were three principal sheep runs, each about 70 metres wide, between Old Castilla and Extremadura.) The crown, perennially in debt, took its cut of the wool profits.

Castilla's monarchs also turned for finance to the old Jewish money lenders, long after they had been replaced by a new breed of "capitalist" banks in Italy, France and even Catalonia. Jews prevailed as royal financiers right down to the days of Fernando and Isabel (Ferdinand and Isabella), when they were summarily expelled.

Cracks in Spain's traditional tolerance, the old society of three religions, began to appear after 1300. Muslims were required to wear certain clothes and hair styles, and Jews were blamed for various troubles, especially economic crises. Persecution increased proportionately with society's ills, though Spain at the time was still less anti-semitic than many other countries. During the same years when Spanish Jews held positions of power and married freely into the aristocracy, their French and English co-religionists were having property confiscated and being expelled en masse.

But the Jews' plight in Spain worsened with time. By some form of twisted logic, they were commonly blamed for the outbreak of the Black Death in Europe in the 1340s. (The name came from the large black blotches on the skin of the afflicted.) The severity of the bubonic plague is often overlooked, but as much as one-third of the continent's population perished in a few years, causing the virtual breakdown of civilization in many areas. Parts of Iberia were hard hit, especially Aragon.

Anti-semitism heated up during the rule of Pedro (Peter) the Cruel (1350-69) after he surrounded himself with Jewish financial advisers and tax collectors. One of them was Samuel Ha-levi, best remembered as the builder of Toledo's El Tránsito Synagogue. Among the Christian clergy and their flocks, Jews came to represent the hated regime itself.

The diabolical state of Castilian politics is summed up in the story of Pedro the Cruel. After he inherited the throne at age 15, the eldest of five illegitimate brothers, a ruthless struggle commenced. It is generally accepted that Pedro murdered an archbishop, several cousins, brothers and friends, not to mention, in all probability, his own French queen.

Pedro lived in his *alcazar* in Sevilla with his mistress. In this love nest he murdered the Red King of Granada with 37 of his courtiers. According to the story, the Muslim ruler arrived wearing a priceless ruby in his turban which Pedro immediately craved. He invited the group for a banquet, and as soon as they were seated his guards leapt out and murdered them one by one.

Some historians claim these stories were invented later to excuse Pedro's own murder by his half-brother, Enrique (Henry) of Trastamara (also known as Henry the Bastard). In fact, Pedro's own followers never called him "The Cruel" (at least publicly), but used the accolade "The Dispenser of Justice."

Economic historians claim there was much more than sibling rivalry involved, and that Pedro was trying to curb the land-hoarding nobles. When Enrique tried to depose his brother, it was the climax of years of struggle between Pedro and the Castilian nobility. Not one to take things lying down, the king appealed to England's famous Edward, The Black Prince, for help. In response, France sent mercenary Bertrand du Guesclin, head of the White Companies, to support Enrique.

Edward dealt the rebels a shattering defeat, and Enrique fled briefly to Aragon, leaving the humiliated Guesclin behind as prisoner. In gratitude, Pedro presented his famous stolen ruby to the wife of the Black Prince, who shortly after returned to England. The gem now adorns the imperial crown in the Tower of London.

Enrique was down but not out and captured Pedro two years later. To finish the sordid story, there was a notorious fight to the death between the two half-brothers, not on a glorious battlefield but in a wretched tent. Enrique stabbed the king with his own hand as he shouted "You Jew bastard!" He would soon be crowned Enrique II, bringing the House of Trastamara to power in Castilla (and later Aragon) until the coming of the Austrian Habsburgs in 1516.

THE 15TH CENTURY opened with the peninsula's political map — the kingdoms of Castilla, Aragon, Navarra, Portugal and Granada — little changed since 1250. What transpired over the next few decades was by no means foredestined. Individual decisions and pure chance would prove more decisive than historical forces in the creation of modern Spain, and in its phenomenal rise to world power.

The weak and cowardly Juan II ruled Castilla for nearly half a century (1406-1454) in spite of his ineptitude. He soon fell under the influence of a court "favourite" named Alvaro de Luna, and before long the king's sole function was to sign whatever his minister put in front of him. After many years of enduring Alvaro, bitterly jealous courtiers accused him of some trumped-up charge and gained the king's ear. After a sham trial Alvaro was beheaded and his mutilated body displayed publicly. But the vacillating king came to regret his action and died a broken man, wishing he "had been born son of a mechanic rather than king of Castilla."

Faced with ineffective kings until the coming of Fernando and Isabel, the Castilian nobility prospered as never before. Leonor de Albuquerque, for example, could travel the entire breadth of Castilla without setting foot outside her estates. Meanwhile, in Aragon, the death of Martin I brought an end to the dynasty begun with the marriage of Berenguer and Petronilla. Lacking other suitable candidates Fernando (Ferdinand) of Antequera, from a junior branch of the Trastamaras, was awarded the crown. Even though Castilla and Aragon remained separate, they were brought immeasurably closer by this sharing of the same ruling house.

## IBERIA IN THE 15th CENTURY

SANTIAGO DE COMPOSTELA

KINGDOM OF NAVARRA

BURGOS • PAMPLONA

FRANCE

KINGDOM OF ARAGON

VALLADOLID •

ZARAGOZA

BARCELONA

KINGDOM OF PORTUGAL

• TOLEDO

VALENCIA

KINGDOM OF CASTILE

LISBON

CORDOBA •

SEVILLA •

• GRANADA
KINGDOM OF GRANADA

MALAGA

☐ CHRISTIAN STATES
■ ISLAMIC STATE

It was Aragon, more than Castilla, which strongly backed this Compromise of Caspe (1412). The reason may have been survival. These were hard years for Aragon: reeling from a severe manpower shortage caused by the plague, the previously booming economy began to badly falter. The fall of Constantinople to the Ottoman Turks in 1453 was a severe blow to Catalan shipping interests, and a dynastic struggle and civil war added to the woes.

Things were not much better in Castilla. Juan was succeeded by his son Enrique, physically repellent and morally perverted. Enrique IV was incompetent and impotent, a deadly combination in a monarch. Some claimed his youthful debaucheries had impaired his sexual vigour, but tongues also wagged about his Moorish guards and a court "full of Jews in bright shirts." Whatever the reason, when his second wife gave birth to a daughter it was assumed she was the offspring of the queen's affair with the dashing Beltran de la Cueva. Juana, the dubious heiress, was dubbed *La Beltraneja* — roughly translated as "Beltran's bastard girl." However, many claim this was all just vicious propaganda invented by her rivals, namely Isabel, Enrique's younger half-sister.

Born in 1451 at Madrigal de las Altas Torres (Avila), the future queen Isabel was plump, with a fair complexion, chestnut hair, greenish-blue eyes and the round face of a peasant girl. In the right light she could be attractive, and Enrique tried to use his sister to cement marriage alliances favourable to Castilla. Isabel had many suitors, but soon the choice boiled down to king Alfonso V of Portugal and Fernando, heir to the throne of Aragon. Enrique favoured Alfonso, a man twice Isabel's age. Fernando, on the other hand, was handsome, athletic and shrewd — what the Spanish call *listo*. Isabel's choice would decide if Castilla would unite with Portugal or Aragon. In other words, the very composition of modern Spain.

To the eternal delight of romantics everywhere, the princess chose Fernando, and envoys were sent to arrange the marriage. Her decision aroused so much opposition, however, that the Aragonese heir chose to travel incognito to Castilla. Disguised as a servant, he waited on the others in his group whenever they stopped en route. Upon reaching Valladolid, Fernando and Isabel finally met, and the attraction was mutual.

Nevertheless, objections persisted in some quarters. For one thing, the couple was so closely related by blood (first cousins) that a papal dispensation was required. This was obtained in short order, but it later proved to be a forgery concocted by the king of Aragon, the archbishop of Toledo, and Fernando himself. But nothing could stop the marriage of 19-year-old Isabel and Fernando, a year younger and slightly shorter. At a ceremony in the castle of Segovia, the bride was clad head to foot in white brocade and ermine; the groom wore a majestic golden robe lined with sable. On October 19, 1469, the two teenage heirs were married.

But before Fernando and Isabel could make their rendezvous with immortality they had other business to attend to. Their storybook marriage had brought no unity to the peninsula, legal or otherwise. King Enrique for one was irate at the prospect of a union with Aragon and declared that his daughter Juana, not

Isabel, was his rightful successor. Adding insult, the pope excommunicated the couple when he found out about Fernando's forgery. To the church they would later champion, they were living in sin.

Enrique's death in 1474 launched a succession crisis that soon led to outright civil war in Castilla. Parliament proclaimed Isabel queen, and she was easily persuaded that her young niece was illegitimate and her supporters traitors (though the Duke of Alba reminded her, "If we are defeated, *we* shall be the traitors.") The supporters of Juana were led by the previously spurned Alfonso of Portugal, who announced his intention to use force to put her on the throne. This was indeed another era, and Fernando challenged the Portuguese king to a duel. The aging Alfonso wisely declined, and two armies met instead at Toro, where Juana's supporters were routed. Alfonso returned to Portugal and Juana *La Beltraneja* was packed off to a convent.

The treaty of Alcacobaca (1479) confirmed Isabel's inheritance and with it Spain's future: Castilla was wedded to Aragon, not Portugal. In that same year Fernando's father finally passed away, leaving him king and the two medieval giants united by the vows of marriage, if little else.

It was an interesting match of monarchs as well as kingdoms. Isabel could be painfully pious at times, certain she was right by virtue of divine guidance. Fernando survived more on personal charm than willpower or intelligence, yet he could be cool and crafty in diplomatic haggling. He knew his limitations and was usually quite willing to follow his wife's lead. Wrote the royal secretary: "He was given to taking advice, especially that of the queen."

In the beginning Fernando intended to reign as an equal. By law his power in Castilla derived solely from his spouse, but he demanded joint exercise of royal authority. He succeeded in winning all the trappings of power: both names on royal appointments, seals, and coins, and a motto that read *Tanto Monta, monta tanto, Isabel como Fernando*, roughly "He counts for as much as she does; she counts for as much as he does." Later, in the spirit of unity, he resigned himself to a secondary role.

Yet there was no real fusion of the two crowns, and they remained rather strange bedfellows. Despite its wars, Castilla was stronger and more dynamic than Aragon, with five times the population. The centre was growing and expanding while the east, notably Barcelona, had experienced a sharp decline since its halcyon days a century earlier. Even after the marriage, Catalans were treated as foreigners in Castilla, where their arch-enemies, the Genoese, had a grip on banking and commerce. Economically, Castilians looked north to market their wool, while Aragon traded with the Mediterranean.

The two kingdoms were quite different politically as well. The Castilian *cortes* (parliament) was weak, and the nobility kept at bay by the crown, although they had recently been flexing their aristocratic muscles. In Aragon, the nobles had triumphed in terms of real power, and Catalonia and Valencia each had its own parliament and rights.

Despite the marriage of the century, Spain was still — to borrow a phrase — a mere "geographical expression."

## SIGHTS & SITES

**Avila**: *Medieval walls average 10 metres in height, with 88 towers and 8 gates; also Romanesque Cathedral and St Vincent's Basilica.*

**Barcelona**: *Gothic Quarter has many buildings from 13th-15th centuries, including Cathedral; Museum of Catalonian Art has Romanesque and Gothic treasures.*

**Burgos**: *Cathedral started in 1221 and continued for three centuries; here lies El Cid beneath soaring transept.*

**Coca** *(Segovia): One of the best examples of* mudejar *style is the* alcazar.

**Córdoba**: *The Juderia, old Jewish quarter, contains synagogue dating to 14th century.*

**Fromista** *(Palencia): Romanesque church on road to Santiago, erected in about 1066.*

**Guadalupe** *(Caceres): Monastery built after appearance of Virgin around 1300; important symbol of hispanidad.*

**Huesca**: *36 kms. from town is Loarre Castle (1096) with vast panorama of Ebro valley.*

**La Oliva Monastery** *(Navarra): One of first built by French Cistercians (ca. 1100).*

**Leon**: *Superb Cathedral, especially stained-glass windows.*

**Leyre Monastery** *(Navarra): Spiritual centre of Navarra and pantheon of its kings.*

**Málaga**: *Alcazaba; museum of Moorish art; Gibralfaro, ramparts on site of ancient lighthouse.*

**Montserrat** *(Barcelona): Although rebuilt in 19th century, in spirit it belongs to the middle ages; an important pilgrimage site.*

**Palma de Mallorca** *(Balearic Islands): Gothic Cathedral built 1230-1601.*

**Pedraza de la Sierra** *(Segovia): Village retains medieval atmosphere with castle on knoll, narrow streets.*

**Peñiscola** *(Castellon): Stone castle was final refuge of anti-pope Benedict XIII.*

**Poblet Monastery** *(Tarragona): Founded by Ramon Berenguer IV in 1150.*

**San Juan de la Pena Monastery** *(Huesca): Served as pantheon of kings of Aragon-Navarra for 500 years.*

**Santiago de Compostela** *(La Coruña): Cathedral is one of world's finest; famous Door of Glory is Romanesque masterpiece.*

**Sevilla**: *Cathedral is Spain's largest, has tombs of Alfonso X and St. Ferdinand; Giralda Tower and Torre de Oro built by Almohades; mudejar Alcazar; Santa Cruz was former Jewish quarter.*

**Sigüenza** *(Guadalajara): Fortress-like cathedral begun in 12th century but not finished till 1495.*

**Toledo**: *Superb Gothic cathedral features choirstalls, Mozarabic chapel; El Transito Synagogue with Sephardic museum.*

**Zaragoza**: *Gothic Seo Cathedral has* mudejar *decoration; the Aljaferia is a Moorish palace from* taifas *period (11th century).*

## CHAPTER 5

# BIRTH OF THE SPANISH WORLD

R omantic writers like Washington Irving have created a windmill of words describing the glories of Granada. Yet few of the thousands of tourists who visit each year realize that one of history's most important towns lies nearby. Sleepy Santa Fe straddles the road to Málaga in the heart of the highly fertile *vega*, once watered with the blood of Christians and Moors. A signpost at the town's entrance reads *La Cuna de Hispanidad*, literally "the cradle of Spanishness."

Although Santa Fe's drab, heat-hazed streets evoke few images of bygone glory, this dusty market town was the birthplace of the Hispanic world. Here, the newly united kingdoms of Castilla and Aragon slammed shut the book on centuries of Moorish occupation, edging closer to the modern nation of Spain. And here too the man we call Christopher Columbus received permission for his great voyage of discovery. A street called Calle Cristobal Colon and a humble plaque are the sole reminders that at Santa Fe was born an empire that would pale the splendours of Moorish Granada.

Santa Fe ("holy faith") was built in 1491 as a base camp for the final conquest of Granada; hence its dubious claim to be "the only place in Spain not contaminated by Muslim heresy." A plaque affixed to the south gate, one of four at each point of a cruciform layout, commemorates the founding, and inscriptions recall the roles of different Spanish towns in the final act of the Reconquest. Underscoring Santa Fe's military origins, a sculpture of a Moor's severed head sits atop the main church.

Here is a place to ponder time's cruel verdicts. Santa Fe witnessed some of history's most important months in that most famous of years — 1492 — but today it is just a forgotten curiosity.

Before facing the Moors of Granada, Fernando and Isabel needed to consolidate their own precarious power. They turned first to the Castilian nobility, which for years had been chipping away at royal authority. In a series of bold moves, they forced the aristocrats out of parliament, took control of the noble-infested military orders, and ordered the destruction of all castles not vital to national defence. The carrot to match this royal stick was the granting of conquered lands in Andalucia to crown supporters.

To support the royal power-grab, Fernando and Isabel gained control of the medieval *Hermandades*. These brotherhoods of towns had their own police, usually bands of crossbowmen who pursued and shot down suspects, vigilante-style. The new monarchs molded these forces into a feared national police called the *Santa Hermandad* (Holy Brotherhood) serving royal interests.

The next target was the church. The archbishop of Toledo was second in power only to the monarchs themselves, and many other bishops were aristocrats with their own castles and private armies. Corruption and immorality were rampant from Toledo down to the village priest. Concubinage, for example, was an accepted practice among the supposedly celibate clergy. The sons of a priest could even inherit his property. The monarchs appointed Hernando Talavera, Isabel's confessor and a converted Jew, to reform these abuses.

What was perhaps the greatest source of burgeoning royal power was created in 1478 — the infamous Inquisition. This papal institution originated in the 13th century to deal with the Albigensian heresy, chiefly in France, and had become virtually extinct. Isabel obtained the pope's permission for a revamped version. From the outset, the Spanish Inquisition's main business was finding and weeding out "false" Christians, particularly Jews who had converted but were suspected of secretly maintaining their rites and customs. Jews or Muslims who practised their religions openly were not within its jurisdiction and were allowed — at least for a few years — to continue. But the so-called *conversos* were considered unreliable and dangerous to a monarchy obsessed with unity and uniformity.

The Inquisition was a product of the times, born amid Spain's shaky new identity and fears of Jewish-Moorish alliances. Religious persecution was part of the age, in Spain as much as in the England of Henry VIII and Mary Tudor. And in Spain too it served crown interests, shoring up royal power at the expense of the nobles and clergy. The Spanish Inquisition was the one institution, other than the crown itself, common to both Castilla and Aragon.

Jews had suffered persecution since the days of Pedro the Cruel, and things were not improving. Jewish converts suspected of reverting to old ways were called *marranos*, derived from the word for swine. But the Inquisition and Christians generally were not anti-semitic in a racial sense. There were Jewish *conversos* in all areas of power — including Talavera and possibly even the feared Grand Inquisitor, Dominican prior Tomás de Torquemada. The crown's military ventures were financed by two prominent Jews, and King Fernando himself had Jewish blood from his maternal grandfather.

It can even be argued that for a time the Inquisition helped protect Jews by rescuing them from the threat of mob violence. Nevertheless, it struck terror in the hearts of converted Jews because its methods virtually guaranteed the guilt of the accused. Those unfortunate enough to fall under suspicion were secretly arrested and thrown into solitary cells, where they might wait months before learning the charges. Their accuser could remain anonymous, and torture was used to extract confessions from anyone maintaining their innocence.

Punishment was dealt out at a public display called an *auto de fe* (act of faith) which included processions, sermons, confessions, and executions. At the first such event, held in Sevilla in 1481, six convicted heretics were solemnly burned at the stake. The Inquisition's early years were especially bloody, with about 2,000 executions in the 1480s alone. (Of an estimated 12,000 death sentences over three centuries, about half occurred between 1481 and 1516.)

SHORTLY AFTER THE civil war ended, Isabel asked the pope for crusading rights against the last bastion of non-Christian Spain — the kingdom of Granada. Ruled by the Nasrid dynasty, this remnant of the *taifas* stretched about 180 kilometres from east to west and 75 inland from the sea. Swelled by Muslim refugees, the capital had about 60,000 inhabitants; other cities were Málaga, famed for its figs and sweet wine, and the prosperous port of Almeria.

Washington Irving and his romantic cohorts have spun a web of gilded prose around Moorish Granada, "enclosed by two rivers like a necklace of pearls." Supreme embodiment of this vision is the Alhambra, a reddish fortress-palace perched on a hill overlooking the old Moorish quarter, the Albaicin. Part of the Alhambra's glory comes from its superb location, a perfect blending of site and structure. The rest derives from its exquisitely carved rooms and lush courtyards filled with the sound of splashing water. It's said that the royal baths here had three taps, from which flowed hot, cold, and perfumed water.

Although begun much earlier, the "red castle" did not reach its splendour until the 14th century, just as Granada was sliding into decadence. Indeed, the last piece of Moorish architecture may well have been the Patio of the Lions, delicate arcades resting on 124 slender pillars that look as fragile as a pirouetting ballerina.

The centuries of impasse between Christian and Moor had not been without incident. In 1410 Antequera (Málaga) was captured by Fernando, the future king of Aragon. Three decades later, more Christian victories led to a puppet ruler in the Alhambra who paid an annual tribute. But Fernando and Isabel soon realized that war with an outside foe was a perfect means to unify their kingdoms.

In 1476, Sultan Mulay Hassan replied to Castilla's demand for payment of the annual tribute by retorting, "The mints of Granada no longer coin gold, but steel." But the Christians were too busy to pick up the gauntlet until five years later, when the castle of Zahara near Ronda fell. At last they prepared for war, and Christian armies marched under the new regal symbol of the yoke and arrows. This final crusade would last ten years (1482-92).

The chronic instability of Moorish Spain sprang from the harem, which produced numerous sons by different mothers, any of whom might vie for the throne. The Moors' last family feud contributed greatly to Christian victory. Granada was split between supporters of Mulay's wife Aixa and her son Boabdil (called "The Unfortunate One" since birth) on one side and a beautiful Christian prisoner named Soraya on the other. The sultan had fallen for Soraya and forsaken Aixa and her son, and civil war inevitably followed.

This was the stuff of legend. Tour-guides at the Alhambra will point out the "blood stains" (probably rust) on the floor of the Hall of the Abencerrajes, where Mulay had thirty followers of Aixa beheaded. In another story, Boabdil escaped from a tower prison by using a rope made from silk sashes. After Aixa's faction gained the upper hand, Mulay was forced to flee Granada to the protection of his brother, Al-Zaghal, governor of Málaga. Fernando revelled in the spectacle and proclaimed, "I intend to pick this pomegranate seed by seed." (The word *granada* means pomegranate.)

But the Spanish army proceeded with some difficulty, mostly financial. On one occasion Fernando was obliged to cut silver chalices (used at Mass) into pieces in order to pay his men. The queen, who served as army quartermaster, took personal loans and even pawned the crown jewels to pay for the campaign.

A year after the war commenced, Boabdil was captured at Loja and cut a secret deal with Fernando. To assure the defeat of his hated father and uncle, he agreed to surrender Granada once his rivals were vanquished. In 1487, Málaga fell after a four-month siege, and Al-Zaghal was exiled and died blind and impoverished in Morocco. Thousands of Moors also crossed the sea, founding the town of Chechouen in the Rif mountains. (Today it remains, except for the occasional tour-bus, a perfect slice of old Al-Andalus.)

Málaga's fate decided the war; henceforth the capital was cut off from any hope of aid from North Africa. But when Almeria too was captured, Boabdil reneged on the secret bargain and refused to surrender Granada. The stage was set for the invasion of the *vega* and the founding of Santa Fe.

Granada was protected by massive walls and towers, and Fernando chose to throw up a blockade rather than attack. When the queen joined the army she vowed not to change her blouse until Granada fell (her husband soon dissuaded her). One night a fire swept through the tent camp, and in April 1491 combat ceased while a new town — of brick and mortar this time — went up. In the following months, the noose around Granada tightened, but apart from the occasional skirmish the war became a stalemate favouring the Christians.

Into this scene strode that dogged adventurer who changed the world — Cristobal Colón, Cristoforo de Colombo, Christopher Columbus, the Great Admiral himself. Speculation has swirled around Columbus's origins and nationality, not to mention his fascinating if confused life prior to arriving in Spain. One noted historian claimed his name was Colom, from a family of

Mallorcan Jews that had emigrated to Genoa and changed their name to Colombo. Another, more improbable, theory holds that he was the illegitimate son of the Prince of Viana, Fernando's disinherited elder brother. Columbus himself threw a smokescreen over his origins, probably because he was indeed the son of a humble weaver from Genoa and was taking a giant step up in a very class-conscious society. But add to the mystery the fact that he never wrote in Italian, not even letters to his brother Bartholomew, and doubts refuse to go away.

The red-haired, blue-eyed boy went to sea at age 14 and may have later become a pirate. In 1476, he escaped from a sinking ship and swam to the Portuguese shore, there to remain for years working as a sailor and map salesman. He somehow married into a well-to-do family and began to devise a plan to reach the Orient by crossing the Atlantic. His bride's father was governor of an island in the Madeiras, and Columbus may have received important nautical information which lent credence to his theories. In any case, he finally managed to present his ideas to the Portuguese king.

Portugal was then at the vanguard of pushing back the world's maritime frontiers. With the Turks blocking traditional land routes, there was an all-out effort to find a sea passage to oriental spice markets. In 1488, Bartholomew Diaz sailed along the African coast and reached the Cape of Good Hope.

Spaniards too were caught up in the spirit of the age, and a century before Columbus they had conquered the Canary Islands. Stubborn Guanches managed to hold out for a time on Tenerife, but their position was hopeless. Sailors spoke of the "remarkable beauty" of the women, and within decades the pure Guanche strain was hard to find. Spain's possession of the Canaries was confirmed by a treaty that also gave the Portuguese a free hand along the west African coast.

With the islands as a base, sailors began looking toward the setting sun. The existence of land to the west was, contrary to myth, a matter of common speculation; only the most ignorant believed that the earth was flat or the ocean inhabited by sea serpents. Some have speculated that Columbus possessed "inside" information, possibly from a sailor named Alfonso Sanchez, who may have reached the West Indies after a storm blew his ship off course.

After years of futile negotiations in Lisbon, Columbus left in disgust and sailed with his young son for Spain. In the summer of 1485, they landed at Palos near Huelva and sought shelter at the Franciscan monastery of La Rábida. Here Columbus met Fray Juan Perez, the queen's former confessor, who took an interest in the project and arranged an introduction at court. Our hero's luck seemed to be changing.

Meanwhile, however, the Catholic Monarchs were up to their necks in the War of Granada and could not consider another costly endeavour. A special commission under Talavera was appointed to study the matter, and Columbus received an annual retainer of 12,000 *maravedis*, the wage of a common seaman. For years he lived on this stipend, following the court and occasionally taking part in fighting. Talavera and other members of the Council of Salamanca regarded the Italian as a wild visionary, but they were not just ignorant clerics. Not since ancient Greece had any educated person doubted that the earth was a sphere. (Before the birth of Christ Strabo wrote, "If the extent of the Atlantic Ocean were not an obstacle, we might easily pass by sea from Iberia to India.")

The debate centred on the size of the ocean and the feasibility of a voyage. Columbus maintained that the distance between the Canaries and China was about 4,000 kilometres, while the council believed it — correctly, as it turned out — to be much larger. Of course, neither had any idea that lying between Europe and Asia was an unexpected surprise. When Columbus continued to press his case, the council proclaimed his plan "vain, impracticable and resting on grounds too weak to merit the support of the government."

Columbus returned briefly to Portugal for another go at the king, and his brother Bartholomew left for England to try to interest Henry VII in the project. Fortunately for Spain, Columbus was what you might call a hard-head, and he refused to give up on Isabel.

One interesting footnote: The "forgotten" man in this saga was Giovanni Caboto from Genoa, who moved to Valencia about 1490 and, calling himself Juan Caboto, tried to convince officials of the westward route. Finally giving up, he moved to England and received a royal commission for a later voyage. In 1497 the man history calls John Cabot discovered Newfoundland (Canada).

BY THE SUMMER of 1491 even Columbus was losing patience, and he travelled to La Rábida to visit his son. The sympathetic Juan Perez wrote a letter to the queen at Santa Fe, and she agreed to see the Italian again. But Isabel had more pressing matters.

After months of stalemate and secret negotiations, Boabdil surrendered Granada in exchange for generous terms, and an agreement was ratified in November. When this became known a riot broke out in the city, and the Christian army entered earlier than expected, on January 2, 1492. It was an auspicious start for that most famous of years; the last stronghold of the Moors had fallen.

Soldiers carried banners of Santiago and sang hymns as they marched up the Hill of Martyrs to the Alhambra. Here they planted a silver cross and the flag of Castilla on the Vela Tower which could be seen all the way to Santa Fe. On January 6 the Catholic Monarchs entered Granada and received homage from Boabdil inside the Alhambra. Looking out on the silent and secretive city, they prepared to spend their first night in the fabled palace.

As part of the settlement, Boabdil, the twentieth and last sultan of the Nasrid dynasty, was given 30,000 gold coins and a slice of the Alpujarras region south of Granada. Leaving the city for the last time, he looked back and wept for his lost kingdom. As every tour-guide knows, his mother then uttered, "You do well to weep as a woman for that which you could not defend as a man." Because Granada was handed over without a fight, the Albaicin quarter retains its Moorish flavour today, its houses boasting inner courtyards and Arabic inscriptions. Other pre-Christian remnants include a few arcades from the old silk market, the *alcaiceria*, and the *corral del carbon*, a caravansary.

The Treaty of Granada contained 55 articles guaranteeing Moorish rights. The vanquished were offered transit to Morocco, as well as the return trip within three years if they were not happy. These lenient terms were favoured by Talavera, named first archbishop of Granada, but within a few years all this would change. The troubles were far from over for the Moors.

The end came sooner for the Jews: just three months after Granada's fall, an expulsion order was issued for any Jew refusing Christian baptism. Adherence to any belief other than Catholicism became tantamount to treason. All this is ironic in that loans from two Jewish financiers (named Seneor and Abravanel) paid for the Granada war. After the expulsion decree, the pair offered 600,000 *reales* to Fernando and Isabel to have it lifted. According to one story, just as the king wavered, Grand Inquisitor Torquemada burst into the room and demanded that the order be executed. And so it was.

The expulsion of the Jews was a curious action in many ways and has been much debated. Such things were not unknown in medieval Europe: England had expelled its Jews in 1290 and France in 1306. But what stung so much in Spain was the high status, both culturally and economically, that Jews had reached during the middle ages. (Remember, the king himself was part Jewish.)

But consider the background. The traditional anti-semitism of the peasantry had been whipped up in recent years by some sordid incidents and rumours. There was the infamous case of Benito Garcia, a Christian convert who was arrested with a consecrated wafer (used in the Mass) hidden in his knapsack. After six days of torture he confessed to the ritual murder by crucifixion of a Christian child and named five *converso* accomplices. All the accused were burned alive at Avila.

Many Christians regarded Jews — whether baptised or not — as the natural allies of the Moors and potential traitors. It was an interesting coincidence that the crown was bankrupt, and Jews were generally prosperous merchants. Before fleeing, many were forced to sell everything at huge losses — a house for a donkey, a vineyard for a suit of clothes — if they did not suffer outright expropriation. (The crown seized all unsold Jewish property in September.) With its regrettable decision, Spain lost a vital part of its citizenry and most of the urban middle class.

The expulsion order gave Jews four months to pack up and leave. An estimated 50,000 converted and took their chances with the Inquisition as "new Christians"; about 200,000 left Spain forever; another few thousand were killed for refusing to do either.

The majority of these Sephardic Jews (from the Hebrew word for Spain, *Sefaradh*) settled in North Africa, Italy, Greece, Turkey, and the Levant. In their cultural baggage they carried the medieval Castilian language, called *ladino*, and hundreds of ancient ballads which still survive in isolated Sephardic communities around the Mediterranean. It's said that old keys to their Spanish homes, long-since demolished, are passed from one generation to the next.

(A final footnote to this story occurred in 1982, when a law was passed inviting Sephardic Jews to become Spaniards again after 490 years of exile.)

1492 WAS QUITE a year; less than a month after the expulsion order, Columbus finally got the royal nod, but not without plenty of drama. Upon Granada's surrender, the intrepid Italian approached Fernando again, but the answer was still no. With an encouraging letter from the French king in hand, Columbus rode off to Palos, where Father Perez persuaded him to wait. The old fray then hopped on a mule and rode to Santa Fe, where a tear-filled plea convinced the queen to see Columbus once more. Even then, the explorer shot himself in the foot again with his extravagant demands, and the royal couple balked.

Columbus rode off a final time and only the eleventh-hour heroics of a friend at court, Luis de Santangel, convinced the queen. She vowed to pledge her jewels to finance the expedition (it proved unnecessary). A rider overtook Columbus a short distance from Granada, and on April 17, 1492, a pact was signed at Santa Fe which raised the curtain on a new world beyond even the Grand Admiral's wildest dreams.

In an age before refrigeration, Eastern spices were in great demand for preserving and flavouring meats. Pepper fetched 40 times its original cost and a pound of cloves was worth two cows. But Isabel was motivated by the chance to gain souls as well as gold. By sailing west to the Orient, she reasoned, Christians could attack Islam from the rear and even regain the Holy Land. The Reconquest could go on and on until the last infidel perished. Let us not forget that the first title inscribed on the Queen's tomb in Granada's Cathedral reads: "Extirpator of the Muhammadan heresy."

With the fall of Granada, Spain was faced with a decision of truly historic implications — whether or not to carry the struggle against Islam into North Africa. Melilla in Morocco was captured in 1497 (it remains Spanish today), but the idea of an African campaign was postponed for a crucial decade. When it resurfaced it was too late. Spain's failure to follow up in North Africa is one of history's great "missed opportunities." But there were other concerns for the Catholic Monarchs: domestic stability and, eventually, the conquest of America.

On the morning of August 3, 1492, a fleet of three small ships with 120 men, many of them criminals under temporary amnesty, sailed off from Palos. They stopped for final provisions in the Canaries, then pressed on westward. After 31 days without sighting land, the crew grew restless and rebellious, urging Columbus to turn back. Certain of his calculations, he asked for just two more days and promised to give up if land was not reached. Finally, at about midnight on October 12, the thirty-second day, a faint shape appeared on the horizon, "something like a white sand cliff gleaming in the moonlight." The next morning the group landed on a small island that Columbus christened San Salvador. The date is celebrated each year throughout the Hispanic world as *El Dia de la Hispanidad*; within a century Spanish language and culture would be found in most of the Americas.

Columbus spent several months searching for the fabulous cities of Marco Polo, but found only a few primitive tribes and a smattering of wealth. From the timbers of the foundered *Santa Maria* he built a fortress and left 40 men behind before sailing for Spain. Eight months after leaving Palos for the great unknown, Columbus strode into the royal court at Barcelona. With him were six natives (called "Indians," the greatest misnomer in history) laden with gold and pearls, strange fruits, and exotic birds. In a carefully rehearsed speech, he lay a world of untold riches at the monarchs' feet. When he finished, everyone fell to their knees in thanksgiving while solemn strains of the *Te Deum* poured forth.

It can be argued (especially by Americans) that the discovery of America in 1492 was the greatest single event in the history of mankind. With one stroke it put an end to the middle ages, opened the colonial era, and shifted the centre of gravity from the Mediterranean to the Atlantic. Most important, the discovery altered forever the concept that a man's station in life was inextricably linked with the class into which he was born. Men of action and enterprise replaced those of high birth as leaders. For "go-getters" everywhere, America became an illusion, a hope for better things in both material and idealistic realms. And so it remains to this day.

During the next few years, Columbus made three more voyages to the Indies. The second expedition, in September 1493, was quite different — 1,500 men in 17 vessels led by the triumphant Italian sailor. They carried seeds, plantings, livestock... everything for a proper colony. But troubled winds were already blowing, for when the group reached San Salvador, nothing was left of the Spanish colony. The natives told of incredible avarice and lust which caused them to massacre the settlers just a month after Columbus left. The Conquest would not be peaceful, after all.

In one of history's cruelest tricks, the dreamed-for lands of India and China continued to elude the great explorer, and he never recognized his actual accomplishment. When Columbus reached Cuba, for example, he imagined himself in the kingdom of the great Khan, and sent two "ambassadors" with letters from the queen off into the jungle searching for the fabled capital. Columbus founded the city of Santo Domingo on the isle of Hispaniola (Haiti/Dominican Republic), and he later explored Jamaica, Puerto Rico and the coast of Honduras on the mainland. But it was not an easy road. A far better dreamer than administrator, he was charged with incompetence and shipped home in irons (he was later released). Aside from a few trinkets, there were no riches for Columbus, and on returning from his last voyage, he was not even invited to court.

Still muttering about the Cipango (Japan) of Marco Polo, he died bedridden and poor in Valladolid in May 1506 at the age of 55. His funeral was simple, and the official chronicle failed to note his passing. (His remains rest in the Cathedral of Santo Domingo, *not* in the ornate casket in Sevilla.) For another decade his discoveries would be shrugged off as essentially worthless.

One final ignominy: the New World received its name from an Italian with a better gift for public relations named Amerigo Vespucci. Sailing under the Castilian flag, this Italian adventurer charted the coastline of South America. Vespucci's widely read letters described "lascivious women healthy as fish" and "cannibals with smoked human legs hung from the rafters of their huts." These images captured Europe's imagination, and one German cartographer decided to call the new continent "America" after Amerigo. The name stuck.

Another, less heralded, event of 1492 was the election of a Spaniard from a famous Italian family, Rodrigo Borgia, as Pope Alexander VI — the most corrupt pontiff in history. He became a close ally of Fernando and Isabel, naming them *Los Reyes Católicos* (The Catholic Monarchs), and his famous "line of demarcation," 370 leagues west of the Cape Verde Islands, conferred virtually all the new lands on Castilla. (Portugal was allowed to conquer Brazil.)

DURING THE REIGN of the Catholic Monarchs, Spain retained an essentially antiquated social structure, whose iniquities were questioned by few. The grandees were addressed as "cousins" by the king and allowed to keep their hats on in his presence. The *hidalgos* jealously guarded the appellation "Don" and their family coat of arms. In a world where heraldry was the key to status, vast time and effort were spent on finding or inventing aristocratic ancestors in the family tree.

Landowners comprised about 2% of the population but owned 97% of the land, while the vast majority of Spaniards were landless peasants. The Duke of Infantado, for example, lorded over 800 villages and 90,000 vassals. This concentration of landed wealth was exacerbated toward the end of the Reconquest, when huge tracts of Andalucia, the *latifundios*, were handed out to important nobles. Soldiers of the military orders received smaller parcels in Extremadura and La Mancha.

The economy remained medieval, each kingdom a world unto itself. Before the wealth of the Indies began to trickle into Castilla, sheep raising was the chief source of income. Aragon's economy was equally weak, having suffered numerous setbacks since the glories of its medieval empire.

On the bright side, peninsular commerce seemed to thrive at traditional fairs, like the one at Medina del Campo (Burgos). People flocked to these colourful markets for the luxuries of medieval life: woollens and silks, perfumes and cosmetics, spices and honey, the only sweetener at the time.

Towns remained medieval in appearance, with garbage thrown into a ditch running down the middle of the street where the pigs fed, and both men and women squatting in the street for bodily functions. (One thing Spaniards in the New World noted was the cleanliness of Indian towns.) Life was brightened by the weekly market and by frequent religious festivals and pilgrimages.

The joint monarchy continued its efforts to reform the indolent and immoral clergy. They succeeded in gaining some royal control over church coffers and the appointment of bishops — essentially the same battle Henry VIII waged in England. In these struggles they were aided by Cardinal Mendoza, chief royal adviser during the crucial dozen years after 1482.

Mendoza's successor was the even more remarkable Cardinal Gonzalo Jimenez de Cisneros, known to history as simply Cisneros. Although coming from a poor background, he was named to the pivotal position of confessor to the queen. Isabel proceeded to get him appointed archbishop of Toledo, and he launched more clerical reforms, such as enforcing the vows of celibacy. More than a thousand friars fled to Morocco with their mistresses rather than conform.

But Cisneros was much more than a bishop. Among other things, the soldier-cardinal oversaw the Inquisition, developed the core of the Spanish navy, and personally led armies against Oran and Tripoli. One of his less-admired roles was ruthless persecutor of the Moors. The previously lenient policy underwent an abrupt switch under Cisneros, who sponsored forced conversions and burnings of Islamic books. These strong-arm tactics provoked a revolt in Granada, and fighting quickly spread to the Alpujarras and Ronda mountains. Spanish armies led by the king and Gonzalo de Córdoba quickly crushed the uprising. (Boabdil emigrated to Morocco and later died fighting for the sultan of Fez.)

In 1502, a decade after the Jewish expulsion, an order went out demanding conversion or exile for all practicing Muslims in Castilla. (In Aragon the powerful landowners, dependent on cheap labour, blocked expulsion of the Muslims until 1525.) Only a few hundred Muslims chose to leave. The rest decided that "Spain was worth a Mass" and took part in huge communal baptisms, like one in Granada at which water was flung from a mop twirled above the crowd. An estimated 300,000 Muslims converted in one year. They were henceforth known as Moriscos.

Cisneros tried to erase centuries of Islamic culture by decree, and the last remnants of Moorish Spain were ground into the dirt. The Arabic language was outlawed, Moriscos forbidden to wear traditional dress, and their public baths closed. Bathing itself became suspect; a common phrase used by the Inquisition was "the accused was known to take baths." For Cisneros and Isabel, the only acceptable water was holy water.

Cardinal Cisneros was a complex figure. For all his militant Christianity he also embodied the learned humanism of the Renaissance. He founded the University of Alcalá de Henares near Madrid and sponsored the Polyglot Bible, which included the text in Hebrew, Latin and Greek for the first time. (The preface stated that the Latin was like Jesus between the two thieves at the crucifixion).

The reign of the Catholic Monarchs was an era of cultural exuberance as well as military glory. In 1492 (that year again!) Nebrija published the first grammar text of a modern language, *Gramática del Castellano*. When the queen asked the purpose of such a book, one adviser remarked, "Your majesty, language is the perfect instrument of empire."

Fifteenth-century literature witnessed the decline of lengthy epics in favour of short poems called *romances*, ballads which form one of the world's great bodies of folk poetry. Passed on orally by a thousand heirs to Homer, many were first collected around 1500. They describe the Moorish wars, El Cid, the murder of Pedro the Cruel, and moving love stories. The equally popular novels of chivalry cast a further mist over peninsular life with their idealized landscapes of enchanted islands, jousts and magical swords, hulking giants and long-bearded wizards.

Closer to the modern novel (called the first European novel by Gerald Brenan) was a masterpiece entitled *La Celestina* (1499) by the *converso* Fernando de Rojas. Written in powerful Castilian as lean as the land itself, the story involves an old hag who sells her wisdom and love potions to encourage seduction and romance.

Exuberance in architecture created the Plateresque style, a strange blend of Gothic and *mudejar* with ostentatious flourishes foreign to Renaissance ideals. More in step with the times, but still unmistakably Spanish, are three Renaissance churches built in the early 16th century at Granada, Málaga, and Jaen.

SPAIN — CASTILLA AND ARAGON to be precise — was preparing to take its place in Europe. By choosing Fernando over other suitors, Isabel had fated the nation to a future of embroilment in Aragon's Italian affairs, with a corollary hostility to France. For the next two centuries, Spain's basic foreign policy would be to encircle its Gallic neighbour.

Fearful of losing their Mediterranean influence, the French invaded Naples. However, in 1504 this important Italian kingdom was confirmed along with Sicily and Sardinia as part of a growing "Spanish lake."

The wily Fernando used his son and daughters to cement desired alliances. Princess Isabel was wed to Alonso, heir to the Portuguese throne. At a famous double wedding, Juan, the Spanish heir, married Habsburg princess Margaret, and his sister Juana took the vows with archduke Philip (Margaret's brother), the Habsburg heir. Another daughter was Catherine (Catalina) of Aragon, who married Henry VIII of England and gave birth to Mary Tudor, the future queen. When Henry renounced the marriage years later, Catherine refused to submit and was imprisoned until her death in 1536.

Fernando's matchmaking formed a clever plan, but a series of tragedies conspired to prevent any of the Catholic Monarchs' children from actually ruling. Prince Juan died, in effect, from sexual excess. He deeply loved his passionate, red-haired wife so much that doctors encouraged the newlyweds to sleep apart temporarily. But Isabel replied, "I cannot separate those whom God has joined." Within a few weeks Juan collapsed and died, profoundly changing the course of Spanish history. (One writer called his sarcophagus in Avila "the tomb of Spain.") Rather than look to its own affairs, the new nation would become hopelessly entangled with Europe's squabbles.

Juana became first in line to succeed Isabel. Her spouse, Philip (Felipe) "the Fair" of Burgundy, was a notorious womanizer, and she "who could boast few personal attractions" was plunged into deep despair during his trysts. Soon the royal heiress acquired the moniker *Juana la loca* (Joanna the Mad).

When the queen died in 1504, the thirtieth year of her reign, it was with the bitter realization that Castilla would go to an unstable daughter and her playboy husband. (Fernando retained Aragon.) In her last testament she appointed her husband as regent for Juana in the event of her incapacity to rule, until the maturity of her son. Isabel made clear the fragility of the much-heralded union of Castilla and Aragon by also stating that "all those lands discovered and yet to be discovered, conquered or yet to be conquered, shall remain in possession of *my* kingdoms of Castilla and Leon."

In effect, the union was temporarily dissolved, but while Juana and her spouse resided in Burgundy, Fernando was ratified as regent. Philip threatened to assert his wife's claims, with force if necessary, and Fernando wisely withdrew. In Toledo heralds proclaimed the accession of Juana to the crown of Castilla. To complicate matters, Fernando soon married the beautiful Germaine de Foix, teenaged niece of the French king.

Fortunately for everyone, except poor Juana, Philip died suddenly just two months later, leaving the six-year-old Charles of Ghent — Philip and Juana's son — heir to Castilla. Upon hearing the news of her husband's death, Juana seemed to collapse mentally. Following the advice of a monk who claimed Philip would revive, she started touring the country with his body. This strange funeral cortege travelled by night for the next few months, the hearse drawn by eight black horses, followed by torchbearers, a train of attendants and the queen. In another gruesome touch, Juana occasionally opened the casket to inspect the deteriorating corpse.

At last she relinquished the body for burial at Tordesillas and went into seclusion at a nearby palace. Here she would spend the next 46 years, bouncing from periods of lucidity to deranged melancholy, as dead to the world as Philip's body lying in the monastery beside her. And through it all, until her death in 1555, she remained queen of Spain.

Cardinal Cisneros persuaded Fernando to return as regent. Fernando, the man whom Machiavelli chose as the perfect prince, adroitly played one foe off another to serve his ends. When the French king complained the Spaniard had lied to him twice, he boasted, "I lied to him not twice but ten times."

In 1512, Fernando annexed the independent kingdom of Navarra, completing the unification of the lands that today comprise Spain. (Henry VIII, still a son-in-law, lent a hand in the conquest.) The mighty Castilian army, modernized and led by Gonzalo Fernandez de Córdoba, was making its presence felt. It would not lose a pitched battle for more than a century.

This decade was also a fabulous one for the conquest of America, or *las Indias* as the new lands were called. During the first stage, the only settlements were on Hispaniola and Cuba. A second wave began to push back the frontier. Searching for a fountain the Indians claimed had remarkable medicinal powers, "the fountain of youth," Ponce de Leon sailed west from Cuba and hit the mainland at a place he called Florida. A year later, Vasco Nuñez de Balboa and his expedition were hacking their way through the snake and insect-infested jungle on the narrow isthmus linking North and South America.

Nuñez, or Balboa as he is commonly known, was an unsuccessful planter who evaded his creditors by hiding in a barrel on a ship bound for Panama. There his fortunes improved dramatically, and he was named to lead an expedition inland.

In one of history's most dramatic moments, Balboa climbed to the top of a ridge, looked down, and shouted *"Coño!"* (a Spanish expletive). With the sighting of the "great southern ocean," there was no doubt that Columbus had discovered a completely new continent. (One sad footnote: Balboa was later arrested by a jealous governor and beheaded like a common criminal.)

Contrary to legend, Balboa did not name his discovery. That honour belongs to the great Portuguese explorer Fernao de Magalhais (Ferdinand Magellan), who sailed for the crown of Castilla. In 1519, he left San Lucar in Spain with five leaky vessels and 265 men to launch history's greatest voyage. After six months spent crossing the Atlantic and following the American coast southward, Magellan found the passage that bears his name and rounded Cape Horn. Upon entering the calm waters of a huge ocean, he christened it *la Pacifica*. Three months and thousands of kilometres later, Magellan landed in the Philippines, where he was killed by the natives. Command passed to his Basque pilot, Juan Sebastian del Cano, who carried on through the Indian Ocean and around Africa before returning, with just one ship and 18 men, to an astonished nation. The expedition proved beyond any doubt that the earth was a sphere.

THE RECONQUEST, with its crusading spirit and military values, was the perfect training ground for the conquest of America. For centuries Spaniards had been lured south by the promise of land and riches won at swordpoint. For such a society, the glories of war could not stop at Granada. Indeed, Spaniards would not halt until they had girdled the globe.

While other nations had their explorers, the *conquistadors* were a unique Spanish archetype, a combination of reckless adventurer, daring idealist, and ruthless overlord. Most of them were from the poorer regions of Extremadura and Andalucia. They sprang from a hard and unforgiving part of Spain, which provided traits that helped them survive. The notorious Spanish tendency to improvise rather than plan also proved invaluable. The audacious exploration of the Amazon, for example, took place without the slightest preparation. Had the explorers insisted on guarantees of success, the project might never have been started. Spaniards needed only about 50 years to discover, explore, and subdue the lands and oceans of an entire hemisphere — an amazing feat.

Even so, all was not "gain, gold, and glory," as our history teachers once told us. There were enormous administrative concerns involving the new lands, and to deal with them the *Casa de la Contratacion de las Indias* (India House) was set up in Sevilla to regulate commerce. For more than two centuries, this city on the Guadalquivir monopolized American trade and grew fat in the process. One important detail: because Columbus had received his commission solely from Isabel, Castilla insisted on all rights to the new lands; the Aragonese were excluded.

There was also the question of what to do about the "Indians" once conquered. Early on, Columbus had sent slaves, properly baptized, back to Spain, but the clergy protested and slavery was curbed. Queen Isabel herself became involved in protecting the natives and helped set up the *encomienda* system, which legalized forced labour but established a wage for the Indians. The new approach itself led to abuses, however.

Fernando died in 1516, and his remains were taken to Granada and deposited in the royal chapel beside Isabel. Together they left Spain on the threshold of world power and cultural glory. Ever since, many Spaniards have looked back at the reign of *Los Reyes Católicos* as an era of innocent grandeur, before the burdens of empire came crashing down on a nation ill-prepared to face them.

According to rumour, the medications Fernando took to increase his virility hastened his death. Moreover, the results were disappointing: his only son with Germaine de Foix died at birth. As fate would have it, both Castilla *and* Aragon would fall to the same heir, Charles of Ghent. Until his arrival, the irrepressible Cisneros took charge as regent, hoping to head off any attempts by the nobles to rally round mad Juana. When his authority to do so was questioned, he pointed to a row of cannons and bellowed, "There's my authority!"

Charles (known in Spanish history and henceforth in our story as Carlos I) was born in Flanders in 1500. In his veins flowed the blood of most great European dynasties, and for four of them — Burgundian, Habsburg, Aragonese, and Castilian — he was the only heir. As a boy Carlos was left in the care of an aunt and received a French education proper for the heir to Burgundy. At 15, he was given a rose of wrought-gold from Pope Leo X, sent "because he was soon to be the most important man in the whole of Europe." Spain too would soon find itself thrust into centre stage.

In September of 1517 a fleet of 40 ships anchored off Santander, and residents fearing attack fled into the hills. Carlos disembarked with a large entourage and marched south to find his mother and determine the extent of her madness. The stately procession was led by thirty falconers to impress the commoners. But all the pomp could not disguise the fact that Carlos cut a poor figure as a youth; he was clumsy and had the huge Habsburg jaw and a mouth that hung open, giving the impression he was stupid. Worst of all, he spoke no Spanish.

After visiting his mother at Tordesillas, Carlos became convinced of her madness and ordered her kept under house-arrest. Although Juana was provided with everything befitting her position, including a staff of 155, her internment created a perennial scandal for Carlos. The Castilian parliament would only recognize him as co-ruler with his mother; on royal documents her name appeared first, followed by her son as "executor."

When the Habsburg emperor died, Carlos inherited the Austrian domains of his grandfather and became a leading candidate for the title of Holy Roman Emperor, still an elected position. His rivals included Francis I of France, and bribes to electors reached unprecedented levels. With the help of the Fugger banking house, he was elected in 1519 as Emperor Charles V (he was Carlos I in Spain).

At the age of 19 this ungainly youth controlled the largest empire since Charlemagne, and perhaps the most powerful since ancient Rome. It encompassed Castilla and Aragon, several Italian states, the Spanish colonies in America, parts of France, the Low Countries (Belgium and the Netherlands), Luxembourg, Austria, Bohemia and sections of Germany. For the first time,

Spaniards had to learn to consider themselves part of Europe. The Pyrenees had ceased to exist.

Unfortunately, warfare was part and parcel of having an empire. First Carlos had to worry about pacifying his Iberian kingdoms. Spaniards resented their foreign king and the influx of outsiders, mostly Flemish, to high posts. (The Flemish courtiers came to be identified with anything flashy, and left their name with Spain's traditional music, *flamenco*.) When Carlos tried to extract money to pay for his election bribes, nobles erupted in the Revolt of the Comuneros. This full-scale civil war saw the razing of Medina del Campo, Castilla's medieval commercial centre, and other atrocities. But the revolt petered out when it threatened to become a social movement and the nobles, as they are prone to do, backed down. The rebels were crushed at the Battle of Villalar (1521).

Fortunately for Carlos, the Comuneros received no support in Aragon. However, an unrelated conflict called the Germania broke out in Valencia led by the mysterious *rey encubierto*, supposedly an illegitimate grandson of Fernando. After this too withered away, Spain could look forward to centuries of internal peace.

Just as well, because Carlos's forty-year reign, of which he spent only sixteen. in Spain, involved an endless series of foreign conflicts. The self-proclaimed "defender of the faith," even made war on the pope; all Europe was shocked when imperial troops went on a rampage and sacked Rome in 1527. One group of soldiers even camped out in the Vatican and built fires that permanently damaged the Sistine Chapel.

This remarkable event sprang from Spain's ongoing problems with France, now worsened by the equally perennial rivalry between the Habsburg and Valois dynasties. Milan was the main object of contention; each side considered it vital to their interests. In a typically medieval gesture, Carlos challenged the French king to personal combat, but it was the Battle of Pavia that decided the conflict. Francis was captured and briefly imprisoned in Madrid, where he remarked, "All is lost but honour."

The sacking of Rome occurred later, after the pope created the Holy League of Cognac, not a drinking society but an alliance concerned with curbing the Habsburgs' awesome growth in power. But just three years later, Carlos dazzled all Europe when he was crowned Holy Roman Emperor by the pope himself at a lavish ceremony in Bologna.

The second great front for Carlos was the struggle against Protestantism in northern Europe. The same year Carlos stepped on Spanish soil for the first time a renegade priest named Martin Luther had nailed his "ninety-five theses" to the door of the Wittenberg cathedral. A few years later Carlos presided over the historic Diet of Worms, a council of German princes where Luther expounded his reasons for revolt against the Roman church. The emperor was not impressed, remarking "It is not this little monk who will make a heretic of me as yet." Nevertheless, many German princes eagerly joined the Protestant revolt, for political as well as spiritual reasons. If the empire hoped to maintain its control, it was vital to suppress Lutheranism. But the final showdown would have to wait.

After a settling-in period, Spaniards began to take a strong liking to Carlos and to enjoy their status as heart of the empire and defender of Catholicism against the hated Luther. Their king had survived adolescence and now looked every inch a regal figure, with a high forehead, alert blue eyes, an aquiline nose and a short beard. We can see this imposing visage in several portraits by Titian, in which Carlos appears clad in full armour beside his horse or in the thick of battle. Among his treasures was an immense collection of arms, including a 115-kilo jousting suit he once wore. (Much of the collection resides in Madrid at the *Real Armeria*.)

The marriage of Carlos to Isabel, beautiful daughter of the Portuguese king, further endeared him with Spaniards. They would have three children, including future king Felipe (Philip) II. (One of the king's infrequent extramarital affairs resulted in Don Juan of Austria, a great figure later in the story.) Carlos also impressed his subjects when he learned Spanish and insisted on speaking it. Once, when he was interrupted by a French bishop, he retorted, "Do not expect to hear from me any language but Spanish."

Spain was ruled as part of a larger dynastic order in which each unit kept its own laws and customs. Except for the Inquisition there was no unifying institution; Carlos was king of Castilla and king of Aragon, not king of Spain. Unfortunately, Castilla ended up footing the bill for the empire's endless wars and the emperor's personal extravagance and incessant travels. The money came from ever-higher taxes and the rapidly growing income from the Indies, which reached phenomenal figures by the 1540s.

The financial and human investment in war begun by Carlos continued for two centuries and became the major reason for Spain's ultimate decline. The enemies seemed endless: yet another threat to Catholicism came from the Ottoman Turks and their allies along the Barbary coast, the old Muslim foes again. Throughout the century, the east and west Mediterranean were two political zones under two banners — Spanish and Turk — and great battles occurred where they met.

Turkey was ruled by a larger-than-life figure named Suleiman the Magnificent, who took charge in 1520 and ruled for 46 years, almost the identical period as Carlos. The struggle commenced when Turks swept up the Balkans to the gates of Vienna, seat of the Habsburg inheritance. Here they were halted in a heroic defence involving thousands of Spanish troops. The Turks were even more fearsome at sea, especially after linking up with Barbarossa, leader of the Barbary pirates. In 1529 he seized Algiers, and Tunis fell five years later. The Spanish coastline itself was under constant threat from the resurgent Muslims, compounded by the presence of Moriscos of questionable loyalty. Spain was paying the price for not carrying the Reconquest into North Africa.

Travelling the Spanish coast today, especially in Andalucia, you will notice scores of watchtowers on hilltops a few kilometres apart. Most date from this period to about 1600 and were designed to form a network of fire and smoke to warn coastal residents of attack. Most of the original *pueblos* are lodged in the hills well away from immediate danger.

Spain's battle-hardened army was Europe's best. The introduction of the *tercio* — 3,000 soldiers divided into pikemen, swordsmen, and arquebusiers — was as significant for military history as the birth of the Roman legion. But the Spanish navy was relatively weak until the reign of Felipe II. Nevertheless, in 1535 Carlos assembled one of the century's greatest expeditions — involving 400 ships and 30,000 troops — to attack Tunis. The daring move was a resounding success, as Barbarossa fled and thousands of Christian slaves were freed of their shackles. It was the high water mark for Carlos.

Unfortunately, his follow-up assault on Algiers six years later ended in disaster, with the loss of 150 ships and 12,000 men. The western Mediterranean remained in the grip of the Barbary pirates, whose leadership passed to the ruthless Dragut.

Among those at the Algiers debacle was a man of some experience — Hernando Cortes, conqueror of Mexico.

THE FIRST 25 YEARS after 1492 were occupied with initial probings of the New World. The next stage (until about 1540) saw the real conquest, when Spain won an empire in almost miraculous fashion. It was built on the ruins of two native empires: the Aztecs of Mexico and the Incas of Peru. From these bases Spaniards fanned out in all directions searching for the fabled El Dorado.

In 1517, Hernandez de Córdoba fought his way to Mexico's Yucatan Peninsula and came across the once great Mayans, now in their final decline. The news inspired Cortes. Born at Medellin in Extremadura he came, like so many other conquistadors, from a family of impoverished *hidalgos*. He left Spain at 19 and took part in the conquest of Cuba. As a handsome and renowned ladies' man (played perfectly in the movies by Caesar Romero), he married the governor's daughter and was chosen to mount an expedition to Mexico.

Eleven ships, with 700 men and 16 horses on board, sailed in February 1519. Upon landing at a spot he named Vera Cruz, Cortes ordered the ships destroyed so that his frightened men would have no chance to retreat. The Spaniards quickly defeated the local tribe, and Cortes took an Indian mistress who served as translator. He learned of a great empire in the interior with its capital city of Tenochtitlan built in the middle of a lake.

Soon an envoy from Montezuma, the Aztec ruler, appeared and seemed friendly. By an incredible stroke of luck, Aztec legends spoke of the god Quetzalcoatl, who had instructed them in agriculture and other things before departing to the east with a promise to return. He had been tall, with white skin and a beard. To the natives it seemed that Cortes could be this god. When they discovered their mistake it was too late.

The Indians had never seen horses, and the sight of the Spaniards' cavalry, not to mention dogs, muskets, and artillery, filled them with awe and terror. Leaving a small garrison behind, Cortes and his force made their famous advance on the capital and, backed up by Indian allies who hated the Aztecs, entered without opposition. The Spaniards were welcomed by Montezuma, and they marveled at the palaces, exotic gardens, and pillars of solid gold. But problems soon arose, and Cortes and his men had to fight their way out of the capital amid horrific bloodshed. Many drowned under the weight of the gold they tried to carry away. Eventually they recaptured the city and made it capital of New Spain. From here, Spanish power rapidly expanded throughout Mexico and into central America.

Not until Cortes did Spaniards realize the full implications of the conquest. The sight of Aztec treasure — rooms of solid gold and jade carvings — stunned the conquistadors and filled them with wonder. Before long, adventurers were swarming to the Indies in search of riches, often fanciful but often very real.

The conquest of Peru was even more incredible, perhaps the most astonishing military feat in history. Led by Francisco Pizarro, 167 soldiers and a few horses set out to conquer an empire of about six million people — and they accomplished it with the loss of a handful of men. Despite popular myth, the Spanish harqebus — a primitive gun — did not seal the Inca's fate; reloading was very slow and it often blew up. The Incas were conquered with swords and spears, not to mention unbelievable courage and panache.

Pizarro was born at Trujillo in Extremadura, about 80 kilometres from the birthplace of Cortes, but was illiterate and quite unlike his polished compatriot. After learning of the Inca empire, sprawling over present-day Peru and Ecuador, Pizarro set out in 1530 in a single ship with his four brothers and other adventurers. Finally, after two years of fitful progress, the Spaniards entered the Andean valley of Cajamarca. Here the Inca ruler, Atahualpa, lived with an army of forty-thousand warriors. For reasons never made clear, the king and his unarmed entourage walked into a trap, and the Spaniards pounced on them in an orgy of bloodletting that left Atahualpa alive, but a prisoner.

Some historians claim that the king was just incredibly naive to have fallen into Pizarro's net. According to another story, he somehow understood the Basque spoken by some of Pizarro's men and, believing it to be the "language of the ancients," reckoned they were gods. In any case, with their leader imprisoned the Incas did not attack. Atahualpa filled a room with gold and silver to obtain release, but Pizarro had him baptized and then garrotted nonetheless. Spanish troops then took the capital of Cuzco without a fight and in 1535 founded Lima, "city of kings." In a true gesture of the times, a royal notary drew up the proper documentation to prove that Spain had legally taken possession.

Pizarro fit — or perhaps inspired — the harsh stereotype of the cruel and avaricious conquistador. When a priest reminded him of the spiritual mission of Spaniards in America he said, "I have not come here for such reasons. I have come to take away their gold." But he was also a very religious man and embodied that frustrating duality shared by most conquistadors. When Pizarro was assassinated by a rival group, he drew a cross on the ground with his own blood and murmured the word "Jesus." Hollywood could not have written a better script.

These were heady times. Orellana and his party crossed the Andes from Peru, built a few rafts, and floated 5,000 kilometres down the Amazon. In North

America, de Soto (also from Trujillo) discovered the Mississippi River, Coronado marched up from Mexico as far north as the Grand Canyon, and Cabeza de Vaca tramped thousands of miles around North America, then went to Brazil and walked across the jungle to Paraguay.

The hardships of these men were almost inconceivable. They suffocated in the desert under their armour and froze to the bone in high mountain passes. They were attacked by hostile natives, wild animals, poisonous reptiles, and swarms of mosquitos. Lacking surgery, they dressed their wounds with boiling fat taken from Indian corpses. What made them do it? As one of Cortes's men explained, "We came here to serve God and the king, and also to get rich."

THE AMERICAN LANDS were divided into two huge "vice-royalties," New Spain and Peru, which formed the basis of government that lasted almost three centuries. They were also two more pieces in Carlos's sprawling domains, each ruled by a viceroy.

During the king's frequent and lengthy absences, Castilla was virtually governed by an Andalusian from Ubeda named Francisco de los Cobos, secretary of finance for 30 years. It was a time of domestic peace and prosperity while war raged in the rest of Europe. With money being spent much faster than it came in, Cobos foresaw trouble and repeatedly warned the king of the situation.

Carlos was no despot, and he still depended on parliament to finance his wars. Sometimes parliament refused. Constant demands for more money from the regions tended to entrench his subjects behind their *fueros*. It was clear that the medieval Spanish institutions could not cope with the demands of an aggressive, money-squandering empire. Wealth from the Indies helped some, but just like a leaky bucket, the more that came in the more poured out.

The Protestant problem came to a head late in the emperor's reign. In 1547, he won a great victory at Muhlberg (pictured in a famous Titian portrait), but just five years later Protestant forces drove him out of Germany. Protestantism never had much appeal in Spain itself, largely because the clergy had been reformed and the crown had stood its ground against the pope. Vaguely related to Protestant ideas were those of the Illuminists, a mystical aberration that many adherents found compatible with sexual indulgence. The movement was led by a reputed nymphomaniac named Francisca Hernandez, "of whom the men spoke with fanatical veneration, and the women with not so much respect."

One of those jailed for suspected Illuminist leanings was a man who came to spearhead the Spanish Counter-Reformation — Ignatius of Loyola. Several years earlier, this Basque soldier was lying wounded in hospital when he received a heavenly sign to "follow the path of Jesus Christ." He made a pilgrimage to the famous Black Virgin at Montserrat, followed by a confession that lasted three days. Living in a cave, Loyola outlined his great book, *Spiritual Exercises*, cornerstone of the Society of Jesus — the Jesuits.

The Jesuits came to be Catholicism's most controversial religious order, especially for their military-style organization and special vow of loyalty to the pope, which did not sit well with Spanish monarchs. With their elitist attitudes about education, they also gained the hostility of the regular clergy and other orders. But they would become a major force in Spain and stood firm against the rising Protestant tide. (A century after his inspiration, Loyola was canonized as St. Ignatius.)

Humanism and other aspects of the Renaissance made some tentative inroads into the Spain of Carlos I. Erasmus of Rotterdam, the leading humanist, actually served as a royal counsellor until he became identified with heresy. Humanist scholars were later exiled and their works appeared in the first Index of prohibited books. After opening briefly, the window onto Renaissance Europe was closing. Under Carlos's successor it would be slammed shut.

The flowery excesses of Renaissance poetry spilled over into Spanish letters, and Garcilaso de la Vega created an original style with rich imagery. (He later died in battle.) Spanish Renaissance architects and sculptors produced the regrettable Palace of Carlos V inside the Alhambra and the spectacular tomb of two famous couples — Fernando and Isabel, Philip the Fair and Juana — inside the royal chapel at Granada's cathedral.

Juana The Mad, queen of Castilla, finally died in April 1555. Her death helped simplify the royal succession. Carlos was prematurely old after a life of intense activity and indulgence in the pleasures of the table. (He belonged to the Order of the Golden Fleece, an aristocratic club whose members took the oath of the Mystic Pheasant and gorged themselves at unending banquets.) In the same year as his mother's death, Carlos shocked all Europe by announcing his abdication of the imperial crown to his brother Ferdinand. A few months later, he handed over the Low Countries and Spain, with all its possessions, to his son Felipe. Though he had ruled for 40 years, Carlos was officially king of Castilla for just nine months. He retired to the monastery of Yuste in Extremadura to live out his final days.

With this turn of events, the Habsburg Empire was permanently divided into its Austrian and Spanish wings. Along with Carlos went the ideal of a universal order based on one empire and one religion.

Almost toothless and plagued by gout, Carlos settled at Yuste with his cat and parrot to enjoy his art collection and indulge his appetite for anchovies and beer. He spent countless hours trying to synchronize his huge collection of clocks and once exclaimed, "How could I possibly have hoped to unite all my dominions when I cannot make these clocks strike the hour together?"

Two years after his retirement, Carlos insisted on attending a rehearsal of his own funeral. After Mass he caught a chill and soon expired, clutching a crucifix to his breast and with the name "Jesus" on his cold, dead lips. He was fifty-eight.

## SIGHTS & SITES

**Barcelona:** *Reproduction of the caravel* Santa Maria *in which Columbus sailed to America, near Plaza de la Paz; on square is the 60-metre-high Columbus*

*Monument (1888).*

**Cáceres**: *The old town includes mansions such as the Palacio de los Golfines.*

**Granada**: *The Alhambra and Generalife, climax of Moorish architecture; Renaissance Palace of Carlos V inside Moorish structure; Albaicin quarter; Cathedral with reliefs of Moorish surrender, royal chapel and its elaborate tombs.*

**Huelva**: *Franciscan monastery of Santa Maria de la Rábida, which first welcomed Columbus to Spain.*

**Jarandilla de la Vera** *(Cáceres): Yuste Monastery, final refuge of Carlos V.*

**Madrid**: *Royal Armoury at Palacio Real contains pieces spanning Habsburg era; the Prado Museum has early Flemish, Renaissance, Italian schools i.e. Bosch, Durer, Raphael, Titian.*

**Palencia**: *Interior of cathedral features Isabeline, Plateresque and Renaissance styles.*

**Salamanca**: *Patio de las Escuelas at old university is surrounded by fine examples of plateresque architecture and sculpture; New Cathedral completed by 1560.*

**Segovia**: *The cathedral was built during reign of Carlos V.*

**Sevilla**: *Casa de Pilatos palace is a fine example of Renaissance-Mudejar blending.*

**Ubeda**: *Buildings around Plaza Vazquez de Molina are mostly Renaissance in style.*

**Valencia**: *Silk exchange, La Lonja, from late 15th century.*

# CHAPTER 6

# ECSTASY AND AGONY

S ome call the famous El Escorial palace-monastery the "eighth wonder of the world." Others speak in harsher terms: foreboding, frightening, "a granite and slate rectangular monster."

Whatever the truth, San Lorenzo del Escorial, 48 kilometres from Madrid, can be appreciated on many levels. First, there is the imposing building itself, with its massive grey-granite façade broken only by narrow, prison-like windows and pointed gables. Inside are 134 kilometres of corridors, 16 courtyards, 15 cloisters, 86 staircases, 1,200 doors and more than 2,000 windows. There is a sumptuous royal crypt, an extremely well-endowed library, and an unbelievable collection of human body parts.

On another level, the Escorial is also the supreme monument of the Counter-Reformation: Spanish Catholicism embodied in solid, unyielding stone. Designed and built by Juan Bautista and Juan de Herrera in a heavy, austere style, it could only have been created in the Spain of the 16th century.

It is also a near-perfect reflection of the man behind it — King Felipe (Philip) II.

Felipe built El Escorial (the name means "slag heap," a reference to nearby mining scoria) to fulfill a vow taken after a Spanish victory on the feast day of Saint Lawrence. Some claim the grid iron design, complete with handle, was based on the martyred saint's death: he was roasted alive on a grill. The first stone was laid in 1563, and work went on for 21 years, a remarkably short period for such an enormous project. Felipe took a deep personal interest in every detail of planning and construction, and signed off on all documents with *"Yo, El Rey"* (I, the King). He sat for hours on a stone bench overlooking the works and watching daily progress. (The spot today is called *La Silla de Felipe II.*)

Indeed, El Escorial became a giant metaphor for the empire itself, which the king also tried to control in the most minute detail. The building was completed in 1584, just at the high water mark of Spain's power and influence, a magnificent symbol of imperial grandeur. The royal abode also served as a Hieronymite monastery, reflecting Philip's own intense religious faith as well. From his spartan quarters he could look down through a small window to the altar of the main church.

Besides paintings (the nucleus of the Prado collection) and books, the king also snapped up religious relics with characteristic obsession. Among them: a hair of Christ's beard, 103 heads including that of St. Lawrence, and an extensive collection of arms, legs, fingers, and toes. With later additions, this bizarre assemblage today numbers more than 7,000 pieces.

Deep in the bowels of the Escorial, the ornate royal mausoleum contains several rooms of tiered coffins for Spanish rulers, starting with Carlos I, as well as assorted family members and select royal bastards like Felipe's half-brother Don Juan of Austria. Of course, Felipe himself is there, resting with a calm that eluded him during his 39-year reign.

He began that reign far from Spain and at war with the pope, who was in league with the French as usual. The exhausted powers were merely going through the motions of warfare, however, and would soon sign a treaty. Felipe inherited his father's hostility to France, but that would soon change, along with many other things. The domains of emperor Carlos were a vast geographical monstrosity. With the loss of Austria (to his uncle Ferdinand), Felipe's inheritance was a streamlined version of the empire, nearly as immense but quite different in character. It became entirely Spanish in orientation after he returned from abroad to rule from the heart of Castilla. Nevertheless, the foreign commitments handed down by his father, especially the Netherlands, would haunt Spain for decades to come.

Encirclement of France was basic Habsburg policy. As part of this strategy, Felipe had married Mary Tudor at Winchester Cathedral in 1554. (His previous wife, Maria of Portugal, died giving birth to Prince Carlos.) The Spanish sovereign became royal consort of the Tudor queen and was regarded as king of England by everyone but the English. They disliked his personality as much as his Catholicism, even though he tried to restrain Mary's pious persecution of Protestants. The loveless marriage ended with Mary's sudden death, and their failure to produce a child assured that Spain and England would go their separate ways. Although Felipe tried persistently to woo Elizabeth, the new queen, Mary's death meant the end of the brief Anglo-Hispanic alliance. The following year he reversed traditional Spanish policy by wedding Elizabeth of Valois, 14-year-old daughter of the French king. Spain's new enemy would be England.

Ceaseless conflict under Carlos had left Spain virtually bankrupt upon Felipe's accession. Huge sums were owed to banking houses which charged up to 50% interest per year. Heavy taxation had helped raise some funds, but not enough, and taxes acted to discourage investment. As a result, prosperous merchants abandoned business and joined the ranks of the idle and indolent *hidalgos*. Since so many of the wealthy and privileged were exempt from taxes, the poorer classes paid the most.

The crown's *quinto real* (royal fifth) of all American treasure was a source of badly needed income, especially after the fabulous discovery of a veritable mountain of silver at Potosí (Bolivia) in 1545. The flood of new wealth was far from Spain's salvation, however; much of it went directly to paying off debts or was squandered in new European ventures. State finances were so bad that the new king tried to balance the budget by putting his father's jewels up at auction. Moreover, the influx of bullion brought high inflation, with prices doubling between 1510 and 1550. This in turn hurt Spanish products in the export market. Even at the height of Spain's political power, the economic underpinnings were already rotting away.

Carlos had fancied himself champion of the Catholic religion against Protestants and Muslims alike, and it was a role that Felipe, heir to his father's worldview as well as his crown, played to the hilt. Although a glimmer of Renaissance culture reached Spain under Carlos, it was snuffed out by his dour son. Suspect foreign books were systematically banned, and Spanish students were forbidden to travel abroad. Spain and a reactionary breed of Catholicism were continuing to merge, and many Spaniards believed it was their mission to stamp out all heresy and convert the unconverted.

NOWHERE WAS THIS MISSION more evident than in the Indies, teeming with heathen souls awaiting "salvation." This religious zeal was important in the conquest from the very beginning, as Spaniards found Indian civilizations which they considered backward and inferior. It was the same "superiority complex" of every colonial power through history, and not completely unfounded. The overly romanticized Incas, for example, had no writing, measured years by knots tied in cords, were not acquainted with the wheel and had markets for human flesh. This was not a highly advanced civilization destroyed by avaricious Spaniards, as many have claimed.

With the inevitable exceptions, most priests and monks sincerely believed they were doing the right and good thing for the Indians, even if this sometimes meant their inadvertent destruction. Spaniards conquered the Americas with memories of the Reconquest still fresh. Cortes, for example, reported that Mexican Indians wore clothes similar to the Moors' and even had mosques. Before being conquered, Indians were usually given a chance to convert, just like the Muslim infidels.

The cruelty of the conquistadors has been exaggerated, but it did exist among many individuals (as opposed to being state policy), especially when precious metals were at stake. Indians became so resentful of this gold-lust that on one occasion they poured molten gold down the throats of captive conquistadors. Missionaries scandalized by their compatriots' greed soon became the Indians' protectors, and they could call on the church's considerable power. Their passion for justice can best be seen in the early work of the Franciscans, who founded the first American colleges. And their compassion for their new flocks did much to balance the evil side of the conquest.

It can be fairly asserted that the Spanish Empire was one of history's most humane. Atrocities were publicly criticized by the clergy, and the crown often listened. The New Laws (1542) prohibited enslavement of Indians, lashed out at the *encomienda* system and granted wide protection of Indian rights. In 1550 Carlos even suspended all further conquests until a debate could be held about ethical questions in Spain's new possessions. The common belief that Spain's conquest of the Americas was *uniquely* barbarous is simply not borne out by the facts.

Nevertheless, the myths persist for one important reason: Spain's "Black Legend" (*la Leyenda Negra*). Ponder this 16th-century English description of the Spanish: "... a craftie fox, a ravenous wolfe, and a raging tygre; theyr filthy, monstrous and abominable luxurie, theyr lustfull and inhumaine deflouring of theyr wives and daughters, matchless and sodomiticall ravishings of young boys... a filthie heape of the most lothsome, infected and slavish people that ever yet lived on earth."

In brief, the Black Legend is the historical and literary tradition of smearing Spain, Spaniards, and anything Hispanic as evil, inferior, and *uniquely* cruel. This jumble of cliché and error has slid with curious continuity down through the ages in stereotypes marching through Anglo-Saxon literature and movies.

In this "cape and sword" fiction, the Spaniard is the swarthy fellow with black pointed beard and wicked Toledo blade, who is not only cruel and greedy, but treacherous and lecherous to boot. There are variations, of course, in the sadistic inquisitor turning the screws, the slippery gigolo, or the cruel viceroy signing death sentences. But whatever the costume, the literary dice are always loaded against the Spanish.

The seeds of the Black Legend were planted during debates over Indian treatment by Bartolome de las Casas, the first priest ordained in the new world. Prone to wild exaggeration, he began a campaign to prove Spanish crimes with publication of his tract *Brevisima relacion de la destruccion de las Indias*. From this polemic came the still-repeated figure of 20 million Indians killed by the conquistadors. This included 3 million on Hispaniola alone, an island that could have supported only a fraction of that population. Las Casas killed more Indians with his pen than all the conquistadors in history.

The chief victim of the Black Legend was Felipe II, who rarely received a kind word from historians until centuries after his death. He is usually pictured stroking his pointed beard with "a thin smile that cut like a sword." He is the "spider of the Escorial," ruling a malevolent empire from the centre of his evil web. Behind this simplistic image was a much more complex figure.

Son of Carlos I and Isabel of Portugal, this eternal symbol of imperial Spain was only one-quarter Spanish. He was a "grave and silent child," and grew up to be a man who terrified even his own ministers with his icy manner and fixed, emotionless stare. Felipe was modestly handsome, with fair hair, pale blue eyes and the pronounced Habsburg jaw of his father.

From the dying Carlos he also received one final piece of advice: "Never trust anyone but yourself." Felipe particularly disliked those with strong personalities, such as the Duke of Alba and Don Juan of Austria, and only felt completely safe among stacks of state papers, which he tirelessly read, annotated and amended. He was forever trying to live up to an idealized version of his father and for-ever failing, at least in his own mind.

Felipe was a passionate youth and had many leisurely pursuits such as music and chess. His first marriage to his cousin Maria was reasonably happy, but she left him a widower at age 18. Nine years later he married Mary Tudor for reasons of state. He married twice more after becoming king — to Elizabeth of Valois, whom he adored until her tragic death, and to Anna of Austria in a desperate attempt to sire an heir. Felipe spent much of his reign in mourning: 17 members of his immediate family died during his lifetime. It was enough to extinguish the youthful optimism of any man.

As the king grew older, he became oddly detached and devoted himself to state affairs. No one could guess what he was thinking; whether he was giving or-ders for an execution or for a *fiesta* his countenance was the same. It was said that his expression was identical after receiving news of both the stunning victory at Lepanto and the stinging defeat of the Armada. A cool head and cold blood — sinister signs for some observers, for others proof of Felipe's greatness.

Carlos had set up a complicated system of government involving councils and viceroys. These survived more in theory than practice under Felipe, who tried to direct everything personally, to sign every paper with his own hand. There is a story that Carlos once asked for pen and ink but none was to be found in the entire palace; the new king, eyes permanently red from overwork, spent his life shuffling papers as the "world's first crowned bureaucrat." From behind his cramped and cluttered writing desk he guided the destiny of half the world. The overworked king had several lifelike statues of himself made, some with moveable limbs. These would be hauled out whenever a crowd or foreign delegation was deemed unworthy of his attentions and propped up at a safe distance from the throngs, who never suspected that they were cheering a dummy. The trans-formation from "warrior king" to the ultimate civil servant was complete.

Despite his reputation as a royal kill-joy, Felipe enjoyed the deep love and respect of his subjects. His outlook was intensely Castilian, and he embodied its espoused ideals — religious faith, personal honour and heroism. But Felipe also shared the Castilian's sometimes unbearable arrogance, and came to regard himself as the source of all wisdom and justice, answerable only to God.

FELIPE II's REIGN began with a spectacular *auto de fe* in Valladolid at which several suspected heretics were burned at the stake. The king used the Inquisition to increase his power over the bishops and regions, and this alliance added plenty of juicy material for Black Legend pamphleteers. But how much is "legend" and how much really *was* evil? After all, we are talking about the despised Spanish

Inquisition. Felipe was unquestionably a religious fanatic and once remarked, "I would rather reign in a desert than over a country peopled with heretics." He later added, "If my son were to oppose the Catholic church, I myself would carry the faggots to burn him."

The Inquisition's original reason for being was to root out suspected "false converts," but with the Protestant Reformation it gained a new role and new life.

Everything about the Inquisition, including its secrecy and slowness, offends our *modern* concepts of legal justice. The case of Bartolome de Carranza, a *converso* and archbishop of Toledo, was one notorious example. Carranza was arrested for admiring the Humanist scholar Erasmus and disappeared into Inquisition dungeons. After 18 years without a verdict he died, it was said, from despair.

A typical case went something like this: arrest was based on a *denuncia* made by at least two anonymous persons, and the accused was placed in solitary confinement and not told any specifics of the charges. He was assumed to be guilty, and it was the inquisitor's job to obtain a confession. In his own defence, the accused could make a list of his enemies, and if any of the accusers appeared on it, their testimony was discounted and they were punished. The Edict of Grace was a period during which the accused could confess and avoid harsh penalties if he also named all accomplices. Torture was used only as a last resort, possibly because the *threat* of torture was enough to jog most memories. If required, harsher forms of persuasion were the rack, the hoist, the garrote, and the harrowing "water-torture."

A confession was only the beginning of a wild search for accomplices, who might in turn reveal more suspects. Once guilt had been established, there were a number of punishments geared to the severity of the crime. These ranged from wearing the *sanbenito* (a yellow robe with a red cross) in public to being burned at the stake. Anyone convicted of heresy a second time was usually doomed to the flames, but repentance brought the privilege of being strangled first.

All of this seems abominable to our modern sensibilities. However, by the standards of the time the Spanish Inquisition was not particularly unfair or brutal. Religious intolerance was rife in Europe. Witchcraft and other offences were commonly punished by death. According to experts, the total numbers of persons executed for religious reasons was fewer in Spain than in contemporary England. One English historian (Hugh Trevor-Davies) even stated that the Inquisition was "the most fair legal system in Europe at the time." So much for the Black Legend.

One of Felipe's most enduring decisions was to move the Spanish capital from Toledo to Madrid (1561), then a squalid village of a few thousand souls. It was selected because of its location at the peninsula's geographical centre and the fact that Felipe could mould it to his tastes. Madrid was as Castilian as a roast suckling pig, but had no troublesome regional or aristocratic loyalties as did other cities.

Spain's population was overwhelmingly rural, and to foreign travellers life seemed strange and primitive, the dress and customs noticeably medieval. The largest towns were Sevilla, Valladolid, Granada, Toledo and Barcelona, but none had more than 50,000 residents. Spain's total population was about nine million at the start of Felipe's reign, compared with sixteen for France and England's four.

After a few early trips, Felipe remained on the peninsula the rest of his life. He maintained an elaborate court where he could keep an eye on the nobles, many of whom were reduced to the status of official servants — First Gentleman of the Bedchamber or Chief Steward — who would fight for the honour of handing the king his shirt. Large numbers of new noble positions were created and became dependent on the crown for their existence, but real power gravitated to about a hundred of the top grandees.

Felipe's first domestic crisis involved his son and heir, the infamous Don Carlos. The boy began life with two genetic strikes against him — his mother and father were cousins and both were grandchildren of Juana the Mad. His frail body could barely support his oversized head, and at a young age he displayed a fondness for disgusting acts of cruelty, such as roasting hares alive and flogging horses to death. At 17 he fell down a flight of stairs and injured his head so badly that doctors had to remove a piece of his skull. Thereafter, his behaviour worsened, with uncontrollable fits of fury and wanton violence. Once he flew into a rage at a bootmaker and forced him to eat a pair of boots, and he was known to wander Madrid streets shouting obscenities and spitting at respectable women.

All Europe began to take an interest in the fate of the Spanish throne. When Carlos's erratic behaviour was compounded with plots against his father, Felipe finally acted, and Carlos was locked up in the old *alcazar* (fortress). When he died under mysterious circumstances a few months later, the king's enemies assumed the worst. The cause of the prince's death was never proved, but historians doubt that Felipe was directly involved; more likely Don Carlos collapsed under confinement from his own physical weakness, compounded by his alternating hunger strikes and gorging and his habit of consuming huge quantities of ice on hot Castilian days.

But Felipe became his own worst enemy by refusing to disclose any details of the affair. Don Carlos became a hero for hispanophobes, climaxing in Verdi's opera.

The year of Prince Carlos's death was a bad one for the king. His French wife also died and a revolt broke out among the Moriscos of Granada. They had been restless for years, suffering under the arrogant and oppressive "old Christians" who settled in the south. For example, one village complained about its parish priest: "All our children's eyes are as blue as his." In 1567, a slew of restrictive laws cracked down on persistent Muslim customs. Then, on Christmas Day, Moriscos paraded through Granada shouting their loyalty to Mohammed.

A revolt spread like brushfire through the Alpujarras and Málaga mountains, and Spanish troops under Don Juan of Austria, Felipe's dashing illegitimate half-brother, were called up. Spaniards were especially terrified of Moriscos linking up with fellow Muslims from Barbary. The campaign was unusually brutal, with about 60,000 killed before the rebels gave up. Moriscos were shipped off en masse to a thousand Castilian towns, and much of Andalucia remained depopulated for decades. (Thus the degree of Moorish blood in areas like the Alpujarras is much less than imagined.)

The Morisco revolt was only one indication of how precarious Spain's own unity really was, in spite of its imperial successes. Concern over secret apostates among Muslim and Jewish converts whipped the Inquisition into even greater frenzy. "Proofs" of traitorous activity multiplied, so that wearing better clothes or failing to light a fire on Saturday (the Jewish Sabbath), washing a corpse in warm water, giving children Hebrew names and cooking with oil instead of lard were all used as evidence.

The uglier side of Spanish society raised its head with the concept of *limpieza de sangre* (pure blood). No longer was it good enough to be a Christian — one had to be an *old* Christian with documented proof that there was no "tainted" blood in the family. Extensive investigations were conducted to uncover blemishes in family pedigrees, and Spaniards lived in fear that some skeleton in the closet might ruin their lives. Names were changed and ancestries falsified to throw professional snoopers off the trail.(Lineage was normally traced back four generations in search of Jewish or Moorish ancestors.)

At first "purity of blood" was required to enter most religious orders and brotherhoods of knights, but the concept spread to the colleges and government posts. Ultimately the testing failed, however, because impurity was found to be too widespread, especially among persons of wealth and power. Untainted blood became a "poor man's honour."

FELIPE'S REIGN BEGAN with a sigh of relief throughout Europe at the breakup of the awesome Habsburg domains, and there was peace for several years. Not one to be denied his taste of glory, the new king turned in a different direction to a deadly serious foe — the Ottoman Empire. The last century had witnessed the decline of powerful city states. Inevitably, the vacuum was filled by the rise of sprawling empires, huge leviathans such as Spain and Turkey which controlled the western and eastern Mediterranean respectively. In the areas where the two met, friction and war usually followed.

Turkish power reached its zenith under Suleiman the Magnificent, with a victory at Djerba near Tunis in 1560. Five years later, news that the Turks were at Malta hit Europe like a hurricane, but a heroic defence by the Knights of St. John turned back the attack. (Malta's knights were the boldest of the Christian pirates and raided the Levant with impunity.) A year later Suleiman died, and power passed to his weak son Selim, who was fonder of wine than of battle. The tide was turning. Spurred on by events, an alliance formed between Spain, the papal states and Venice to seek out and destroy the Turk. Twenty-four-year old Don Juan of Austria was named commander of the fleet.

"On that day the insolent pride of the Ottomans was broken forever... It was the greatest occasion the centuries had ever seen." The young Spaniard who penned these words about October 7, 1571, thought victory was well worth three wounds and losing the use of one arm. His name: Miguel de Cervantes.

The Spanish fleet, larger than the Great Armada of 1588, had 208 warships and many smaller vessels carrying an army of 28,000 men. The Turks boasted 230 ships and a nasty reputation. Although each side had been seeking out the other, dawn of October 7 found them unexpectedly face-to-face at the entrance to the Bay of Lepanto in Greece. The day ended with a breathtaking Christian victory from which only 35 Ottoman ships escaped; and lest there be doubts about who had won, the Turkish commander's head was stuck to a pike. With Lepanto the Ottoman threat was curtailed for decades, and the mystique of their invincible sea power broken.

Don Juan of Austria was one of the century's great figures, a born leader who was brave, cunning and ruthless in equal measures. He was also charismatic and hence a threat to his half-brother in Madrid, and when he proposed carrying the fighting on to Constantinople or North Africa, the king refused. Although Don Juan did recapture Tunis a few years later, open warfare between the two empires subsided. Henceforth, threats to Spanish shipping came from pirates based in Algiers.

In addition to sibling rivalry, another concern prevented Felipe from following up after Lepanto. That problem was the Netherlands, Spain's "Fatal Inheritance." With the death of Carlos V, the Low Countries (17 separate provinces roughly encompassing modern-day Belgium, Luxembourg and the Netherlands) were no longer one part in an empire of equals; Spain would try to rule them as it did Italy or the Indies. The Low Countries formed Europe's richest area, with a full- blown capitalist economy centred in Antwerp. Their material worth for Spain was immense. Indeed, Felipe considered Flanders (the southwestern counties) the key to his empire — without it Spain would cease to be a *European* power.

Although the Low Countries were still Catholic, Lutherans and Calvinists were making much headway in the north. As everywhere, local nobles used Protestantism as a means to assert their waning power and independence. These Dutch nobles were deep in debt and had a vested interest in rebellion and war. Their leader was William of Orange, essentially a corrupt figure mouthing liberal principles to advance his own interests.

The two nationalities were a study in contrast: the Dutch were pleasure-loving businessmen while Spaniards were abstemious and devout. Attempts to transform this urbanized, industrialized country into another Spain — trying to stop students from travelling to Paris, for instance — were futile and foolish. Resistance in the form of riots, church burnings, and other violence began in the mid 1560s and continued for decades. The feared Duke of Alba arrived in Brussels to squelch the bubbling revolt with a hard hand, sending hundreds to their deaths. He remarked, "It is far better to preserve by war for God and the king a kingdom that is impoverished and even ruined than ... preserve it entire for the benefit of the devil and the heretics, his disciples."

Soon a state of open rebellion existed, and Spain was forced to fight on two fronts: Protestants on land and the Turks at sea. The corresponding financial obligations forced Felipe to suspend all payments (a polite form of declaring bankruptcy). As a result the Spanish army was not paid for months, and in a horrific incident called "the Spanish Fury," soldiers in Antwerp erupted in an orgy of mindless destruction that left thousands of innocent citizens dead. This final humiliation united all 17 provinces in a common effort to drive out the Spanish.

Amid this background Felipe sent in Don Juan "the miracle worker" to attempt a solution. Said the departing Alba, always a great one for a quote, "Kings treat men like oranges. They go for the juice, and once they have sucked them dry, they throw them aside." Don Juan arrived with some farfetched schemes for ending the trouble. Elizabeth of England was blatantly aiding the rebels, and the prince concocted a plan to conquer England and wed Mary Stuart. But Don Juan too succumbed to the "fatal inheritance," dying of typhus at the age of 33. His body lies in the Escorial's Pantheon of the Infantes, beneath a lifelike effigy that once moved female visitors to tears.

Ever since the breakup of the Habsburg empire (and loss of land routes), Spain's control of the Netherlands depended on the neutrality of England and its navy. Thus the Spanish king actively supported Elizabeth against the pope's threats of excommunication and the machinations of Mary of Scots, a French ally. These attempts to cement the Anglo-Spanish alliance belie Felipe's reputation as a rigid religious fanatic. Protestant England counted more than Catholic France when Spain's political interests were at stake.

Inevitably, war and rebellion took their financial toll on Spain's precarious economy and debt payments were periodically suspended. American silver served as a temporary stopgap, but it was a mere palliative to a fundamentally unsound economy. Castilla exported raw materials, such as wool and iron, but suffered a large trade imbalance because it imported far more finished goods. The difference was made up with any American bullion left after paying foreign creditors.

Sevilla became a raffish boomtown at the hub of Spanish-American trade and grew in size to rival Paris and Naples. It was a city of corruption and prevaricating officials, a city in which silver-lust wreaked havoc. To Sevilla came adventurers and thieves, impoverished gentlemen and husbands fleeing shrewish wives — all hoping for a slice of the American pie. There were many foreign merchants, who soon outwitted locals and gained control of trade.

Disdain for business was but one reason Spaniards failed to seize the moment. There was also a shortage of skilled labour and capital: rather than being used on investment, money was spent to build churches, palaces, and monasteries. (Spaniards had discovered the dubious formula for transforming gold and silver into stone, it was said.) There was no coherent government planning to infuse American wealth into the economy in some productive way.

With a few exceptions, such as the Guadalquivir Valley, agriculture was also a disaster. Much of the country lived on imported wheat. Poor soil, a harsh climate, stifling institutions such as the Mesta and *latifundia*, and too much government regulation combined to produce rural areas that were ill-cultivated and underpopulated. Travellers invariably mentioned the emptiness of the landscape,

*Above, English ships battle the Spanish Armada in 1588. Following pages, the Escorial palace/monastery, a reflection of the man who built it, King Felipe II (ABOVE: NATIONAL MARITIME MUSEUM, LONDON; FOLLOWING PAGES: AGE FOTOSTOCK, BARCELONA)*

Top, Velázquez's portrayal of a
Spanish victory at Breda, the Low
Countries. Left and above, Titian's
portraits of King Carlos I and of
Felipe II. (PRADO MUSEUM,
MADRID)

the solitude of deserted roads. Inns along the way served foul food to guests who ate at a long wooden table with a single carving knife chained to it.

Perhaps the most important factor in Spain's economic plight was the utter lack of commercial values. For a Spaniard with ambition, the road to success meant "church, or sea, or royal service." In 1626 there were 9,088 monasteries in Spain. Naturally, this huge group devoted to "spiritual matters" was unproductive, as was the immense class of nobles and would-be nobles. By the end of Felipe's reign, more than 100,000 persons claimed nobility in Spain, as the cash-strapped crown sold titles like lottery tickets. The payoff was honourable indolence for a lifetime.

Commoners were in a state of perpetual restlessness, longing to move up in class through church service or military enterprise. The humblest peasant, "pure of blood" precisely because he was a peasant, sensed that he was somehow a member of the ruling caste. *Hidalguia* (squirehood) became a state of mind. A true gentleman's income could be as meagre as his pride was great; he instinctively abhorred trade and industry and never soiled his hands with manual labour, lest he be associated with Jews or Moriscos. In Madrid, foreign merchants and technicians, mostly French, took over most productive positions, and this community remained vital to the economy for centuries.

Madrid became a town of rich and poor, the latter sleeping in the streets rolled up in their cloaks. In the 1590s, a visiting Italian priest reported that the city was full of squalid mud houses without chimneys or toilets. Vagrants flooding in from the provinces formed their own brotherhood, whose headquarters lay at the Puerta del Sol square in the heart of old Madrid. In the country, the unemployed wandered from one monastery to another in search of free soup. Too often they found it.

In this world of beggars and scoundrels the picaresque novel was born. *La Vida de Lazarillo de'Tormes* (1554, authorship disputed) presented a character with just the proper combination of poverty and pride, a poor squire living a life of semi-starvation who scatters a few crumbs of bread on his clothes to prove he has eaten. Lazarillo is a poor boy who must live by his wits amid this world of rogues and hypocritical priests. The picaroon — forever trying to cheat the system and sworn to keep up appearances at all costs — became a Spanish archetype, in life as well as in literature.

Another literary light at this dawn of the Golden Century (*Siglo de Oro*) was Fray Luis de Leon from Salamanca University, who was imprisoned for five years by the Inquisition before being cleared. When he returned to the lecture hall, this poet and scholar began with the words, "As we were saying yesterday..."

The most essentially Spanish of "literary movements" was the exalted mysticism of St. Teresa of Avila and St. John of the Cross (Juan de la Cruz). At the age of 18 Teresa joined a convent. One day she slipped into an ecstatic trance in which a voice told her to shun further dialogue with mere mortals and converse only with angels. She wrote of the union of her soul with her heavenly bridegroom, "like two candlelights merging," and of her longing for death. Fellow nuns believed she was possessed.

Teresa founded the secret order of the barefoot Carmelites (they actually wore rope sandals), who slept on straw, ate no meat, and lived a cloistered life of prayer and contemplation. Her practical guide to salvation stressed prayer, self-mortification and humility. "The Lord walks among the pots and pans," she said. After Teresa died in 1582, it was reported that the fragrance of violets wafted up from her gravesite. Forty years later she was canonized, and a fervent monk cut off one of her hands, which supposedly had the power to perform miracles.

Teresa's protégé from Avila was Juan de la Cruz, a priest who became one of Spain's great mystics and poets. He had also helped found the barefoot order and was kidnapped by angry Carmelites and held in solitary confinement for eight months. There, in his gloomy cell, his spiritual ecstasies blossomed.

Spanish mysticism found its ultimate expression in painting with the work of a foreigner, a man from Crete named Domenico Theotokopoulos, otherwise known as El Greco. After studying in Italy, "the Greek" moved to Toledo and its lively cultural milieu, which included the baroque poet Góngora. El Greco explored the typically Spanish form of brooding, religious realism which pushes its subjects into mystical realms, as in his transcendent "View of Toledo" and "The Burial of Count Orgaz." In the latter he captured the meeting of spiritual and material worlds in the elongated bodies spiralling up to heaven, with their other-worldly expressions and "winged hands." It is a masterpiece that embodied on canvas the Spanish Counter-Reformation just as the Escorial did in stone.

Felipe's architectural masterpiece was completed in 1584 as the ultimate expression of a peculiarly Spanish style. Ornateness would later return with the baroque, a grandiose style in keeping with imperial times by its sheer mass and volume. Baroque architecture would dominate tastes until the French launched the classical revival in the 18th century.

Felipe settled into the Escorial to run his empire and live his tortured life, and within its walls were embodied all the complexities and contradictions of the man. He lived in a modest room overlooking the church, yet kept Bosch's wildly wicked *The Garden of Earthly Delights* above his bed (he also bought many nudes by Titian and Rubens). Book collecting, another of his obsessions, resulted in the stunning royal library, a triumph of both scholarship and architecture. With 14,000 priceless volumes, it was the largest private collection in Europe.

With the passing years, the empire's arteries seemed to harden along with Felipe's. He continued to fight a losing battle against all the paperwork the empire could produce, strangely unable to distinguish between the trivial and the important. The details of some religious procession or the bridging of an obscure stream occupied the king's time while crucial issues lay unresolved. He even corrected spelling as part of the routine. Towns in America felt free to write directly to the Escorial about local matters, knowing that an answer would eventually come. As unsettled affairs piled up, Felipe tried to solve them by procrastination; often by the time he made a decision the basics had completely changed. As one Italian minister remarked, "If death came from Spain, we should all live a long time."

Nevertheless, Felipe's empire continued to grow in spectacular fashion, as if by the strength of its own momentum. When the Portuguese king was killed while leading an invasion of Morocco, Felipe claimed the throne through his mother's family. His position was strong, stronger still when backed up by Spanish troops, and in 1580 he realized a centuries-old dream of uniting the entire Iberian peninsula under one ruler. Said Felipe of Portugal, "I inherited it, I bought it, I conquered it."

The joint Spanish-Portuguese empire was awesome in size and wealth, taking in most of the western hemisphere and a good deal more, including the Philippines, Guinea, Angola, Mozambique, Cape Verde, and Madeira. In America, the overthrow of native empires was only the first stage of Spanish conquest; they still had to take possession of this vast land and administer it. By 1580, a permanent colony at Buenos Aires completed the founding of cities which now form the capitals of Latin America. At the end of Felipe's reign, 130 Spanish families crossed the Rio Grande and settled in *Nuevo Mexico*, the land that today forms the southwestern United States.

About 120,000 Spaniards had emigrated to America by 1570. They came with the idea of establishing "new Spains," and soon most of America was dotted with signs of Spanish administration. Towns had municipal institutions like those of Castilla, and belonged to vice-royalties, which were on an equal footing with all others in the empire. Spanish America reminded visitors of Spain itself, with fields of vines and cereals, peasants riding burros or tending flocks, sprawling *plazas*, and baroque churches. In the cities, colonial architecture was often monumental in size and sumptuous in detail, designed to awe the natives as the Romans had done in Iberia centuries earlier.

If Spaniards conquered the Indies with the horse, steel and gunpowder, their most precious gift was wheat. From America they brought back tobacco, maize, tomatoes and potatoes (thought to be an aphrodisiac). Spain's initial economic relationship with its colonies was a monopoly that involved supplying products and extracting precious metals. In time, the colonies developed economies dangerously similar to Spain's and became competitive rather than complementary. The gap between them was filled by English and Dutch traders, who soon made a shambles of the Spanish monopoly.

Legitimate commerce was not the only foreign threat, as outright attacks on Spanish shipping — both pirate and government sponsored — multiplied in the late 1500s. To counteract these assaults, scores of vessels would sail in gigantic convoys once or twice a year, often with priceless cargoes in their holds. Despite legend, however, very few Spanish treasure ships fell prey to the likes of Drake and Hawkins. Violent storms sent many more ships to the bottom than did the pirates, and even so an estimated 95% of all Spanish treasure ships reached Spain without incident — a remarkable achievement of maritime skill.

Treasure arrived at Sevilla and was registered at the Torre del Oro on the Guadalquivir. Nearby lies the fabulous Archive of the Indies, a vast depository of paperwork covering the entire colonial period: shipping logs, maps, charts — some 50 million documents in all. Many a treasure-hunter has uncovered crucial information regarding sunken ships at this archive.

Europe's first great colonial venture led to colossal deeds, both good and bad, but native populations were decimated largely by the unintentional introduction of new diseases, not by the sword. Nor was overwork in the mines and plantations a factor. On Jamaica, for example, where there were no mines, the Arawak Indians had largely disappeared by the 18th century. (In any case, before long Spaniards began to import Negro slaves, who were considered harder workers and "naturally servile.") But disease and cultural shock were very real and proved too great for the Indians. There is little room for debate regarding the extent of the demographic catastrophe. After two devastating epidemics, the Indian population of Mexico had dwindled from about 11 million in 1520 to 2 million at the end of the century. Populations fell similarly in Peru and elsewhere, causing economic catastrophe as a result of a severe labour shortage.

The Spanish took their own approach to native Americans, freely interbreeding with them and trying to provide both religious and cultural instruction. The English colonists, on the other hand, stood aloof and rarely intermingled in any way with the Indians; a "half-breed" became the lowest form of human life. For three centuries Spain ruled America without a standing army and without any serious native rebellions. Invariably, revolts started with the Creoles (*criollos*), colonials of Spanish descent who wanted more local control. Today, native cultures are present everywhere in Latin American society, and Indians have served as presidents and leaders in all fields of endeavour. In areas settled by the English or their descendants, the handful of native survivors live out their pathetic lives on reservations. This is the ultimate refutation of the Black Legend.

New techniques for refining silver from America produced a startling increase in bullion imports by the late 1570s. This encouraged Felipe to pursue a more aggressive imperial policy against his northern foes, among them William of Orange. The Dutch leader had been busy, officially kicking off the Black Legend with his anti-Spanish tract *Apologia* (1580). His attacks on Felipe included the charge that he poisoned Don Carlos because he was having an affair with his stepmother, Elizabeth of Valois. The story would be picked up by hispanophobes over the next two centuries, each adding grisly details of the crime.

In 1581, the United Provinces declared their independence while the south (Belgium) remained loyal. Three years later William was assassinated by a fanatical Catholic. Shortly after, England and the United Provinces entered into an accord, prompting Felipe to order the seizure of English ships. Elizabeth countered by sending Francis Drake to maul Spanish colonies in the Caribbean, and he even swooped into Cádiz and "singed the beard of the Spanish king." Step by step, outright war was approaching.

IN MARCH OF 1587, word reached the Escorial that Elizabeth had executed Mary Queen of Scots, the great Catholic hope. Partly to punish this act and partly to stop English raids on shipping, Felipe began planning the Great Armada for the invasion of England. Elizabeth meanwhile pursued an alliance with the

Turks, stating that both Muslims and Protestants hated Spanish "idolitries."

The great expedition, in retrospect, seemed doomed from the start. Problems started at the top with the king, who insisted on reviewing every detail of planning, and with the Duke of Medina Sidonia, chosen as commander though he had never been to sea. Felipe viewed the Armada as a religious mission and commanded sailors to "refrain from swearing and blasphemy." About 200 priests went along to tend to the men's spiritual needs, but there were not prayers enough

## SPANISH POSSESSIONS
## IN THE NEW WORLD

SAN FRANCISCO

MEXICO

TORDESILLAS
DEMARCATION LINE

BUENOS AIRES

to save the Armada from disaster.

Trouble had already started in Spain at La Coruña, where a sudden summer storm destroyed about a quarter of the fleet. Due to inept planning, provisions were already running low, and half the men were ill. Finally, in July 1588, about 130 ships and 29,000 men set sail for the English Channel, where the plan called for them to take on more troops in Belgium. The Spanish fleet went into its feared crescent formation and moved up the channel with little opposition. But the English under Lord Howard and Drake lay waiting at Plymouth Sound, then slipped out and got windward of the Spanish. (Much credit for the victory goes to the disarming self-confidence of Drake, who really *did* play that famous game of bowls.)

From their superior position, the smaller and faster English ships began snapping at the lurching Spanish galleons like dogs at a sick bull. The Armada's fate was sealed by a fatal strategic flaw: the Spanish had no port capable of handling their huge ships for re-supplying or boarding their land-based army. They were forced to operate on the high seas, far from home or any hope of aid. In anchorage off Calais, the Armada became a perfect target for fire ships, which caused the Spanish to panic and break formation. It was the beginning of the end, as the retreating fleet headed north into a flurry of storms. Finally, after rounding Scotland and skirting the Irish coast, the remnants of the "Invincible Armada" limped home; 63 ships and 9,000 men were not among them.

It was a great victory for England, but not the turning point some have claimed, that is, the end of Spanish sea power and the beginning of English. Spain's overall fleet advantage — 300,000 tons to England's 42,000 — was far too great to be smashed with a single defeat, even one so shattering as that of 1588. Moreover, Spain used its failure as a chance to build a better navy. Over the next few decades, more ships and treasure reached Spain safely than ever before. In fact, it can even be argued that the defeat of the Great Armada marked the *beginning*, not the end, of Spanish sea power. (Few people are aware that Felipe, angered by Lord Essex's daring attack on Cádiz, sent two more armadas against the English — in 1596 and 1597 — both of which were dispersed by storms.)

The decade of the Armada, which began so auspiciously for Felipe, also turned sour at home, culminating in the Antonio Perez affair and a revolt in Aragón.

The shrewd son of a priest, Perez was the king's trusted secretary, but a bitter rival of Juan de Escobedo, Don Juan's aide in the Netherlands. Perez raised eyebrows at court when he linked up (in several senses) with the Princess of Eboli, a beautiful widow who wore a black patch over one eye and was famed as an irresistible seductress. She was also skilful at political intrigue, and Escobedo suspected the pair of collusion with the Dutch rebels. When three attempts at poisoning failed, Perez had him murdered by thugs on a Madrid street.

After waffling for a time, Felipe had his secretary arrested and tortured, and on the eighth twist of the rope Perez confessed. He languished in jail for years, then escaped (by changing clothes with his visiting wife) and fled to Aragón, where he claimed sanctuary. When the Aragonese government refused to arrest the fugitive, the Inquisition stepped in (as the crown's only effective regional force) and grabbed Perez. This set off aristocratic protest and popular rioting, and Perez managed to escape to France amid the turmoil. There he peddled state secrets and penned a scurrilous exposé about Felipe, which added more fuel to the Black Legend.

Peeved by the king's increasing demands for money as well as the Perez affair, the nobles of Aragón barricaded themselves behind their medieval *fueros*. These were aristocratic privileges rather than popular liberties, but the nobles managed to gain widespread support. The brief revolt was crushed, but even then Felipe did not dare outlaw the *fueros*.

The impact of Felipe's long, difficult life is revealed in the portrait by Titian when he was 20 and the one done near the end, in which he appears withered and feeble, a mere shadow of a once great king. Among his other concerns, the death of Don Carlos had left Spain without a royal heir. Kingly duty running in his veins, he had married a fourth time back in 1570 — to his niece, Anne of Austria. She bore him five children, but only one survived beyond the age of eight, a feeble son who would become the next king. Said Felipe, "God, who has given me so many kingdoms, has denied me a son capable of ruling them."

SPANISH POSSESSIONS
IN EUROPE (1600)

In the seventh decade of his life, Felipe was afflicted with a variety of ailments and was carried to the Escorial to die. He held on for 53 days, making elaborate funeral preparations and lengthy confessions of "a lifetime of errors." (On display at the Escorial are the macabre skull and crossbones vestments priests wore at his funeral.) On September 13, 1598, Felipe II finally expired in his little room overlooking the church, clutching the same crucifix his father had held on his own deathbed.

Bells began to toll throughout Spain and continued for nine days before an uneasy quiet fell over the land. Felipe was loved by his people, but his reticent ways made him an enigma to all who knew him. And so he remains. But whatever his mistakes, Felipe had been a great king. His heir had big shoes to fill.

FELIPE'S DEATH AFTER 40 years as king changed everything and yet changed nothing. His weak and inexperienced son, crowned Felipe (Philip) III, resembled his father in little but physical appearance and religious convictions. He was twenty years old when he became king, devoted to hunting, the theatre and religious festivals. Felipe III abandoned the role of royal administrator his father had found all-consuming.

The new king inherited an empire that was virtually intact except for the not-yet-official loss of the United Provinces. He also assumed an empty treasury and a 100 million ducat debt. From the outside the Spanish Empire still appeared mighty, but Castilla was mired in debt, poverty and growing self-doubt. The enormous facade of imperial Spain was like an elaborate setting hiding a great empty stage. The coming century would be one of political and economic disasters, overseen by a parade of feeble and debauched kings. Yet it was also a time of spectacular cultural brilliance, the brightest glow of the luminous Golden Century begun under Felipe II. This bitter contrast has haunted Spaniards ever since.

The new century began with some unfinished business with the old nemesis, England. Still smarting from the defeat of the Invincible Armada, Spain tried to stir up a rebellion in Ireland. In 1601, a force of 3,000 men landed near Cork to link up with Irish rebels, but the plan was betrayed, for a bottle of whiskey it's said. Nevertheless, the death of Elizabeth and accession of James I (1603) ended Anglo-Hispanic tensions for quite some time. A few years later, Spain gave tacit recognition to the independent United Provinces of the Netherlands and seemed satisfied to hold Flanders along the French border. Encirclement of France returned as the number one priority.

Felipe III began the tradition of rule by select ministers, the "favourites," (*validos* in Spanish). By pandering to the monarch's weaknesses, the Duke of Lerma (Francisco Gomez de Sandoval y Rojas) rose to the position of favourite and became Spain's virtual ruler. It was an unfortunate turn of events. Spain urgently needed economic reforms, but Lerma often stayed away for days while pressing business lay unattended. Foreign diplomats complained that they could not gain audiences or conduct affairs while in Madrid.

The only act of resolution under Philip III and Lerma was the expulsion of the Moriscos from Aragón (1609). Spain had struggled for more than a century to assimilate these nominal Christians, stubborn in their Muslim ways and suspected of aiding Barbary pirates. The fact remained that the Catholic religion was the national catalyst, and there was no room for non-conformity. Hence, there was little debate when the archbishop of Valencia persuaded the king to act.

Several hundred thousand Moriscos (estimates range from 150,000 to 500,000) were expelled over a five-year period. Although the economic effects have been exaggerated, such a population loss in an underpopulated country of 9 million hurt, especially the farms of Valencia where Moriscos formed 40% of the work force. Most of the fugitives headed for Morocco where, ironically, they were considered "Spaniards"; many were murdered or sold as slaves. (In Rabat refugees founded their own republic and turned to piracy, the famous Sallee Rovers mentioned in *Robinson Crusoe*). In France, Cardinal Richelieu called the expulsion "the most barbarous stroke in human annals." But there was one notable result: pirate raids along the Spanish coast suddenly ceased.

The affable and easy-going Lerma was mainly concerned with his own wealth and power. Almost any event was greeted with extravagant displays at court, and royal expenditures rocketed. In order to make ends meet, the government decided to debase the coinage with copper, the equivalent of printing more paper currency today. The result was the same — inflation — and huge wagons were soon needed to transport any large sum. (For a century Spanish coins — gold *escudos* and silver *reales* — had been the universal currency in the Mediterranean world and America. From the eight-*real* coin came the expression "pieces of eight.")

The ostentation and morals of the Spanish capital during the 17th century shocked visitors. By mid-century there were 800 brothels in Madrid, and "public women" moved freely in higher social circles. Laws passed to curb immorality — carriages could not be used with the curtains drawn, for example — proved inadequate. Madrid's population swelled with the influx of beggars and vagabonds, and the gap between rich and poor widened. The middle class was lured by the easy-money of investment and hungered for the titles of their social betters, the idle aristocracy. Unlike the burgeoning middle classes of other countries, here the young dandies were disinterested in commerce, industry, technology and science — all the things that were propelling Europe into a new age. Instead, a sense of fatalism and decadence began to creep over the land.

It was amid this setting that *Don Quixote*, Spain's universal masterpiece, sprang from the pen of Miguel de Cervantes. Born at Alcalá de Henares in 1547, Cervantes was a contemporary of Shakespeare. (The two writers died on the same date, April 23, 1616.) Cervantes led a full life: after fleeing Spain following a duel, he joined the army and fought at Lepanto; later, he was captured by Muslims and held for five years in a fetid Algerian prison, to be ransomed at the age of 33. Next Cervantes worked as a tax collector, but was imprisoned for malfeasance in a Sevilla jail (a plaque marks the spot); along the way he managed to have affairs with several actresses.

Cervantes struggled as a writer and did not even begin *Don Quixote* until he was 56. His life spanned two ages, the glories of Lepanto and the decline and disillusionment of the early 17th century. The book deftly dances between comedy and tragedy, optimism and pessimism, idealism and realism, humour and bitter irony. It is the story of a befuddled knight named Don Quixote on a mission to correct all the world's evils. Taking up a rusty lance, shield and broken helmet, he mounts Rocinante, his ungainly nag, and marches boldly across the desolate plains of La Mancha in search of adventure. The Don's sidekick is Sancho Panza, an unpolished but perceptive squire, and the novel works so well because of the contrast between these two characters. It was a brilliant parable for a crusading nation that had found itself tilting at windmills, just like the lovable but pathetic knight-errant.

FELIPE III, FULL of unwarranted contrition for his inconsequential life, died in 1621 at the age of 43. His teenaged son was heir to a wasted estate; although in appearance still Europe's greatest power, Spain was on a collision course with disaster. The new king, Felipe (Philip) IV, became a notorious libertine who entertained an endless procession of mistresses, whom he promptly packed off to convents once he tired of them. He became tormented by guilt and confessed his sins in a series of extraordinary letters to a nun named Sor Maria de Agreda. Obsessed with death, he spent hours lying in his burial niche at the Escorial. But all this did not stop him from fathering some 30 illegitimate children.

While the king frittered away his time, Spain was governed by a remarkable figure named Gaspar de Guzman, the Count-Duke of Olivares. This wily statesman, every bit the equal of France's Richelieu (who ruled for Louis XIII), was the son of a Spanish ambassador and led a privileged life befitting a member of the great house of Guzman. (While a law student in Salamanca, for example, he had 19 servants.) In Madrid, he insinuated himself in the royal household, then bowed and scraped his way to the top. (He once kissed the prince's chamber pot as a sign of submission.) When the prince became king, Olivares was ready.

The great Count-Duke appears in a magnificent portrait by Velazquez, larger-than-life astride a fine steed, with a swirling moustache and huge floppy hat. For 22 years he tried through the strength of his personality to reverse Spain's slide. In a flurry of energy he cut royal extravagance, purged the bloated bureaucracy, and took other measures to transform Spain into a modern nation-state. The manic Olivares could be seen roaming the corridors with state papers bulging in his pockets, surrounded by scurrying secretaries as he dictated correspondence in several languages. He was "the maestro who moved all the wheels of that great clock" called the Spanish Empire.

Olivares believed firmly in the rightness and inevitability of Spanish hegemony in Europe and tried to maintain it at all costs. But times had changed: the Mediterranean was no longer at centre stage. The first shots of the Thirty Years War (1618-48) were far away, but the Netherlands were involved and Spain would soon become entangled in this sordid struggle. In 1621, Olivares deliberately violated the standing truce with the United Provinces and war followed. Seven years later an entire treasure fleet was captured by the Dutch, and its hoard carted off to Holland.

Spain was flirting with financial disaster. War broke out with France again and expenditures climbed. Spain had grown used to its annual "fix" from the Americas, but in the crucial year of 1639 no treasure fleet arrived. The high costs of war prompted the Count-Duke to seek more revenue from the tight-fisted provinces. A tax on salt, along with universal conscription, caused riots in Catalonia. For quite some time the crown had been losing its grip on this northeastern region. Olivares was facing the fundamental problems of the Spanish monarchy: too much financial burden on Castilla and too many antiquated privileges used to defend entrenched social élites.

It's said that in 1640 Olivares lost two kingdoms in one week. In Catalonia, a mob murdered the hated Castilian viceroy, the corpulent count of Santa Coloma, and the Catalans asked for French aid, naming Louis XIII Count of Barcelona. Later, a combined French-Catalan force defeated the Spanish army on Montjuich hill in Barcelona. Fortunately for the crown, neither Aragón nor Valencia lent a hand to their Catalan "brothers," which might have put a final end to the work of Fernando and Isabel.

The situation in Portugal was analogous. Resentful of the Count-Duke's centralising, the Portuguese turned to the Duke of Braganza. Things were surprisingly easy for the rebels: 400 of them rushed a Lisbon palace and proclaimed Braganza king Joao IV. Although Portugal's independence was not officially recognized for 25 years, it was a fact by 1641, just six decades after Felipe II had created history's greatest empire.

The provincial revolts led to the fall of Count-Duke Olivares in 1643. He retired to his sister's palace in Toro, where he died half-mad a few years later. A man of great plans but inept execution, he himself remarked, "We were trying to achieve miracles and reduce the world to what it cannot be." In a few years the Count-Duke's policies were in shreds.

The 1640s were a terrible decade for Spain. Sicily and Naples also revolted, and a new offensive against France led to the disastrous battle of Rocroi, which marked the end of Spanish military prestige in Europe. In 1648 the Peace of Westphalia ended the Thirty Years War and recognized what long had been a fact: an independent Netherlands (excluding Flanders). Spain's 80-year northern nightmare was over.

War with France dragged on until the Treaty of the Pyrenees (1659), the official end of Spain's European power status and the emergence of France under Louis XIV. To drive home the point Louis married Maria Teresa, daughter of the Spanish king. The marriage turned out to be a crux of history. (One odd remnant of the treaty is Llivia, once capital of Catalan Cerdanya, now an island of Spanish territory completely surrounded by France.)

Historians have drawn a correlation between Spain's declining fortunes on the battlefield and the declining silver cargoes from America. The unfavourable trade balance (raw wool was still the only major export) meant that the little treasure that did make it to Sevilla passed on to foreign bankers like water through a sieve. Reform was imperative, but no one seemed willing to face the task. The mines of Potosí and Mexico had always saved the country, so why plan or save? Money would be plentiful again once the fleet arrived, it was reasoned. Many Spaniards held the belief that Spain was richer and more fertile than other countries, hence entirely self-sufficient and without the need for foreign trade.

Looms fell silent as industry choked from under-investment and over-taxation. Further crippled by inflation, over-priced Spanish goods could not compete on the world market. Furthermore, by 1650 foreign entrepreneurs controlled almost all the nation's external trade and about 80% of its internal trade and industry. The Fuggers of Augsburg, for example, monopolized wool, timber, mercury and iron exports, and the entire colony of Venezuela was briefly sold to Hamburg bankers.

Spain's fossilized social structure and feeble work ethic only worsened matters. The best men continued to enter the military, church, or government, all honourable but essentially unproductive positions. As one writer lamented, "So many men without posts, so many posts without men."

The church offered the population an unending succession of masses, processions, and religious festivals, which took up about a third of the year. Spain's most important institution also influenced society in other ways. Thus a group of priests summoned to consider a projected canal could flatly declare, "If God had wanted these two rivers to be navigable, He could have effected it simply by a fiat, and it would be an infringement of the rights of providence to improve that which, for reasons not to be understood, it had wished to remain imperfect."

In the midst of all this, however, Spaniards were creating a cultural golden age with few rivals. Spanish painting in particular exploded with the incredible genius of Zurbaran, Murillo, Ribera and especially Velazquez. Diego de Silva y Velazquez was both insightful and technically brilliant, and his talents won him a position as court painter. Over several decades, the artist produced one superb canvas after another depicting the homely and troubled king, Prince Baltasar Carlos (who died at 17 from debauchery), Princess Margarita (who also died young), and other members of the royal family. With the dispassionate mastery of his brush, Velazquez dominated the Habsburg world more completely than even Count-Duke Olivares could have wished. A visit to the Velazquez rooms at the Prado is an enlightening journey into the 17th century. Here are the riveting portraits of Felipe and Olivares and the painter's undeniable masterpiece, "*Las Meninas*" (The Maids of Honour), a multi-dimensional look at court life.

Although a royal employee, Velazquez never abused his artistic powers in service of kingly egos. His vision at times is unnerving, and Spain's disillusionment with itself seeps through. Both Cervantes and Velazquez reflected on a country that had climbed to heights and sunk to depths, achieved and lost everything, conquered the world but was vanquished by itself. Scholars still debate the meaning of the painter's treatment of Mars, mythical god of war. In contrast to classical renditions, Velazquez's Mars is an ordinary-looking man seated uncomfortably on the edge of a couch. He is naked except for a blue cape and a helmet that casts his glum face into shadow, looking more dejected than divine. Is it Velazquez's metaphor of Spain's decaying military might?

Spanish painting of the era went far beyond other European schools by infusing a penetrating realism that embraced everything from life's most depressing aspects — dwarfs, drunkards, bearded women — to the most transcendent spiritual realms. Somehow this realism managed to bridge the deep cleavage between the worlds of spirit and flesh. Murillo, for example, painted mostly religious themes, but also delighted in tattered peddlers and street urchins. Zurbaran's canvases of luminous monks, dressed in stiff white and brown habits, combine stark realism with intense spirituality, capturing the poverty-induced ecstasies of cloistered life.

Spanish sculpture of the Golden Century was as ultra-realistic as its painting, using wood instead of stone or marble as a perfect medium for conveying the violent emotions of grieving Christs and martyrs. Among the masters of polychromed wood sculpture were Becerra and Cano.

Cervantes was but the brightest of many literary lights during Spain's Golden Century. Lope de Vega was an incredibly prolific playwright, with 1,800 known plays of which about 500 survive. Said Lope of his speed, "More than a hundred of my comedies have taken only 24 hours to pass from my brain to the boards of the theatre." His observations on war, religion and love were always entertaining though rarely profound, but he did more than anyone to create Spain's national theatre. Drama often revolved around the concept of honour, the gentleman's code that was pushed to ridiculous extremes in 17th-century Spain. According to the rules of *pundonor*, the true gentleman was willing to risk his life in an instant to defend his good name in a duel or other test.

Other first-class writers included Tirso de Molina, Calderon de la Barca, and Francisco de Quevedo. In *The Deceiver of Sevilla*, Tirso (*nom de plume* of a friar named Gabriel Tellez) created the classic figure of Don Juan the seducer, who embodied Spanish daring and masculinity in the battle of the sexes. The Don Juan character would go on to seduce foreign authors from Moliere to Bernard Shaw. Calderon appeared in the sunset glow of culture during Felipe IV's final years as the poet of decline and decadence. He epitomized the baroque style, with a love of extremes and marvellous effects, and greatly influenced later Romantic writers.

Quevedo was perhaps the best of all; his style is acerbic and savagely pessimistic about the decay all around him. "I am strong like Spain, for lack of sustenance," he wrote. Quevedo looked back to the days of Spain's greatness, but realized with anguish that his country was slipping into inexorable decline. Yet he managed to dissect Spanish life with humour. In *La Vida del Buscon*, the hero goes to school and is served a bit of lamb that "between what stuck under our fingernails and what lodged between our teeth, it was all gone, leaving the belly excommunicated from participation."

It is ironic that Spain's great cultural flowering would occur at precisely the time when the Inquisition supposedly had a stranglehold on intellectual life. One explanation for this enigma is that few *important* books from Spain or abroad were ever banned, even though the Inquisition had the power to do so. (Many more obscure works appeared on its Index.) Nevertheless, the Inquisition continued to meddle in daily life, using spies called *familiares* to keep a sharp eye out for abnormal behaviour. Among their special interests were subversive public discussions, usury (lending money at interest), and sexual misconduct. Rooms at Spanish inns could not be bolted from inside so that agents could enter at any time to pounce on any unmarried, hence illicit couples.

The Inquisition found its way to the Americas too, but was less influential; only about a hundred persons were executed in 250 years. During the 17th century colonial administration was formalized to replicate Spanish models, but because government in Spain itself was breaking down, the seeds of decay were transplanted to new soil.

Jealous rivals also continued to pick away at the empire; in 1654 the English took Jamaica, the first permanent loss of Spanish territory. The scourge of piracy swept through the West Indies, climaxing with Henry Morgan and his pirate army. This band of brigands ruthlessly sacked Panama, and the English crown rewarded Morgan with a knighthood and the governorship of Jamaica for his deeds. Despite these incidents, however, the Spanish empire remained a colossus long after Spain itself lay prostrate.

Spain was the first to feel the sting of the printing press in the propaganda wars among rival European powers. Fray Las Casas's *A Brief Relation* pro- liferated, including one edition subtitled: "The Tears of the Indians: Being an Historical and True Account of the Cruel Massacres and Slaughters of Above Twenty Millions of Innocent People... the cry of their blood ceasing at the noise of Your [Majesty's] great transactions, while You arm for their revenge against the Bloudy and Popish nation of the Spaniards."

After about 1660, enemies of Spain plainly saw an enfeebled nation lying south of the Pyrenees. Castilla was dying and hopeful mourners were gather- ing. Felipe managed to hang on a few more years before succumbing to a skin disease. Mariana, his Austrian niece and second wife, had borne him a son and heir, Carlos (Charles), only four when his father died and the final hope for a beleaguered nation. Instead, he became what one historian called "the last stunted sprig of a degenerate line."

Carlos II was a tragic victim of royal interbreeding: four generations of pre- decessors had married cousins or nieces, and their offspring suffered from a variety of physical and mental ailments. Carlos was so weak he had to be presented to the nobles at court held up by strings which his nurse worked like a puppeteer. Until he "came of age" at 15, Spain was ruled by Felipe's widow, the queen-mother Mariana, who ushered in a confused period which often took on aspects of a comic opera.

Mariana engaged an Austrian Jesuit named Father Nithard as confessor, and he soon became an all-powerful force at court. His archrival was Juan Jose, bastard son of Felipe and actress Maria Calderon, who rallied legions of intriguers around him and personally led two coups. One succeeded, and he ruled for two years, albeit no more competently than his predecessors, before dying mysteriously (historians suspect poison).

In view of his feeble physical condition, it was remarkable that Carlos managed to survive to the age of 39. His huge Habsburg jaw stuck out so far that his teeth did not meet, making it impossible for him to chew properly and adding indigestion to a long list of ailments, which included fainting spells, fits, rashes, discharges and eruptions. Exorcists and visionary nuns employed every trick to free him from "the devil."

Nevertheless, Carlos "The Bewitched" was not the monster his name implies. His mind was clear if limited and his character kindly. But he was weak-willed and became the focus of intrigue and conspiracy. Even as a young man he spent only a few minutes a day on state affairs, the rest of his time going to childish games. He liked to pick strawberries, then spend hours counting and recounting them with glee. Spain needed a saviour but got poor Carlos instead.

Both the triumphs and disasters of the Golden Century rest on the shoulders of Castilla, and the heartland reached its nadir around the year 1680. Two-thirds of American silver imports were going directly to foreigners, and the economy was in ruins, with wild inflation and worthless currency causing a large-scale return to barter. Adding to the dismal picture was a serious decline in population throughout the century, from about nine million in 1600 to six million a hundred years later. Plagues, emigration, expulsions, high infant-mortality, and a high incidence of celibacy all took their toll.

The final years of the last Habsburg king were a pathetic spectacle of degradation. Said the Venetian envoy: "From the poor to the rich, everyone devours the state of the king, some taking little bites, the nobility large ones, and the greatest enormous portions." All the important posts went to men of rank, who proceeded to do as little as possible — ministers like the Duke of Medina de las Torres, "who spent all his life in Madrid in total idleness, almost exclusively shared between eating and sleeping."

In foreign affairs, all the chickens would come home to roost as Spain became caught up in the last act of the lengthy duel between France and Austria. Carlos was married off to Marie Louise, niece of the French king, but the union soured when no children arrived, apparently because of a mutual ignorance of the sex act. It soon became clear that Carlos would be the last of his regal line, and foreign diplomats and intriguers began gathering like vultures.

Rival French and Austrian factions formed under Cardinal Portocarrero and the queen-mother respectively. The Austrians convinced Carlos that his fits (probably epileptic) were the work of demons and persuaded him to try an exorcist, who then attempted to plead the Habsburg case. When a rival specialist turned out to have French sympathies, both exorcists had to be driven out of court, and Portocarrero literally camped out in the king's chambers to fend off intruders.

Carlos first named the prince of Bavaria as heir, but he died suddenly a year later. Numerous other claimants came forth, but the choice boiled down to Leopold of Austria or Philippe, the Duke of Anjou. Finally, on his deathbed in 1700, Carlos signed documents handing over his crown to the French duke and the Bourbon dynasty. The Spanish Habsburgs were no more.

## SIGHTS & SITES

**Alcazar de San Juan** *(Ciudad Real): The supposed site of Don Quixote's battle with the windmills (still extant) lies 8 kms. from town.*
**Alpujarras** *(Granada): The mountainous region south of Granada retains traces of its history as final Morisco bastion.*
**Baeza** *(Jaen): Superb architectural centre includes Lion's Square and Plaza Santa Maria.*
**Barcelona**: *Montjuich Castle, built during revolt against Felipe IV in 1640, offers excellent views.*
**El Escorial** *(Madrid): Felipe II's masterpiece includes royal apartments, museums, church, library, and royal pantheon.*
**Granada**: *Carthusian Monastery features splendid baroque decoration.*
**Madrid**: *Convent of the Descalzas Reales, founded by daughter of Carlos V, Joanna of Austria, as religious retreat for women of nobility; the Prado has magnificent collection of all Golden Age artists; El Retiro Park is from the epoch of Felipe IV; Plaza Mayor was heart of old town in 17th century.*
**Sevilla**: *Fine Arts Museum is one of Spain's best, with outstanding works by Murillo, Velazquez and Zurbaran; Archives of the Indies houses millions of documents from Spanish Empire, including letter from Columbus, America's "birth certificate."*
**Toledo**: *Santo Tomé Church contains El Greco's masterpiece "The Burial of the Count of Orgaz"; El Greco House and Museum; Santa Cruz Museum has 18 works by the painter; Hospital of Tavera has more.*
**Valladolid**: *San Gregorio College now serves as National Museum of Polychrome Sculpture.*

# CHAPTER 7

# THE FRENCH CENTURY

Madrid's Palacio Real (Royal Palace), home to several generations of Bourbon monarchs, stands regally on high ground overlooking the Manzanares River. From the Plaza de Oriente, you can scan the imposing east facade, four stories of granite from the Guadarrama mountains and white limestone from Colmenar. This palace is Madrid's finest example of neo-classical architecture, a symphony of pilasters, pediments and corinthian columns, topped by a balustrade lined with statues of Spanish kings.

Inside are hundreds of rooms, riots of sumptuous decor and exquisite detail. Visitors enter the palace via a monumental bronze staircase, then proceed through rooms straining to hold the riches — hundreds of tapestries, chandeliers, diamond-studded clocks, lustrous damask work, mosaics, antique furniture and delicately painted ceilings.

And yet there is something wrong, a piece of the historical puzzle that does not seem to fit. This magnificent architectural creation, a confident statement from a wealthy and powerful monarchy, is not a product of the Golden Century or the glorious heyday of the Spanish Empire. Begun in 1738 by Felipe V, Spain's first Bourbon king, it was built at a time when the nation and its empire had supposedly fallen to incredible depths of inertia and poverty.

Until a recent flood of research, the 18th century was the "missing" one for Spanish historians. They saw it as an aberration, "the French century," and pushed on impatiently toward the War of Independence and the birth of modern, "genuine" Spain. Many even blamed this period for the "ruination" of their country by its fawning mimicry of foreign ideas and customs.

It can be argued, however, that modern Spain really arrived with the first Bourbon. Habsburg glories had withered away. Their last king, feeble in mind and body, had become a pathetic metaphor for a royal line gone sour. The Bourbons brought hope again. The new century that began in 1701 was far different from the pessimistic, religion-haunted era of decline that preceded it.

SPAIN'S FAR FLUNG OVERSEAS empire remained intact, the ballast for a proud nation that would enjoy true world "superpower" status for another century. The loss of its European possessions in the late 1600s became the silver lining which ushered in an epoch of recovery, reform, and progress. Ironically, despite the losses Spain became *more* European under the Bourbons.

"There are no more Pyrenees," proclaimed Louis XIV.

France's "Sun King" was grandfather of the new ruler of Spain (still known as *Castilla y Aragón* ). Restless, powerful, "modern" France was about to shake static, traditional Spain to its bootheels. This was the century of omnipotent despots, "enlightened" and otherwise, and the Bourbons — armed with new ideas and methods of government — would try to yank Spain into the European mainstream.

Carlos II had made nonsense of the previous 30 years of military struggles by naming Philippe of Anjou, second in line to the French throne, as his heir. (Philippe was actually one-quarter Spanish Habsburg through his grandmother, Maria Theresa, and inherited the family's melancholia and odd chin.) Shortly after creating havoc in diplomatic chambers with this decision, Carlos died.

In December of 1700, a mild, docile 16-year-old French boy reluctantly departed the gardens and salons of Versailles and rode south on a white mount toward the Pyrenees. After a journey of 50 days, he entered a jubilant Madrid as King Felipe V, the first of a new royal line from a barony south of Paris. Bourbons have remained on the Spanish throne most of the two hundred and ninety years since Felipe arrived, right down to King Juan Carlos I. (The Spanish Bourbons are distinct from the senior line of French Bourbons, who have not ruled France since 1848. There are also junior lines of Italian Bourbons.)

Louis XIV advised the new king of Spain: "Be a good Spaniard, but remember that you are French by birth..." The sentiment was unnecessary; Felipe longed for the French crown and was appalled at the "backward" Spanish court, where nobles insisted on wearing starched white collars and their own hair (French periwigs had not reached Madrid). Other European powers were gripped with fear that the two monarchies might one day unite, creating a colossus that would straddle the Pyrenees and control most of America.

It is doubtful if Louis ever intended to respect Spanish independence, and all pretences vanished the moment his grandson arrived at Madrid. Felipe, it soon became clear, was both lazy and moody in addition to being young and inexperienced. Hunting was a passion, and he would throw tantrums or sulk if interrupted for state affairs. Everything about his character encouraged French meddling, and the king soon found himself with a Paris-approved wife, 13-year-old Maria Luisa of Saxony. Key to Louis' plans to control Spain was the Princess des Ursins, who was named lady-in-waiting to the queen. Tall and attractive, intelligent and wily, Ursins was a born intriguer.

Austrian Emperor Leopold, France's archrival, objected to the cozy Bourbon arrangement in Spain. Like Louis, he had married a daughter of Felipe IV and proposed his own son, the Archduke Charles, as legitimate heir to the Spanish throne. By 1701, England and the Netherlands joined Austria in the Grand Alliance to dispute Felipe's inheritance, and within a year Spain would witness the first major fighting on its soil since the Reconquest.

The War of Spanish Succession was Europe's first great modern war. Its causes were not religious or even dynastic in the strict sense. The stakes were the balance of power in Europe; neither France nor Austria could tolerate Spain and its empire going over to the other side. England, which held the deciding cards, would become the war's chief beneficiary.

In 1703, the Austrian archduke was proclaimed King Carlos III of Spain at a solemn ceremony in Vienna and shortly after he landed at Lisbon to begin his regal quest. An Anglo-Dutch fleet under Sir George Rooke harassed Cádiz, then took Gibraltar in the name of Queen Anne. The Bourbons responded by assembling a large Spanish-French fleet, but it was badly mauled at the Battle of Málaga (off Marbella), the war's largest naval action.

Felipe and his queen had the support of most Spaniards. However, the Bourbons' well-known centralizing policies were feared in the regions, and Aragón and Valencia soon sided with the Austrian Charles. Using Barcelona as his base, the archduke marched on to Madrid and forced Felipe to flee.

Things were going so bad, in fact, that Louis XIV began to secretly wheel and deal with the enemy at the expense of his grandson, promising to dismember the Spanish Empire. But Felipe stood firm. Shortly after, everything suddenly changed: the archduke's elder brother died, leaving Charles heir to the emperor's throne. England promptly switched sides; a Spain united with Austria would mean a virtual re-creation of Carlos V's 16th-century empire, something the English wanted even less than a dual Bourbon monarchy. When Felipe renounced his claims to the French throne, the stage was set for peace.

As every schoolboy used to know, the Treaty of Utrecht ended the War of Spanish Succession in 1713. Spain lost Flanders and several Italian territories to Austria and was forced to confirm British occupation of Menorca and Gibraltar. The treaty marked the dawn of Britain's control of the Mediterranean and its rise to world-power status. Felipe likened Gibraltar's loss to "thorns in the feet," and so it has remained for Spaniards to this day. Spain and France would spend the next century trying to undo Utrecht.

Meanwhile, Spain had other concerns: namely the rebellious Catalans outraged at being stripped of their medieval privileges. In one stroke, the new king abolished the *fueros* which even Felipe II had not dared attack openly. (Navarra and the Basque lands retained their rights as a reward for their loyalty.)

After a heroic defence of Barcelona, with savage fighting, the city fell to royal troops in September 1714. In order to keep closer watch on the rebel city, Felipe ordered the building of *La Ciudadela* (the Citadel) overlooking Barcelona. It became for Catalans a much- hated reminder of defeat and a symbol of the new Spain — united at long last as a nation called *España*.

The 46-year reign of Felipe V was the longest of modern Spanish history. It was a time of interminable warfare with little or no lasting effects. (As Samuel Johnson remarked, 18th-century European politics was much too complicated to understand or bother with.) Although he managed to break the gloomy Habsburg spell, Felipe was a poor symbol for a new age. Even as a young man, he became a hopeless hypochondriac, spending days in bed staring into space and granting midnight audiences to his ministers. Increasingly indolent and melancholic, he often refused to shave or change his stinking clothes for months on end. At other times palace life became the scene of wild and infantile games, with the king and his dwarfs chasing the queen and her ladies in waiting, snatching their wigs, tearing their clothes and ripping out handfuls of hair in glee.

Maria Luisa died in 1714, worn out by her eccentric and over-sexed albeit totally devoted husband, who had to be stopped from crawling into his wife's bed for his marital rights the night before she died. One cynical minister said that all Felipe needed to keep him happy was "a couch and a woman's thighs." Faced with the king's mercurial moods, the Princess des Ursins immediately sought a successor to Maria.

Meanwhile, an Italian priest named Giulio Alberoni turned up at court and managed to worm his way into the inner circle, mostly with the gourmet meals he relished preparing for friends and victims alike. Together with Ursins, he selected as queen-to-be Elizabeth Farnese, niece of an Italian duke. She later remarked, "The Spanish do not like me, but I fully detest them also." Not a healthy attitude for the queen of Spain.

Ursins was soon outmanoeuvred at court by Alberoni, who became the new queen's adviser. Farnese was a woman of extraordinary energy and will, ir- resistibly attractive it was said, at least to Felipe, who became a docile servant to her political and sexual whims. Foreign policy became the queen's plaything. Her main ambition was to provide thrones for her sons, and for the next 40 years Italy (still a loose collection of independent states) became the centre of Span- ish intrigues.

Alberoni busied himself reviving the crippled Spanish army and navy and dreaming up bizarre schemes. Among them was a grandiose plot to persuade Sweden and Russia to invade Scotland on behalf of the Stuart pretender, James III. Although the two countries backed out, Alberoni readied an invasion fleet at Cádiz. James arrived from Rome in March 1719 and was welcomed with honours worthy of a reigning monarch. The hare-brained expedition actually put to sea, but was battered by storms off Cape Finisterre. A counterpart con- spiracy in Scotland, known in British history as The Nineteen, also failed. Not long after, Alberoni was deposed.

Yet despite all the antics at court, Bourbon Spain was different — stronger, better governed, more prosperous, more attuned to the rest of Europe. Most important, the centuries-long Castilian push for one unified nation — with Madrid supreme — became a reality. During this period the red-and-gold national flag was adopted, a national anthem chosen, and a regular army formed. In fact, Spain under the Bourbons was more unified than Britain or even France. The ghost of Count-Duke Olivares had reason to smile.

Under the new order, Aragón and Valencia became subject to Castilian laws and language in all official matters. After two centuries of struggle, the quasi-independent status of these regions abruptly ended. A military governor reporting directly to the king replaced the old viceroy, and financial officers, mostly French functionaries, made sure that the regions were paying their share of taxes.

The great Louis XIV had proclaimed "I am the state." His nephew agreed, often using the phrase "for such is my will" in royal decrees. Bourbons saw it as their "divine right" to rule. Having dealt with the regions, the new regime embarked on its twin goals of centralizing authority in the crown and unifying the morass of antiquated legal statutes and customs.

The main power struggle involved the monarch and the high nobility, who traditionally controlled government councils. In place of these, the Bourbons created "departments" run by career bureaucrats who enjoyed privileged and aloof positions and remained loyal to the crown. Resentful nobles had no immediate means of resisting, with the stubborn regional parliaments now defunct and the Castilian *cortes* a feeble body that would convene only three times during the century.

The mass arrival of French and Italians profoundly affected Spain's static insularity, especially after the coming of Farnese and her entourage. Feeling their new home intellectually and culturally backward, the Bourbons brought in foreign technicians and sent young Spaniards abroad. Royal academies based on French models were founded, such as the Academy of Good Taste, which tried to establish neo-classical standards.

This was the century when intellectuals were obsessed with cataloguing, describing and systematizing. They produced dictionaries and encyclopedias rather than masterpieces. A history of Spanish literature by Mohedano reached ten volumes and took 25 years to write, though it did not get beyond Seneca. Nothing could have been further from the transcendent genius of the *Siglo de Oro*. For about a century official art became totally French and Italian, until Goya arrived on the scene. Having failed to "hispanicize" Europe the previous century, Spain now experienced a Bourbon campaign to make it European. France's domination gave rise to the popular expression, "When France sneezes, Spain rejoins 'Bless You!'"

The king despised the sombre Escorial and decided to create a mini-Versailles at La Granja de San Ildefonso near Segovia. Strolling around the perfectly symmetrical, manicured gardens and through the ornate rooms, visitors today find it hard to believe they are not in France. Felipe succeeded in re-creating the palace of his childhood, right down to the imported chestnut trees. La Granja's 26 spring-fed fountains, designed by French sculptors, are among the world's finest. After Madrid's old *alcázar* was destroyed by fire, work started on the Royal Palace; when finished it amazed European visitors as a worthy rival to Buckingham and Schonbrunn. The magnificent abode at Aranjuez south of Madrid was also completed to please Bourbon tastes, and the court moved between the various palaces with the regularity of a travelling circus.

Nevertheless, with the passing years Felipe grew more despondent and homesick for France. Even La Granja was not good enough. During several lengthy periods he refused to leave his room and, though rarely violent towards others, he would bite and scratch himself viciously. Elizabeth tried to frustrate his attempts to abdicate, but during one spell of black melancholy in 1724, the 40-year-old king stepped aside for his son, then 16. He became the little-known King Luis I of Spain. Unfortunately, Luis died of smallpox just seven months later, and Felipe resumed his royal duties for another two decades.

Largely through his wife's efforts, the king's depression was kept under control. She sent for the greatest singer of the day, the Neapolitan *castrato* Farinelli, whose job it was to entertain the king and soothe his nervous tension. Felipe was so enchanted by the singer's ethereal voice that Farinelli stayed on at court, singing the same four arias nightly for the next ten years.

By the end of Felipe's reign, Spain's prestige and military might were almost as great as in its days of glory. French and Spanish Bourbons signed the Family Pact, and Britain re-emerged as Spain's chief enemy for the entire century. The idea was to frustrate English ambitions in the Mediterranean and in the Americas, where merchants coveted the vast Hispanic market.

One curious conflict occurred in 1739: the War of Jenkins Ear. By treaty, Britain enjoyed a monopoly of the American slave trade and its ships were exempt from examination or duty. Naturally, this produced a lively contraband trade and piracy in the Caribbean, mostly out of Jamaica. Weary of incessant infractions since the days of Henry Morgan, Spain began searching British vessels.

In the midst of this tension, a Mr. Jenkins turned up in London with a box containing his severed ear, claiming that it had been lopped off years earlier by a Spaniard. Both Parliament and the public were outraged and made Jenkin's ear the symbol of Spanish "harassment". All this poppycock led to war. Spanish victories soon proved that the Bourbon reforms were working, at least in rebuilding the military. After a year, the conflict merged with the War of Austrian Succession and became an odd footnote to a confused era.

THIS WAS THE CENTURY of the Enlightenment, when ideals such as rationalism, natural law and scientific progress became the rage in intellectual circles. Writers like Voltaire pointed an accusing finger at Catholic, traditional Spain as the epitome of backwardness and intolerance. Their invective did much to carry the Black Legend into modern times; Voltaire even concocted an "order" from the Spanish king to exterminate the Indians.

By mid-century the new ideas were trickling into the peninsula, brought in part by French families living in Spain. A few Spanish adherents came forth to promote the new ideas (*luces*) through local societies called Friends of the

Country. One notable spokesman was a Benedictine monk named Feijoo, who attacked astrology, magic, false miracles and other forms of popular superstition. Wrote one admirer: "Thanks to the immortal Feijoo, spirits no longer trouble our houses, witches have fled our towns, the evil eye does not plague the tender child, and an eclipse does not dismay us."

Standing squarely in opposition to "enlightened" progress was the Catholic church and its dreaded Inquisition, living symbol of how far out of step Spain remained. The church, especially the Jesuits, fought with all its considerable powers, not only banning and burning books, but also hauling up suspects to face the grand inquisitor. Wrote one critic, "The frightful caverns of the Inquisition open up to swallow the poor wretch who has incurred the indignation of the priests and hypocrites. Spain is a thousand leagues from Europe and ten centuries from the eighteenth."

All the intellectual ferment affected only a tiny minority. Devotion to the Catholic religion remained the strongest social force in Spain, especially among superstitious commoners. There was no shortage of miracle workers, such as the Beata of Cuenca, who claimed her flesh had been transformed into the body and blood of Christ. A fierce intellectual struggle broke out between those wanting to share in European progress and those afraid that Spain was losing its unique identity to the onslaught of francophiles. Conservatives blasted the masonic lodges, known for spreading Enlightenment ideas, and appealed for the return to true "Spanishness."

Many customs today regarded as typically Spanish sprang from the widespread hostility to France at this time. In spite of (or because of) several royal bans, the bullfight became popular and evolved into its modern form: when aristocrats on horseback abandoned the sport, footmen working with short sword and cape took centre stage. (The aristocratic version survives with the *rejoneo* style.) The first of many large rings was built in Madrid in 1756.

Likewise, religious festivals and processions such as *Semana Santa* (Holy Week) took on new fervour, and young people adopted the folkloric style of dress and manners seen in Goya's paintings of the *majos y majas*. These lower-class idols were intensely anti-French young bullies who wore long capes and broad-brimmed hats. The fashion spread, and it was said that "a Spaniard might be willing to go around without shoes, but without a cape, never. They are even buried in them."

Another reason the new ideas met resistance was that Spain really *was* different. A census in 1797 put the unproductive classes, from grandees down to vagrants, at 30% of the male population. Mendicants subsisted on a free pittance from the church and spent their lives in idleness and rags. Even worse, two classes, the nobility and the church, held about two-thirds of the land, most of which lay fallow. About half-a-million Spaniards claimed noble birth (more than in France, which had twice the population), and they shared contempt for farming and the "vile trades."

The grandees derived their power from their *señorios*, rights dating back to the Reconquest. The dukes of Alba, for instance, were *señores* of one quarter of

Salamanca province, 168 towns and villages in all. The dukes of Osuna, Alba and Medinaceli controlled vast tracts of Andalucia. Beneath them came the *hidalgos*. Their mansions can be seen throughout Spain, especially in Andalusian towns such as Ronda and Baeza, where social life centred on horse breeding and other gentlemanly pursuits.

Enlightened bourgeois values threatened the very concept of an unproductive nobility and met staunch resistance. In Spain, the minor gentry still preferred beggary to work, and a royal proclamation that trade and manual labor were not incompatible with honour had little impact. Much of the nation's essential work was not getting done.

As a prop of the old order and old ways of thinking, the church's influence was pervasive, percolating down to every level of life. The numbers were staggering — about 250,000 Spaniards were priests or members of religious orders. The power of the parish priest went unchallenged, especially in the stable peasant societies of the north, where Catholicism was not just a faith but like a second skin. Educational institutions also resisted the Enlightenment for a simple reason: the Jesuits controlled Spanish schools, where the guiding principle was still the unenlightened *la letra con sangre entra*, "it takes a little blood to let learning in."

Spanish scientific progress has never kept pace with the rest of Europe, a fact which some blame on Spaniards' extreme individualism, unsuited to "teamwork" and methodical research. While other countries excelled in mathematics and science, Spain produced theologians and painters. In the age of Bacon and Descartes, the study of science languished and theological problems were endlessly debated at the clergy-riddled universities. While the rest of Europe advanced in technology, Spaniards were discussing which language the angels spoke and whether the sky was made of bell metal or a wine-like liquid.

On the positive side, the second half of the century witnessed some progress in the biological and natural sciences. A botanical garden was founded in Madrid and scientific expeditions were sent to America.

FERNANDO (FERDINAND) VI, Felipe's eldest surviving son by Maria Luisa, succeeded his anguished but long-lived father in 1746. Everyone was eager for peace — and to be rid of Elizabeth Farnese. The new consort was Barbara of Braganza, a homely but strong-willed Portuguese princess who shared her husband's desire for neutrality and reform. Fernando replaced French advisors with Spanish and under the sure hand of ministers like Ensenada finances were reorganized, the navy expanded and the Inquisition's feared *autos de fe* stopped. (The Inquisition's last victim, an old crone accused of "having carnal converse with the Devil and laying eggs that had prophecies written on them," was burned at the stake in Sevilla in 1780.) Under Fernando, a concordat was signed with the pope placing the Spanish church largely under the king's authority, capping a long struggle.

These were years of tranquility and recuperation. The royal couple were devoted to each other and to good music (their "royal master" was Domenico Scarlatti) and enlightened prosperity. For diversion, they enjoyed sailing in the "toy fleet" of barges that cruised the Tajo River at Aranjuez. Unfortunately, this dream world began to crumble after just a few years. Devastating earthquakes rocked the peninsula in 1755-56, and several cities (including Lisbon) were destroyed. After Barbara died two years later, Fernando lapsed into the typical family melancholia. At times he sat motionless on a stool for hours; at others he lay in bed screaming and throwing dishes at the servants. Fernando was a broken man and died a year after his wife.

And yet, despite the monarch's collapse Spain was once more a prosperous nation with a powerful fleet. By mid century the Spanish economy was undergoing a remarkable transformation as Basque shipyards bustled and Catalan looms hummed. By the end of the 1700s Catalonia was second in textile production only to England; once again Barcelona became a great Mediterranean port and Spain's leader in commerce and industry. Ironically, the Bourbons' destruction of Catalonia's medieval rights may have helped push the region toward economic modernization.

In Castilla there was reason for concern: the peninsula's coastal areas were outstripping the centre in population, economic growth and standard of living. While Bourbon centralization was trying to pull everything to the capital, economic realities were doing just the opposite. Something had to give. Two vastly different Spains were emerging: the centre and south — arid, sparsely populated, with large landholdings — and the coastal areas of the north and east — with small farms, growing industries and open ports. A line drawn between the two areas roughly corresponds (except for Madrid) with the front lines during the first year of the Spanish Civil War in 1936. That is not mere coincidence.

Spain's crucial economic problem was land, its distribution and use in a staunchly conservative society that was trying meekly to reform. There was corresponding agricultural diversity, from the poorest type of unirrigated cereal farming on the *meseta* to the verdant gardens of Valencia, from the handkerchief plots of Galicia to the sprawling untilled estates of the south. Perhaps the most important impediment to progress was the land itself, with its poor soil and erratic rainfall. For these reasons, Spain did not achieve the dramatic rise in agricultural production seen elsewhere in Europe, a rise that helped lead to the Industrial Revolution.

There was another essential split developing in Spanish society — between the cities and countryside (and its villages). Spain was still overwhelmingly rural, with only a few cities of more than 100,000 inhabitants. Generally, the great unwashed and untitled masses lived in isolated, backwater towns and shunned anything that smacked of novelty. Everything revolved around the *pueblo* (village), whose very name in Spanish also means "the people." The typical Spaniard saw himself belonging first to his village or town, then to his province or region, and lastly to his nation. The language is full of contemptuous references to other regions, like "rather be a tart than a Galician."

The persistence of the *pueblo* phenomenon sprang from poor roads and communications. The countryside was often underpopulated and dangerous.

Early travellers, such as a British major touring Spain in 1774, reported that Andalucia was a land of smugglers and bandits chased by the *migueletes*, predecessors of the civil guard.

Most cities were squalid. Madrid was the worst of all, with about 150,000 residents living on narrow, dark streets where slop was hurled from the windows onto unsuspecting passers-by. People fled to the cafés where (believe it or not) laws prohibited smoking, reading newspapers, talking politics, or playing cards. The capital's medieval panorama began to change with the Bourbons (especially Carlos III), who endowed Madrid with new buildings, the first sewage system, and street lighting. Order improved after neighbourhood watchmen called *serenos* were introduced. With the wider, more pleasant streets, the *paseo* (stroll) became a mandatory evening social activity. For literary types, the *tertulia* was a conversational gathering in a bar or café, where the drink of choice was chocolate, considered one of life's necessities. The state lottery was also introduced in this era.

For the upper crust, elaborate carriages became the rage. This aristocratic means of transport reached a remarkable level of sumptuousness, with gilded panels, monograms, and decorative shells to dazzle humble observers. The Carriage Museum next to the Royal Palace in Madrid contains an impressive display of these delightful vehicles from another era.

WHEN FERNANDO DIED childless in 1759, his half-brother (son of Farnese and Felipe V) succeeded him as Carlos (Charles) III. The new king came well prepared, having served 24 years as king of Naples, and he is considered a bright star in the dark sky of the Spanish monarchy. Carlos was one of Europe's new "enlightened despots," whose attitude might be summed as "Everything for the people, but nothing by the people." Indeed, with all his good intentions, Carlos governed more despotically than even Felipe II would have dared. He once remarked, "My subjects are like children; they cry when they are washed."

Goya's portrait of Carlos which hangs in the Prado is sympathetic if not flattering: a narrow face creased with wrinkles, piercing blue eyes, a prominent nose and drooping mouth. (It was said that Princess Adelaide of France refused to marry him after one look at his portrait.) Carlos was not a brilliant man and comes off as something of a yokel in Goya's work — in a simple hunter's costume, musket in hand. His main diversion was deer hunting and he lived an untypically modest life as a widower.

Carlos ruled through a series of astute ministers, often Italians or Spanish francophiles. For example, his trusted aide from Naples, the Marquis of Squillace, became minister of finance and war. Together they unleashed an offensive to crush the foot-dragging church and sheath the sword of the Inquisition. Even though Carlos was a pious Catholic, he targeted the Jesuits in particular for royal discipline, mainly because of their fanatical loyalty to the pope. Moreover, they were generally a nuisance in a society painfully trying to make intellectual headway. For example, Jesuits claimed that such events as the great Lisbon earthquake was "punishment from God" and opposed any relief efforts.

An odd series of events led to the expulsion from Spain of this "fighting order" of priests. (The unpopular order had already been booted out of France and Portugal). First, the government tried to outlaw the traditional cape and brimmed hat on the grounds that criminals used them to hide weapons. Troops patrolled the streets of Madrid, accompanied by tailors brandishing shears to cut the offending capes and pins to fold back hat brims into the acceptable French tricorn. Matters were made worse by the high price of bread at the time, and riots ensued. (Later, the ingenious Count of Aranda made the cape and brimmed hat the costume of the public executioner and popular support melted away.)

An investigation blamed the Jesuits for inciting the riots. The Count of Aranda, friend of Voltaire and member of the Freemasons, ordered several thousand priests and novices rounded up and shipped off to Rome. Ironically, the pope himself did not allow the Jesuits to land, and when their boats arrived in Italy papal troops threatened to open fire. Most of the fugitives went to Corsica, but were later allowed into Italy.

The three decades of Carlos III's rule were much more positive in tone, however. For the first time in memory, Spain entered the European mainstream. Madrid was transformed with the royal palace, the future home of the Prado Museum, the Alcalá arch and Cibeles fountain, and grand avenues like the Paseo del Prado, all in the neo-classical style. Spanish-baroque architecture also continued to flourish in the 1700s, as many older churches and mansions received new façades or interiors. The exuberance of the age outdid itself with the gushingly ornate Churrigueresque style, named for three architects: brothers Jose, Joaquin and Alberto Churriguera.

"Enlightened" public works took precedence over church building for the first time. Spanish roads had outraged travellers for years, but a new corps of road engineers began a highway network shooting out from Madrid like the spokes of a wheel. Regular coach service soon linked major cities. The great Canal of Aragón (begun two centuries earlier) was finally completed and, true to the times, the king even built a model port near the mouth of the Ebro.

Carlos thought big and acted decisively, usually with success. He called for Spain's first census in 1768 (Britain's first was in 1801), which counted 10.2 million residents, a healthy increase after the decimation of the final Habsburg years. To deal with underpopulation in the bandit-riddled Sierra Morena, the king arranged for about 6,000 Bavarian immigrants to settle in 13 new villages. To bolster the army, one man in five was drafted for eight year stints. In another decisive measure, the king ended the ancient privileges of the Mesta. One area in which even Carlos had to struggle was agrarian reform. Here he met with virulent opposition from landed interests.

Foreign policy under Carlos set off on the wrong foot. Spain's late entry into the Seven Years War between Britain and France had led to humiliating defeats in Cuba and the Philippines, followed by a treaty which stripped Spain of several American possessions. The tension heated up under the anglophobic Carlos. Sources of hostility lay in Gibraltar and Menorca, which Spain claimed, and in Britain's lust for the Spanish empire. And there was already friction over the Falkland Islands (Las Malvinas) after the arrival of some English "settlers" in the 1770s.

The American Revolution gave both France and Spain a chance for revenge, and both nations aided the Americans. A combined Spanish-French fleet took control of the English Channel and prevented Britain from sending reinforcements to the beleaguered Lord Cornwallis, who was forced to surrender to the Americans in 1781. There is a story that money intended to finish the second tower of Málaga's cathedral was diverted to help the American colonists. The church, known as *la manquita* (the one-armed) still has only one tower.

For Spain the war's most notable event was the Great Siege of Gibraltar. The Rock was defended by Lord Elliot and his men, and today you can get a real sense of the siege by visiting the Upper Galleries in Gibraltar. Here, men using hand tools and explosives cut gun positions into solid rock, and installed the heavy cannons that decided the battle. The attackers used enormous, heavily armed floating batteries in Gibraltar Bay, but were driven back by cannonballs raining down from above. After three years of unsuccessful attack, Gibraltar had proved impregnable to the armies of that day.

Nevertheless, when all the smoke had cleared and all the deals were done at the Treaty of Versailles (1783), Spain tasted the sweet grapes of revenge, winning back Menorca and a good deal of pride. Spain's power was its greatest in nearly two centuries, especially in the New World, where the empire still took in all of south and central America (except for Brazil and Guiana), as well as Mexico, Florida and the vast Louisiana territory. (Spain's share of lands that became the United States was far larger than England's.) Soldiers and priests were taming the American south-west (the future Texas, New Mexico and Arizona), and a humble fray from Mallorca, Junipero Serra, was finishing a string of missions in a faraway land called California. Spain, the fallen giant, was still a world power.

IN THIS THIRD century of empire, America seemed oblivious to the chronic crises of Europe. Nevertheless, Spain's loose-knit control could not successfully resist aggressive interlopers forever. British merchants — backed by the royal fleet — rallied round the Black Legend by supporting the "end of despotism" in order to carve a slice of the American market. And they succeeded. As the popular saying went, "Where Spain keeps the cow, the rest of Europe drinks the milk." The opening up of trade to Spain's non-Castilian cities (1778) helped some, but by then much of America had become an economic fief of foreigners.

Moreover, administrative reforms from the enlightened monarchs, the first major changes in two centuries, actually served to undermine Spain's control. Reformers suffered from the delusion that good government would solve colonial problems. Under corrupt and inefficient viceroys, Creoles had grown wealthy and independent, and the new laws merely underscored the inconvenience of the Spanish connection.

Following the American Revolution isolated rumblings of discontent stirred in Spain's colonies. In Peru, Tupac Amaru, supposedly a descendent of the Inca kings, led an uprising of 60,000 Indians that was severely crushed — Amaru's body was mutilated and pulled apart by teams of wild horses — proving that behind every legend (even black ones) is some fact. Rebellions would become commonplace after 1800.

The French Revolution had even greater impact than the American, upsetting the precarious union (achieved by Carlos III) between the crown and enlightened Spaniards. The great reforms of the past few decades sprang from enlightened despots and shrewd ministers who permitted no opposition or debate. Now Spain found itself at odds with the spirit of the times, what might loosely be called "democracy." Spaniards generally were terrified by the French Revolution, especially when moderation boiled over into the Reign of Terror. Minister Floridablanca threw up an unsuccessful *cordon sanitaire* along the border to keep out the revolutionary virus, and every foreigner entering Spain was forced to swear an oath of allegiance to the throne and the Catholic church.

Carlos III had died in 1788 of a cold caught while hunting. His second son, Carlos (Charles) IV, was a simple fellow of 40 with a taste for clocks and fine embroidery. His mushy will and fuzzy intellect did not bode well for dealing with two decades of challenge, and he soon came under the domination of Maria Luisa of Parma, his waspish and randy Italian wife. Goya's portraits show her as strong-willed and modestly attractive, with auburn hair, hypnotic eyes and a sensuous mouth. Carlos was dissolute, but the queen was utterly abandoned to sensuality — and prematurely old. Their advanced state of physical and moral decay comes through well in Goya's dazzling and disturbing masterpiece, "The Family of Carlos IV."

Francisco Jose de Goya y Lucientes was born near Zaragoza and became the official court painter for thirty years. In that position he moved in the highest circles and had a stormy affair with the Duchess of Alba, Spain's richest woman. She was *not* the model for the famous *majas* (naked and clothed), but a portrait of her does exist in which she points to words in the sand at her feet which read "*Solo* [only] *Goya*."

It is from Goya that we enjoy a remarkably clear picture of the era. In addition to royal portraits, he created scenes of typical Spanish life in paintings and hundreds of tapestries, today on display at Madrid's Royal Tapestry Factory. We see common people working or at fiestas and high society living the idyllic life. Later, after a serious illness left him deaf, his art became darker and more biting. A series of 80 satiric etchings called the *caprichos* depicts foppish gallants, pompous priests and ladies of easy virtue. And there was much more to come as the old world crumbled in the coming decades.

Carlos IV was a first cousin of Louis XVI, and after the French king met the guillotine (1793) Spain found itself at war with revolutionary France, which vowed "to help all peoples who desire to recover their liberty." Waves of anti-French and anti-Revolutionary sentiment swept across Spain, including a popular belief that a mortal struggle for control was taking place between Freemasons and Jesuits. In time, liberals and progressives of any stripe came to be seen as traitors to Spain and its traditional values, the origin of the profound split into the "two

Spains" so often blamed for the nation's ills.

At the queen's insistence, Carlos appointed a 25-year-old royal guard named Manuel Godoy to serve as chief minister. This handsome young man from Extremadura had caught the queen's eye and he soon became her lover. It was a common practice among aristocratic women of the time, and Carlos seemed willing to play the cuckold. No one was really sure how much the king knew, but the queen herself referred to the strange relationship as "the earthly trinity." The common people were outraged at such scandalous behaviour.

Godoy was an adventurer with more ambition than brains, and he could be obnoxiously vain, tactless and opinionated. But he was far from being the buffoon of legend; many of his "enlightened" ideas and programmes continued the best work of Carlos III. In any case, the royal couple showered him with honours and gifts, naming him Prince of Peace (which outraged the grandees) and giving him a carriage with his own monogram.

In time Maria Luisa, about twice Godoy's age, treated him more as a spoiled son than a lover, but she also came to regard him as a political genius. The aristocracy and commoners reacted with disgust, and crown prince Fernando (Ferdinand) strongly resented his mother's brazen affair. The idea that Spain was being governed by a cuckold king, a lascivious queen and an empty-headed paramour broke the spell Carlos III had cast over Spaniards. The monarchy would never again be quite the same.

In 1795, with the relatively moderate Directory running the show in Paris, Godoy struck a treaty with France that pledged military cooperation against Britain. Sporadic war raged for the next few years. With Napoleon Bonaparte's coup d'etat in 1799, royalist Spain slept easier, viewing his rise as the first step toward Bourbon restoration. The Spanish king launched a fierce crackdown on liberal ministers. Even Godoy, briefly out of power, fell under the scrutiny of a revived Inquisition for "atheism and immorality." (He was absolved.)

Carlos feared French ambitions in Italy, but Bonaparte wanted Spanish support and flattered the royal couple with presents. His cynical intentions soon became clear, however, when Spain found itself taking part in an invasion of Portugal, England's ally. This "War of the Oranges" inspired Goya's painting of a swaggering Godoy on a mock battlefield with the bombastic title "Generalisimo of the Armies." As usual, Godoy's "crimes" were vulgarity and ostentation.

War with England ceased, but not for long. The same year (1804) Napoleon declared himself emperor. Like the proverbial lamb, Spain went willingly to the slaughter as France's ally. The executioner was none other than Lord Nelson. The British fleet met a French-Spanish navy off Cape Trafalgar (between Algeciras and Cádiz) on October 21, 1805, in one of history's most decisive battles. In Gibraltar, you can visit Trafalgar cemetery, where many of the fallen lie, and see the beach where the fatally wounded Nelson was carried ashore.

This great British triumph destroyed the Spanish fleet, so painstakingly built up during the 1700s and was the real end of Spain's sea power, 217 years after the defeat of the Invincible Armada. It also signalled the end of Spain's ability to protect its empire, either from revolutionaries within or from foreign navies. France too had been badly hurt at Trafalgar, but Napoleon was still in firm control on land and many great victories lay ahead.

Two years after Trafalgar, a treaty between France and Spain arranged for the partition of Portugal, with Godoy receiving the southern section as "Hereditary Prince of Algarves." Bonaparte's troops poured into the peninsula, but what had been agreed as "safe passage" through Spain soon became outright occupation. By March 1808, 100,000 French soldiers were on Spanish soil and they controlled Madrid itself. Rumours began to spread that Godoy was conspiring with Napoleon to deprive Prince Fernando of his rightful inheritance.

Godoy and Fernando had clashed before, as much for the queen's affection as the rights of succession. Fernando had in fact secretly approached Bonaparte with a scheme to overthrow the hated trio, praising him as the "saviour of Europe" and begging the hand of a relative. Someone (one of those great "someones" of history) left a note on the king's dressing table informing him of the plot and Fernando, caught trying to conceal papers, was arrested for high treason. After three days of interrogation he made a humiliating confession: "I crave Your Majesty's pardon for having deceived you, and beg, as a grateful son, to kiss your royal feet." He was promptly pardoned, but his own mother called him "a spiked vine of cowardice."

In the popular mind Godoy, not Fernando, had come to represent collusion with the French, but he had begun to suspect Napoleon's real motives. Sensing trouble, Godoy and the royal couple left Madrid hurriedly, heading south to the palace at Aranjuez. To the hysterical populace it seemed that the "earthly trinity" were trying to escape. In just a few hours, the scene at Aranjuez was uncomfortably similar to Versailles just before the French Revolution, as gangs of malcontents from Madrid descended on the palace demanding "justice."

On March 18 violent riots broke out and Godoy only managed to save his skin by hiding for two days in a rolled-up carpet. When he emerged it was too late: Carlos had abdicated to his son, proclaimed as King Fernando (Ferdinand) VII. Godoy was roughed up by the rabble and made to grovel at his rival's feet. The masses had entered Spanish politics with a vengeance.

A thrill of expectation swept across Spain at the prospect of a new monarch who, ironically, came to symbolize staunch opposition to the French after spineless Carlos. In reality, the fool had been succeeded by the knave: Fernando VII, the most contemptible king in Spanish history.

## SIGHTS & SITES

*Aranjuez* (Madrid): Neo-classical Royal Palace dates from reign of Felipe V; Carlos IV signed abdication in Throne Room.
*Cádiz*: Model of town during reign of Carlos III in Historical Museum; Cathedral, built 1720-1838, has outstanding silver collection.
*Fuendetodos* (Zaragoza): Goya's House (birthplace)

**Gibraltar**: *Upper Galleries and Trafalgar Cemetery date from Napoleonic wars.*
**Madrid**: *National Library founded in 1711 by Felipe V has one of Europe's largest collections, including 800 editions of* Don Quixote; *much of city is a neo-classical showcase of Carlos III: Royal Palace, Cibeles Fountain, Alcalá Arch, etc.; Chapel of San Antonio de la Florida has fresco by Goya; Prado Museum's Goya rooms are superb; Royal Tapestry Factory has display of Goya cartoons; Basilica of San Francisco el Grande has imposing facade by Sabatini and enormous dome.*
**Petra** *(Mallorca): House-Museum of native son Junipero Serra, famous missionary of California.*
**Puerto de la Cruz** *(Canary Islands): Botanical Gardens dating from reign of Carlos III are outstanding.*
**Ronda** *(Málaga): Beautiful bullring built in 1785; scene of annual Goyesque Fair devoted to 18th-century bullfighting.*
**Salamanca**: *The Plaza Mayor, built for the city by Felipe V, is among most beautiful in Spain; designed by the Churriguera brothers.*
**Santa Cruz de Tenerife** *(Canary Islands): Attacking Paso Alto Castle in 1797, Lord Nelson lost his right arm.*
**Santiago de Compostela** *(La Coruña): Baroque façade (1750) of earlier cathedral is a masterpiece by Fernando Casas.*
**Segovia**: *La Granja de San Ildefonso and Riofrio palaces built by Philip V and Elizabeth Farnese, 11 kms. from town.*
**Sevilla**: *Gushing baroque specimens are Chapel of San Jose and San Telmo Palace.*
**Toledo**: *Transparente by Narciso Tome is a controversial baroque island in the famous Gothic Cathedral.*
**Vic** *(Barcelona): Neo-Classical Cathedral (1781-1803) and Episcopal Museum.*
**Zaragoza**: *The older Seo Cathedral has a baroque façade.*

# CHAPTER 8

# LIBERAL SPAIN

Hanging in Madrid's Prado Museum are two of Goya's most powerful canvases, titled simply "The Second of May" and "The Third of May." Together they depict the most important 48 hours in Spanish history, the virtual birth of modern Spain. For the story of Spain and its empire, the year 1808 is the closest in importance to 1492. Events shook centuries of ingrained attitudes, astounded a continent on the verge of collapse before Napoleon, and set ablaze the whole of Spanish America.

On May 2, 1808, a Madrid mob rose with incredible fury against the French army and its Mameluke cavalry. Men and women from the poor neighbourhoods grabbed any weapon they could find — knives, shovels, sticks, axes — and descended on the intruders. Balconies and windows vomited a shower of tiles, bricks, stones, boiling water, wash-tubs and furniture. In *"Dos de Mayo"* Goya painted knife-wielding women pulling the terrified Mamelukes from their horses. Dozens of these Egyptian mercenaries were bludgeoned to death before French regulars regained control. Throughout the uproar wealthy *Madrileños* locked their doors, and the Spanish garrison stayed meekly in its quarters. This was a new type of popular street-rising that would come again.

Those suspected of the massacre were rounded up and executed the following day, a scene Goya witnessed from a nearby window while he sketched feverishly. More than its companion oil, the painting *"Tres de Mayo"* is considered a landmark of modern art, both in its impassioned theme and innovative technique. Goya captured all the emotion of the scene — the ominous firing squad, the terrified but defiant victims with their outstretched arms, the blood-drenched corpses rapidly filling the square. He also preserved for eternity those few frenzied moments that marked the start of Spain's War of Independence (what we know as the Peninsular War).

Goya himself viewed that war with the same mixed emotions felt by many Spaniards. As any good patriot he detested the invader, but he greatly admired French accomplishments championed by Napoleon, which seemed to herald a new world capable of replacing Spain's inert society. In the end Goya came to detest war regardless of its outcome; his series of searing etchings, "Disasters of War" (also in the Prado), contain no marching armies or glorious deeds, only the horror and destruction of warfare. To Goya we owe our visual perceptions of these frightful times. His macabre vision took Spanish realism into realms never imagined by Velazquez or Ribera.

AFTER HIS FATHER'S forced abdication at Aranjuez in March, a triumphant Fernando had returned to Madrid. Here, the new king by acclamation discovered that a French army under Murat had occupied the capital the day before. Napoleon, refusing to recognize Fernando's claims, summoned him together with his father, Queen Maria Luisa and Godoy.

Appearing before the emperor at Bayonne, the royal family put on a degrading spectacle that shocked even the cynical Frenchman, shouting scandalous insults at each other and grovelling for his favour. When Fernando brashly accused his mother of repeated adultery, Napoleon quickly pointed out that if this were true it might compromise his claims to the throne. The French ruler later wrote that Carlos was "a nice man" but his son "very stupid and very wicked." The queen, he observed, "has her past and her character written on her face, which is all I need say. It surpasses anything one dare imagine."

Fernando was forced to abdicate to his father, then Carlos in turn to Napoleon's brother, Joseph Bonaparte. Fernando was detained at the emperor's pleasure and would not see Spain again for six years. Word spread among Spaniards that their "prince charming" was urging resistance, and they dubbed him el deseado ("the desired one"). Carlos, his queen and Godoy — by then political nonentities — were packed off to early retirement and a lifetime of exile in France. Even after their scandalous world came tumbling down, however, they remained loyal and devoted to one other. (The ex-king and his queen died within the same month in 1819, while Godoy managed to survive another three decades, finally dying in obscurity in Paris.) Deposing the Spanish Bourbons was one of Napoleon's most high-handed actions and later, in exile on St. Helena, he traced his own downfall to that one day's events at Bayonne.

While Napoleon conducted his four-ring circus in France, the events leading to May 2nd were unfolding back in Madrid. Crowds gathered outside the palace, and rumours spread that the royal family had been lured away to be murdered. For all their scorn for the "earthly trinity," people were outraged; and their love for Fernando grew more passionate. After some minor incidents the mob grew unruly and French soldiers fired into the crowd, setting off the city-wide mêlée.

In a matter of days, word of the Madrid revolt hurtled though the nation, and men from all corners of the peninsula began to take up arms. Napoleon was livid when he heard the news, but predicted a quick end to the affair.

Great men often make great mistakes.

"Spaniards, after a long agony your nation is perishing. I have seen your ills and I shall remedy them." Thus read Napoleon's proclamation to the Spanish nation, unfurled by his innocuous brother as he launched his brief reign as King Jose I. It was Joseph's mission to replace Spain's medieval remnants with modern French ideas and systems, to complete the work begun by the great reformer-king, Carlos III. But the emperor had misjudged his brother, who has been described as amiable, placid, and soft-spoken — decidedly un-Napoleonic traits. He also misjudged the Spanish temperament. Within months the "intruder king" would write, "My position is unique in history. I have not a single supporter here."

Joseph was exaggerating to make his point. Most Spaniards still listened to fire-breathing conservative friars for political guidance, but the "new order" appealed to many intellectuals weary of Bourbon incompetence and sloth. Many young men had welcomed the French Revolution and its ideals and belonged to republican clubs and masonic lodges. These Spanish supporters faced a profound crisis in having to choose between revolutionary France and reactionary Spain, between head and heart as it were. Those who served Joseph would one day regret their choice and hidebound traditionalists could forever equate liberal thinking with treason.

THE OUTBURST OF SPANISH resistance was spontaneous and reckless, challenging Europe's finest army to combat without a thought of its own strengths or those of the enemy. Napoleon's fatal mistake was to underestimate these ill-trained, ill-equipped bands of patriots fighting for their homeland, and by summer his army had suffered setbacks at Valencia and Bailen (Jaen). Although these battles were fought by regular units, Spaniards soon became famed for their devastating hit-and-run tactics — *guerrilla* warfare in the long Iberian tradition. This often-romanticized style of fighting was perfectly suited to the tough Spanish terrain and to the temperament of its residents.

Napoleon was so upset by the Spanish victories that in November (1808) he arrived with 135,000 men to take personal command. In a month of brilliant soldiering he completely reversed the tide and marched into Madrid unopposed. French troops fanned out across the peninsula, taking control of the important towns despite some fierce resistance. At Zaragoza, for example, starving but defiant citizens threw back loaves of bread tossed over the city walls by the French soldiers.

By the fall of 1810, the nucleus of Spain's loyalist government was cooped up in the seaport of Cádiz, surrounded by French troops. Adding insult to injury, King Joseph made a triumphal march through Andalucia. But the French occupation was illusory, in spite of several hundred thousand troops under a gaggle of illustrious commanders. The peninsula was just too big. Communication lines were easily cut, and sizable armed escorts were required for simple things like delivering the post. *Guerrilleros* struck at will, then retreated to their mountain strongholds.

Britain soon realised the importance of Spain's resistance and dispatched General Arthur Wellesley, the future Duke of Wellington, to Portugal. By the fall of 1810, he commanded about 25,000 British troops and about the same number of Portuguese, compared with a French force at least five times that number. Spaniards have never given the Iron Duke his proper due for helping to win their War of Independence. Madrid boasts no statue or street in his honour, even though he liberated the capital from French occupation. Nevertheless, it was a two-pronged effort. Spanish guerrillas numbering about 30,000 worked in brilliant complement to British regulars in creating Napoleon's "Spanish ulcer." These savvy, ruthless fighters could tie up and harass huge numbers of French troops while Wellington and his aides carefully engineered one triumph after another.

The breakdown of the Bourbon government led to the creation of local and regional authorities called *juntas*, which tended to act with alarming independence and lack of cooperation. (Galicia sent its own emissary to London "as nation to nation," and Sevilla and Granada nearly went to war at one point.) As regionalism approached anarchy, a Central Junta and the famous Cortes (Parliament) of Cádiz convened at the Church of San Felipe Neri. Here, they produced the Constitution of 1812, the birth certificate of Liberal Spain.

The men at Cádiz claimed to represent the nation in its darkest hour. In reality, they were far from typical Spaniards. The city itself boasted Spain's most bourgeois, liberal society, in which business acumen and commercial wealth counted more than aristocratic privilege. For obvious reasons, representatives from the different areas of Spain, especially the conservative interior, could not readily attend. Instead, Cádiz residents from those cities or regions (and the colonies), invariably more progressive than their compatriots back home, sat at the *cortes* to decide the nation's future. They voiced the interests of a tiny minority.

The meeting of a single *national* parliament (as opposed to the traditional regional bodies) was a profound event, but it arrived long after the decline of Spain's medieval political institutions. Hence, there was no real tradition of a unified representative power strong enough to stand up to the monarchy. The celebrated Constitution of 1812 was therefore an even more daring step than one might imagine. Echoing the recent American and French documents, it contained most of the liberal menu: sovereignty of the people; the sanctity of individual property rights; curtailment of aristocratic and church power; uniform laws; centralized government. The policies of enlightened despots such as Carlos III were pushed to their logical conclusion.

Unfortunately, the Cádiz "liberals" (the word itself is of Spanish origin) were building castles in the sand. The admirable but totally impractical constitution humbled Spain's two strongest institutions — the crown and the church — without creating anything strong enough to replace them. The monarchy was treated as a necessary evil; the Catholic church, although acknowledged as the only "official" religion, would have to accept the closing of its monasteries and other galling measures. Inevitably, both monarchs and bishops became instinctive enemies of the Cádiz liberals and their work.

Napoleon's downfall had begun on the peninsula, but the year 1812 brought even more serious problems with his sputtering Russian campaign. In Spain, the allies took advantage of large French troop withdrawals to score a string of victories — at Ciudad Rodrigo, Badajoz, and Salamanca, followed by Wellington's triumphant entry into Madrid, an event painted by Goya. (The artist supposedly had to be restrained from shooting the outspoken general when he criticized his work.)

The final victory came a year later at Vitoria in the Basque region, when an army of 70,000 French was routed. (Beethoven composed "Wellington's Victory" to commemorate the battle.) King Joseph himself was present at the debacle and escaped capture by a whisker, losing his carriage and silver chamber pot in the confusion. Every June 21, in what must be the British army's strangest tradition, the men of the Tenth Hussars unit drink champagne from a replica of the pot. (The original sits in a Manchester museum.)

For all intents and purposes, the War of Independence was over. The struggle had cost the French about 180,000 casualties and sealed Napoleon's fate. Spain "the giant killer" had dished out its revenge for centuries of French interference. Mild-mannered Joseph, "the intruder king," fled, and in the spring of 1814 Fernando, "the desired one," returned to the ecstatic adulation of his people. But Spain's troubles were only just beginning.

Except for the brief Spanish-American War (1898) and some colonial strife in Morocco, the War of Independence was Spain's last foreign conflict. But the war — and the French Revolution itself — unleashed most of the internal conflicts that would haunt Spain for generations, bringing countless political crises and several civil wars. Spanish nationalism was indeed born in this patriotic war against the French, but it was a highly reactionary variety that rallied to the cry of "religion and king" as well as "country." Moreover, the national unity was hollow. Beneath the seeming solidarity, Spain was breaking up into unyielding factions of conservatives and liberals, traditionalists and reformers. From the return of Fernando to the last days of Franco the "two Spains" would grapple with the problem of the country's role in modern Europe.

The war also meant the final demise of Spain as a major power. Much of the country's influence during the last century derived from its French alliance but with this shattered forever Spain was relegated to a second-rate status. When the European powers met at the Congress of Vienna (1815) to decide Europe's fate, Spain was not invited to attend.

WHAT REALLY TOPPLED Spain from its pedestal was the humiliating loss of its American empire during the war and its aftermath. Entering its fourth century of existence, the empire had rarely produced serious signs of unhappiness with Spanish rule. Nevertheless, an American-born economic and social elite of pure Spanish blood, the Creoles (*criollos*), clamoured for more power. Spain's occupation by Napoleon and the collapse of Spanish colonial authority provided the Creoles with their chance to declare independence. Exploiting the myth of Spanish oppression, they stirred up the normally passive natives to fight and die for creole goals.

The new spirit of independence was led by Venezuelan Francisco de Miranda, whom Napoleon compared with Don Quixote "except that he is not mad." He called for the creation of a vast, "enlightened" country uniting all of South America, to be called Columbia. Another prominent Creole and man of the Enlightenment (he studied in Paris) was Simon Bolivar, called "the George Washington of South America" for his key role in the liberation of five future countries: Bolivia, Peru, Ecuador, Venezuela and Colombia.

Strong independence movements formed in Mexico, Venezuela and Argentina around 1810. The Mexican insurgents were led by two rabble-rousing priests whose attempts to foster a social revolution scared off the Creoles and brought a loyalist triumph. Everywhere else the revolts met with success, but by the end of the Napoleonic wars (1814) Spain's position was still salvageable. A year later, a force of 14,000 royal troops under General Morillo arrived to fight the rebels. But force alone would not suffice, and Spain — itself exhausted and divided — utterly failed to offer any constructive solutions to the American problem.

"A Bourbon never learns anything, and never forgets anything," according to a traditional Spanish saying. Champion of Spain's proud and obstinate stance was *el deseado* himself, the restored king Fernando VII. Born in 1785, he was only 29 when he returned as conquering hero, yet he already possessed a markedly debauched look — bloated and bleary-eyed, with a huge lip and drooping nose. Even his own mother called him ugly, and his mother-in-law added that he was "hideous" and "utterly dull." Writer Gerald Brenan remarked that Fernando had all the defects of his people and none of their virtues.

Nevertheless, the vast majority of Spaniards believed him a saviour who had successfully defied Napoleon in captivity while he planned Spain's liberation. No one knew that he had spent these years living in vice and indolence on Talleyrand's splendid estate, forever trying to marry Napoleon's niece. Fernando's return coincided with the comeback of French King Louis XVIII, as a wave of conservative reaction swept across Europe. In Spain, jubilant crowds shouted "Long live our chains!" and "Viva despotism!" as Fernando marched toward Madrid.

Although some naive liberals pinned their hopes on the new king, it soon became clear that he intended to turn the clock back. His first decree declared the constitution null and void, and liberals who had fought the French while the king grovelled before Napoleon were jailed or exiled. About 12,000 reputed French sympathizers were banished, and the Jesuits allowed to return and resume their vise-like grip on education.

To support this power play Fernando relied on his army of mass supporters throughout Spain. In Cádiz, an angry mob sacked the *cortes* building, and in pulpits across the land liberal-bashing clergy thundered out their approval of the king's draconian methods. But in appealing to the masses, the church and crown released a genie that would never go back into the bottle again. Throughout the previous century, "the people" had been politically apathetic. Reforms came from the top or didn't happen at all. The French Revolution, the events at Aranjuez and the War of Independence changed all that. No longer were "the people" mere cannon fodder and tillers of fields. After all, they had dethroned two kings and made another.

In the minds of many Spaniards, the monarchy's prestige had suffered tremendously and would never again enjoy its lofty status. For six years Spain had proved it could live without a king, and the new liberal ideas slowly began to spread. One place they took root was in the Spanish army, where free-thinking officers resented such customs as having to say the rosary in formation. They flocked to masonic lodges and other liberal clubs to discuss change. (The Freemasons became the perennial bogeyman for Spanish reactionaries, long after they were anything more than a harmless social fraternity.)

In 1820, an army of reinforcements was sitting in Cádiz awaiting transport to the Americas. Bored with their condition, eager for advancement and hostile at having to fight — and quite possibly die — in the colonies, the troops revolted in the name of liberalism under the leadership of Colonel Rafael de Riego. This was the first army *pronunciamiento* (a "pronouncement" of rebellion) but definitely not the last. From 1820 to 1874 there was one every 20 months on the average. The liberals had let loose a lion onto the Spanish political scene.

Garrisons throughout Spain rose to support Riego and the king's "people's army" failed to react. A few months later, a thoroughly humiliated Fernando pledged to reform. Riego and his band called for the return of the constitution and other changes, including an end to the Inquisition. Time had already done its damage to this once almighty body; when a mob broke into one of the Inquisition's few remaining prisons, they found just one French priest, comfortably housed in the attic and reluctant to leave.

All Europe was astonished at Riego's daring coup d'etat, the first crack in its post-war conservative monolith. The revolt also assured the independence of the American colonies. The year 1819 had been a pivotal one for the rebel cause, as Bolivar led his ragtag army through high mountain passes to win the battle of Boyaca in Columbia. In the south, Jose de San Martin conducted a brilliant campaign that involved crossing the Andes from Argentina into Chile (where Bernard O'Higgins had already declared independence), then pressing north to Lima, the centre of loyalist strength. Venezuela fell when Riego's army, the expeditionary force that was to relieve Morillo, failed to arrive.

Mexico declared its independence in 1821, and soon almost every other colony had jumped on the bandwagon. In December 1824, two armies clashed at 2,700 metres in the Peruvian mountains at the battle of Ayacucho. It marked the end of Spanish power on the mainland. Only the islands of Cuba and Puerto Rico remained of the empire in America.

When the smoke cleared, there was not one vast country as Miranda had envisaged, but 17 separate, squabbling republics. And there was no social revolution to accompany independence. Instead, power passed directly to the local creole oligarchies. A tradition of alternating despotism and anarchy would plague Latin America from that day forward. Having destroyed Spanish authority and institutions, the rebels did not replace them with anything but the rule of self-interest. Said a bitter Bolivar, "America is ungovernable. He who serves a revolution ploughs the sea."

Back in Spain, the liberals brought to power by Riego were splitting into conservative(*moderado*) and radical (*exaltado*) wings, the classic division between those who wanted slow, orderly change (men of property and position) and those preaching social revolution (the urban radicals). Civil disorder was driving the radicals to despotic measures which alienated the little popular support they enjoyed. Liberal Spain was a hollow façade: when Fernando appealed to fellow monarchs of the Holy Alliance for help, only a handful of Spaniards objected. Said one liberal officer, "The Constitution was made entirely for the people, but they hated it."

Therefore, when the French king sent an army to aid his fellow despot in 1823, the countryside was amazingly quiet. The blatant invasion of the "Hundred Thousand Sons of St. Louis," was more like a military promenade than a war. Although he promised amnesty, Fernando immediately unleashed a reign of terror against liberals that shocked even the French. Riego was taken to the centre of Madrid in a coal cart, there to be hanged, drawn and quartered for public display. The mere possession of his picture carried the death penalty, and hundreds went to the gallows. (The liberal colonel achieved immortality through the military march, "Riego's Hymn.")

The remaining decade of Fernando's reign was an era of knee-jerk reactionism and bureaucratic bungling. The king's ministers were mediocre sycophants, each kept in ignorance of his colleagues' policies. For example, it took the foreign minister four months to find out that Spain had joined the Holy Alliance!

After the war the nation was devastated, its trade and industry in shambles and the countryside depopulated and infested with bandits. Visitors commented on the squalid poverty, appalling roads and wretched inns. This was the golden age of the *bandoleros*, often guerrillas reluctant to abandon their arms and lives of freedom. Most famous of all was Hinojosa Cobacho, better known as Jose Maria "El Tempranillo", who controlled much of Andalucia for a decade. "In Spain the king rules, but in the Sierra I do," he declared.

All this fed Spain's picturesque image, the popular impression that maybe Africa began at the Pyrenees after all. In truth, Iberia did cling to much of the medieval panorama fast disappearing in the rest of Europe. One curious symptom of this was Carlism, the most hopeless of lost causes in that its principal enemy was time itself — and the changes it was bringing to Spain.

THE ULTRA-CONSERVATIVE Carlists took their name from their hero, King Fernando's younger brother Don Carlos, who stood to inherit the throne. They were extreme monarchists who believed even the intransigent Fernando was "too soft" on liberals, having left a handful of them in office after his purges.

Carlists called for the dissolution of the liberal-infested army, exile of all progressives, abolition of public education and restoration of the Inquisition. One Carlist bishop founded "The Society of the Exterminating Angel" to oppose the constitution with any means necessary.

By 1829, Fernando's three marriages had failed to produce children, and everyone assumed that Carlos would inherit the throne from his gout-ridden brother. But a year later Fernando wed Maria Cristina, his Italian niece, who soon became pregnant. The Carlists were outraged, but felt at least partially protected by the law. During the War of Spanish Succession Felipe V had declared the Salic Law, which stated that a woman could not rule as monarch in Spain. Hence Carlos would still become king unless the queen gave birth to a son. But things were not that simple; unbeknown to the Carlists, in 1789 a secret session of the *cortes* had repealed the Salic Law, thus opening the door to a female monarch.

In 1830 Princess Isabel was born and clouds began to form. Three years later, as Fernando lay dying at La Granja, he added to the debate by repudiating his daughter's rights. This caused an uproar in Maria Cristina's faction which led to insults, at least one face slapped, and the king's ultimate reversal of his recent repudiation. Before finally expiring he remarked, "Spain is a bottle of beer and I am the cork. When that comes out, all the liquid inside will escape, God knows in what direction." Spoken like a true Bourbon.

Upon the king's death, Maria Cristina was named regent for Isabel. The Pretender Don Carlos, living in exile in Portugal, simply stated, "Now I am king." The nation braced itself for its first civil war since the Revolt of the Comuneros more than three centuries earlier. The First Carlist War was no mere dynastic struggle. This breach in the royal family can be blamed for most of Spain's subsequent political ills.

The backbone of Carlist support came from the ranks of traditional Spain — clergy, ultra-conservative monarchists, and foot-dragging peasants — especially in areas of the north with long histories of local rights, the persistent *fueros*. These troublesome regions included the strongly Catholic Basque country, Navarra and mountainous parts of Aragón and Catalonia. Don Carlos swore to honour the *fueros* beneath the famous oak tree of Guernica, symbol of Basque freedom. But more than a champion of regional rights, Carlism was a reaction to the modern world. Hence, its predominately rural supporters shared a strong hatred for cities and their "liberal" ways. These masses who answered to the call of "Viva Christ the King" were the same race of peasants who would form the ranks of Franco's army in 1936.

Pious and severe, Don Carlos was a man of some backbone. He alone of the royal family had stood up to Napoleon's badgering. But from the outset his cause was futile, an absurdly romantic, tragic attempt to return to the days of Felipe II. Among other quixotic gestures, he named Our Lady of the Sorrows as *generalisimo* of his armies. The Duke of Wellington called him "one of the silliest devils I ever knew."

Spain's political history in the 19th century was a comic opera in which every act ended in tragedy. The war fought over the next six years (1833-39) cost Spain 140,000 lives. The Carlists' ferocity was legendary, with soldier-priests of the "Exterminating Angel" leading their troops in appalling barbarities. The red-bereted warriors seemed to attract the best and worst types, and their campaigns often became mere excuses for brigandage. One of the more "romantic" heroes was Tomas Zumalacarregui, who gained worldwide fame among schoolboys in the popular illustrated journals of the day, shown wearing his goatskin cloak and red beret.

Almost the entire army remained loyal to Isabel and the regency, but because the Carlists were guerrilla fighters government forces had problems winning decisive victories and often resorted to the same kind of outrages committed by the opposition. In addition, anti-clerical mobs sacked convents and murdered monks to destroy the perceived enemy of the liberal state — the Catholic Church. An outbreak of cholera was blamed on the clergy poisoning the wells, and rumour-gorged mobs killed about 70 priests. Said one writer of the war, "Here lies half Spain, done to death by the other half."

The First Carlist War witnessed the birth of popular anti-clericalism in Spain, which reached ghastly proportions in the next century. Whether as victim or instigator, the church (and one's attitude toward it) lay at the heart of most of Spain's social questions. As a popular expression put it, "Everyone in Spain follows the church: half with a candle, the other half with a club."

Much like the civil war of the 1930s, the Carlist War captured the attention of all Europe, which saw it as a mortal struggle between liberalism and reaction. Idealists, adventurers and journalists descended on Spain to "fight the good fight." This produced its share of bizarre incidents, such as the young Irish aristocrat who used his yacht to seize Málaga briefly in the name of Don Carlos. (Later he was named bishop of Dublin.)

The war reached a stalemate in 1834. Meanwhile, Spain under the Regency of Maria Cristina was undergoing profound changes. Liberals returned from exile in droves to re-light the torch extinguished by Fernando VII. A new constitution granted limited suffrage, centralized government and bourgeois property rights, and was supported by both radicals (by then called *progresistas*) and the *moderados*. Although there would be other constitutions and countless crises and military coups over the next decades, these two "liberal" political groupings divided power and patronage between them for almost a century.

The conservatives usually held the upper hand. They were the oligarchy of liberalism, the bourgeois landowners and aristocrats who championed property rights, the high-placed civil servants and army officers who wished order above all, the lawyers who defended the establishment for handsome fees. Their task was to defend the "ruling class" without resorting to the threadbare arguments of the Carlists. The radicals counted among their supporters a few generals and most of the sergeants, merchants, needy journalists and the aspiring urban lower middle class.

During the height of the Carlist War and anti-clerical frenzy, the regent called on a Basque financial wizard named Mendizabal to head the government. A decree in 1835 closed all religious orders; in Madrid alone 44 churches and monasteries were shut down. Then, in an act of vast impact, this radical banker launched a programme of land reform that confiscated church property and offered it for sale. About one-quarter of all church lands went on the block in the first two years. Naturally, poor peasants did not have the money to buy the land they worked, and most of the bonanza was snapped up by wealthy land-lords and speculators. Thus the largest transfer of property since the Reconquest brought no agrarian reform. In one case church lands farmed by 6,000 fami-lies suddenly supported only 400. Indeed, the Andalusian *latifundia* system of huge estates worked by landless peasants became worse — all in the name of "Liberalism."

Even more important, the reformers put an end to land entailment, which for centuries had prevented the breaking up of family estates and had provided the *hidalgo* class with their reason for being. Land policy drove a huge wedge between the two liberal factions. It also drove vast numbers of landless peas-ants, who regarded collective land-use as a God-given right, into the arms of the Carlists and, much later, to the Anarchists. The centralized state in Madrid became the sworn enemy of both the extreme right and the extreme left, which shared much more in political philosophy than is realized.

Other legislation — based on the French model — created the 49 provinces of modern Spain, often disrupting long traditions of local or regional rule. In their desire to break the back of Carlism, liberals took similar actions which went against the historical grain of a thousand years of custom. Thus well-meaning reformers sowed the seeds of modern regional upheavals in Catalonia and the Basque lands.

In 1837, the Carlists gambled everything on a disastrous march on Madrid. They lost the war because, as one historian put it, "They were even madder and more foolish than their adversaries." At Vergara (1839), two opposing generals embraced theatrically, then signed an agreement which recognized Isabel as Spain's legitimate queen. The pact also achieved a truce between the church and the middle-class values of the *moderado* order.

Don Carlos retired to France with several thousand followers, and there were many suicides in Carlist ranks, including two fanatics who simultaneously skewered each other with their bayonets. After the peace of Vergara, Carlism became largely confined to Navarra.

THE ARMY EMERGED from the war as Spain's most solid institution, happy with its new role as arbiter of the country's destiny. Having stood by the constitutional monarchy against the Carlists, the generals would demand their pound of flesh. In essence, the war and its aftermath allowed them to take command of Spanish politics, and this role became its peculiar feature. As all sides began to accept the new rules, the main question revolved around who would control the army. Liberals of both persuasions were equally high-handed in forcing their programmes on the nation, and *politicos* had no qualms about using military sedition.

The age of "romantic militarism" began in 1840 with a coup by General Espartero which ousted Maria Cristina. She had slowly lost support, especially among the generals, after secretly marrying Agustin Muñoz, ex-corporal of the guard and son of a shopkeeper. Critics started calling him "Ferdinand VIII" behind his back when they noticed he was wearing the deceased king's tie-pins, and they thundered about the "royal whore" when she failed to conceal a series of pregnancies.

Baldomero Espartero was a flamboyant figure with a blustery voice who enjoyed the total devotion of his men, but he was politically naive. His famous taste for the ladies prompted one British lord to remark, "He wore out more sheets than shoe leather." Espartero's coup represented radical interests, which defended local power in the face of *moderado* centralization. It was during a crisis over this issue that the general forced the resignation of Maria Cristina, who had appealed to him for support at one point. Espartero became new head of state, and the departing regent remarked, "I have made you a count and a duke, but I could not make you a gentleman."

With Espartero's coup the militarization of Spanish politics entered a new phase, as governments were made and unmade by the "sword arm" of each political party. The radical-liberals had surrendered their leadership to a general, and the conservatives would soon find one of their own. Espartero's regency lasted two troubled years, during which more church land was nationalized and sold, driving the clergy further rightward. In 1843, another coup led by *moderado* generals Serrano and Narvaez forced Espartero from power. The pattern had been firmly established.

During the 116 years between Riego's *pronunciamiento* and General Franco's putsch, there were more than a hundred military rumblings of varying types: foiled café-conspiracies, sergeants' uprisings, barracks plots, colonels' coups... This figure includes one period from 1874 until 1923 during which plotting virtually ceased. Almost like classical drama, *pronunciamientos* followed a well-defined procedure: first came the preliminary plotting — the *trabajos* to win over supporters — often in a mineral spa or a café; the *compromisos* followed, by which the accomplices were bound to action; finally, at the preordained moment, came the *grito*, the "cry" of insurrection by the leader (*el jefe*) to his assembled troops, explaining his reasons for wanting to overthrow the government.

As the army grew to see itself as a legitimate option to quarrelling factions, there emerged the prototype of the conservative "soldier-politician." By definition he was authoritarian, monarchist, rigidly Catholic and often from a humble background (many generals rose from the ranks) and therefore hostile to aristocrats and intellectuals. In the tradition of St. James the Moor Slayer, he identified his opponents as godless rebels. Narvaez once wrote to general Zurbano, who was planning a coup: "By violating the law, as I once violated it, you are moving straight towards a bottomless pit." He then threatened to shoot him.

The fall of Espartero brought the declaration of the new queen, Isabel II, at the premature age of 13. She was a poor successor to her namesake, prompting one eminent Spanish historian to write, "Her coming of age (to rule) was a pure constitutional fiction. Queen Isabel was never of age, though she died a grandmother."

Isabel was plump, comely, easy-going without pretensions, generous and good-hearted, and above all passionate. Shortly after her accession she lent herself to a hare-brained plot involving a dashing cavalry officer which brought down the government. Indeed, like a reckless teenager who never grew up, Isabel let her passions rule, and she rivals Catherine the Great of Russia as history's most lascivious queen.

Royal councillors began to worry that an heir might arrive on the scene before a husband, so an exhaustive search commenced among Europe's elite. The unfortunate choice for the hot-blooded, 16-year-old queen was her Bourbon cousin Francisco de Asis, who had a high, squeaky voice and was soon dubbed "Paquita" (roughly translated as "Fanny"). Later, Isabel described their honeymoon: "What can I say of a man who on his wedding night wore more lace than I?" To everyone's amazement, especially the consort's, children began to arrive like clockwork. Said one observer, "The queen has plenty of faithful subjects who can replace Francisco in case of need."

The history of Isabel II's reign was largely consumed with power struggles between three rival generals: Espartero, Narvaez and a Spaniard with an Irish surname, Leopoldo O'Donnell. It was a grey period of revolving governments (40 different ministries, 18 coup attempts) dominated by General Narvaez, who based his dictatorial powers on obscure passages of the constitution and sheer chutzpa. On one occasion he appeared at the council of ministers and announced, "Gentlemen, by royal order you have all been relieved of your functions."

Ramon Narvaez was an Andalusian squire who loved power for its rewards: a fine coach, a palace, inside financial tips. He had a violent temper and would put up with no contradiction, once calling his political opponents "filthy mutineers." He led the *moderados* and served as prime minister five times over two decades. During this period electoral fraud became a regular practice, and with the voting machinery in the hands of the governing party, revolution became the only hope for change. Excluded by a corrupt political system, the radicals usually resorted to coups to gain power; the conservatives accepted the change until they decided to return to power by means of their own general.

Narvaez reconciled the formerly anti-clerical upper middle class landowners with the church, who formed an alliance against the lower middle class championed by Espartero. Narvaez maintained power by keeping the army contented, and he used it often to quell dissent and sedition, from radicals to diehard Carlists, who rose again briefly in 1848. He employed any means necessary to defend the monarchy of Isabel from its many opponents. When asked on his deathbed if he had forgiven his enemies, Narvaez replied, "I have no enemies, father. I have had them all shot."

The era of Narvaez, despite the ongoing political carnival, was one of peace and prosperity. To bring the bandit-infested countryside under control, a rural police called the *guardia civil* (civil guard) was set up on the French model.

One rule was that *guardias* could not be natives of the districts they served. This lessened the chance of corruption, but alienated them from the people they served.

This rural police force was also created to stifle local influences objectionable to Madrid, and it served *all* governments against *all* forms of sedition. *Guardias* made the roads safe for travellers but also made things "safe" for landlords by crushing any glimmer of social revolution. Hence they became the sworn enemies of regionalism and, later, of working-class movements.

Foreign travellers wrote of rural banditry and many other aspects of Spanish life during Isabel's reign. Literary apostles of Romanticism, then the rage throughout Europe, found in Spain the picturesque and exotic life — peasants tilling with Roman ploughs or beating laundry along a stream bed — that was fast vanishing elsewhere. They attributed this "untouched" civilization to some intangible "Spanishness" which they hoped would resist the tide of modern "progress."

Among the writers to produce a cluster of classic Romantic travel accounts were Henry Inglis, Washington Irving, Richard Ford, and Theophile Gautier. Ford called Spain "Roman, African or, in a word, un-European" and lamented that "... *mantillas* are going, alas!" George Borrow's eccentric book *The Bible In Spain*, describing his adventures as a bible salesman, became an instant bestseller (1842). Offshoots of this fascination with Spain were a series of gothic novels, complete with dim dungeons and rattling chains, and some pretty wild exposés of life in Spanish monasteries and nunneries. The Black Legend had gone Romantic.

Spanish liberals returned from abroad with the literary Romanticism of Walter Scott in their cultural baggage. This gave rise to the *costumbrista* school of writers, recording strange types and regional oddities with relish. One of the better products of this phenomenon was *La Gaviota* (The Seagull) by Fernan Caballero, considered Spanish literature's first modern novel. Writers could either revel in Spain's uniqueness or see it as symbolic of *retraso* (backwardness). Among those who blasted the mimicking of foreign literary trends was Mariano Jose de Larra, who described Spain as the country of *casi* (which means "almost" or "not quite"). Something was always missing, from institutions recognized by "not quite" the whole nation to canals "not quite" finished and museums "not quite" arranged. What was picturesque for foreign romantics finally drove Larra to suicide.

SPANISH ROMANTICISM got mixed up with revived Catalan "national" pride in a movement called the *renaixenca* (renaissance). As a cultural vehicle the Catalan language virtually died in the 16th century. But when a bank clerk published a poem in Catalan in a Barcelona newspaper (1833) it marked the beginning of a revival. The cultural revival had its underpinnings in Catalonia's remarkable industrial development (mainly textiles) in the first half of the century, which gave Barcelona the moniker "The Manchester of Spain." Favouring high tariffs to keep out English goods, Catalans developed a new hostility to meddling from Madrid that went far beyond the old rivalry with Castilla.

Catalan businessmen were bound with the equally industrious Basques more by trade policies than by authentic regional spirit. They also shared a "reverence for money," which Castilians scorned. Most of the important banks seemed to spring from Barcelona or Bilbao and were housed in massive neo-classical buildings typical of the age. Basque wealth was founded on iron deposits in Vizcaya. Scattered homesteads gave the countryside the appearance of one vast, prosperous village.

There were still many Spains. Galicia was desperately poor, its peasants futilely trying to eke out a living on their "handkerchief plots." Like the Irish, countless Galicians fled their land of gorse and granite to seek better lives elsewhere. Equally impoverished, but for entirely different reasons, were the landless *braceros* of Andalucia, working sporadically during the grape and olive harvests, then suffering in squalid misery the rest of the year.

Dry cereal farming (with the poorest wheat yields in Europe) occupied the farmers of Castilla and Extremadura, a barren land of rock fences with "hardly a branch on which a bird might light." (The destruction of Spanish forests continued unabated throughout the century.) In a complete turnaround from the days of the Mesta, livestock was woefully inadequate to supply Spain's needs for meat, wool and fertilizer. Scattered across this bleak tableland were depressing villages whose streets were alternately dusty in summer and mud-choked in winter. The intense dry cold of the heartland spawned a popular saying about the air of Madrid, "so keen and subtle that it will not extinguish a candle, but can put out a man's life."

Spain's strong regional identities and differences translated into economic fragmentation. Indeed, much of Spanish society's chronic instability stems from very unequal rates of economic growth during modern times. There was no real national economy with common concerns and policies. Railroads, for example, came late and never really developed as in other countries. Even the tracks were a different width than in the rest of Europe.

Railroads were largely financed by foreign (mostly French) capital, the Rothschilds and Pereires. British investors chose minerals such as Almaden mercury and the copper mines of Rio Tinto. English capital flooded into the Jerez area and its burgeoning sherry trade. Spain's economy outside of Catalonia was still based on export of raw materials to more advanced countries, just as in centuries past.

Economic historians have postured a myriad of reasons for Spain's failure to create a modern economy. Backward agricultural methods kept farmers bound to the land, hence freeing fewer workers for industry. The weak domestic market (no one had money to spend) meant little demand for Spanish products at home, and foreigners were not beating down the doors either. The Bank of Spain spent most of its energy furnishing loans to the government rather than on productive investment. Finally, there was the nation's work ethic, still suffering from tradition. In 1830, Henry Inglis described Madrid's Puerta del Sol, with "hundreds of gentlemen standing there with no other occupation than shaking the dust from their cigars."

"There are but two families in the world," said Sancho Panza. "The haves and the have-nots." Foreign visitors were struck by the presence of beggars in every Spanish town, and in Madrid alone convents were dishing out 30,000 bowls of soup daily. Moreover, as in much of Europe the urban poverty of *les miserables* was creeping into Spain, and this new working class would grow into a major force.

Although Spain's middle class remained weak in numbers at mid-century, this was the "age of the bourgeoisie." Middle-class tastes determined styles from the royal palace on down — a prosperous merchant might use the same silver tea service as the queen. The aristocracy clung to its titles and court offices (the Duke of Osuna had over 50 titles), but smart nobles realized that the road to survival meant adoption of bourgeois goals (i.e. money). The two classes began to merge, and the high bourgeoisie allied with the nobility rather than becoming its rival and watchdog, as in other countries. Successful soldiers, politicians, financiers and industrialists were granted titles of nobility to accompany their wealth. These *poderosos* (powerful ones) often ran things at the local level and became staunch pillars of the status quo.

The 38-year reign of Isabel II was punctuated by bizarre behaviour at court which spilled over into the political arena. Wrote the American ambassador: "A safe word whispered by a crawling confessor, an attack of nerves on a cloudy day, the appearance of a well-made soldier at a levee, have often sufficed to make and break administrations." Behind the throne stood Father Claret, Isabel's confessor, and Sor Patrocino, "the bleeding nun," whose hands and feet bore the "wounds of Christ," undoubtedly self-inflicted.

The queen's love life continued to outrage her subjects and husband alike, with a parade of paramours passing through the royal palace. Among them were General Serrano and an American dentist named McKeon, who may have fathered Alfonso, the first Prince of Asturias born in the century and future king. Said the *London Times*: "Isabel is guilty of high treason against the cause of virtue and morality."

Compounding the public outrage were reports of massive corruption in the royal family, especially the shady dealings of the queen mother in railway construction and the Cuban slave trade. Popularly labeled *la ladrona* (the thief), she was even caught trying to switch the palace's silver service for pewter imitations.

Eventually, "the impossible lady" alienated even her few remaining supporters. When the increasingly obese queen took a new lover named Carlos Malfori, son of an Italian pastry cook, it was the last straw. The radical-liberals, excluded from government by the queen, formed a coalition with discontented generals to plot her overthrow. When both generals O'Donnell and Narvaez died, it removed the queen's main props for the past thirty years. Progressive General Prim "pronounced" in 1868 for a "Spain with honour," and 38-year-old Isabel fled to France escorted by an army guard. It appeared that the Bourbons were

Above, the Spanish Bourbon's playground palace at Aranjuez, south of Madrid, pictured by Francesco Battaglioli in 1756. The palace was inspired by French models. Left, Goya's portrait of King Carlos III, considered one of the bright lights in Spain's Bourbon dynasty (PRADO MUSEUM, MADRID)

Goya's "Second of May" (right) and "Third of May" (above) depict events in Madrid in 1808, as the populace rose against Napoleon's Marmeluke mercenaries, only to suffer bloody reprisals the following day. It was the start of what Spaniards call the War of Independence, or what is known in the English-speaking world as the Peninsular War (PRADO MUSEUM, MADRID)

finished in Spain after 168 memorable years.

Prim was a strong-willed Catalan who admired Abraham Lincoln. Together with Serrano, the queen's former lover, he formed a provisional government which granted a liberal constitution. Nevertheless, Spaniards remained monarchists at heart and started looking for a new king rather than considering other options. The honour of obtaining the Spanish throne, once the envy of all Europe, was politely turned down by several candidates before Leopold of Hohenzollern accepted briefly, then backed down. (The affair sparked the Franco-Prussian War of 1870.) Prim remarked that finding a king to rule a constitutional monarchy was "like looking for an atheist in heaven." The name of General Espartero was even mentioned, but somehow the idea of a King Baldomero I never caught on.

Finally, the *politicos* settled on the somewhat reluctant Amadeus of Savoy, second son of Italy's King Victor Emmanuel and known for his liberal views. When parliament approved the choice of Amadeo I by a vote of 191 to 63, he became known as "king of the 191." Amadeo's reign had an inauspicious start: on the day he arrived in Spain, General Prim — his main supporter — was assassinated on a dark Madrid street. Factions of the shaky coalition that had made the revolution of '68 were already at each other's throats, mainly over the perennial prism of Spanish politics — religion. The church had regained much of its power over the past two decades, and the clergy were outraged by the choice of a liberal, hence "godless" monarch.

Moreover, the new king was considered a foreign interloper and treated with outright disrespect at every level. For example, on Amadeo's first day at the royal palace he asked for breakfast at eight, but was curtly informed that he would get nothing until eleven, as was customary. (He went out to a café for breakfast.) He and his wife were insulted at the theatre and given the cold shoulder by the aristocracy, which began to split between supporters of the Carlist candidate and Isabel's son Alfonso.

Realizing it was their big and possibly final chance, the supporters of Carlos VII (24-year-old grandson of the original Don Carlos) began the Second Carlist War in April 1872. This conflict and Amadeo's less-than-cordial treatment convinced the king to abdicate the following February. He thanked Spain "for the great honour it had bestowed on him" and promptly left for Portugal.

SPAIN'S FIRST REPUBLIC could not have been born at a worse time. General Prim once said, "If it was not easy to make a king, it will be even more difficult to make a republic in a country where there are no republicans." The situation was approaching chaos in many parts of the land, with most of the north acknowledging Don Carlos, Barcelona virtually autonomous and anarchist agitators whipping up the peasants in Andalucia.

Amid all this parliament proclaimed a republic, with Catalan Pi y Margall as national president despite the fact that he was a firm believer in local self-government. A few months later, a federal republic of 17 states in a decentralized nation was declared. The Republic lasted just eleven months and had four presidents, all lawyers or professors. Politicians seemed incapable of putting aside their differences to form a strong government, and parliament could not even agree on simple matters of form and procedure.

The federal idea soon degenerated into "cantonalism," a curious theory based on extreme localism in an already centrifugal state. By the summer of 1873 Valencia, Málaga, Granada and other cities and regions had declared their independence from Madrid. The Spanish navy defected to the Canton of Cartagena. The "age of taifas" had returned.

The Carlists stepped up their military campaign, sensing the time was right for Spaniards to choose between monarchy and anarchy. Soon they controlled most of Spain north of the Ebro River and seemed poised to topple the defenceless Republic. But the Carlists' could not follow through, and this failure revealed their fundamental weakness as champions of a traditional Spain that was passing away.

Meanwhile, the "Alfonsistas" plotted. Isabel's 16-year-old son was enrolled at Sandhurst, England's royal military college. Military in education and interests (he knew army regulations by heart), Alfonso seemed an ideal choice to lead Spain out of the mire of republicanism.

The inevitable *pronunciamiento* came in 1874 at Sagunto (the old Iberian village made famous during the Punic War) with the *grito* delivered by General Martinez Campos. In Madrid General Pavia rode his horse up the steps of the Cortes building, where his men shot a few rounds into the air that scattered the delegates. Pavia declared for the new king, Alfonso XII, and delirious crowds received him in the capital on January 12, 1875. The army had knocked the Bourbons off the throne seven years earlier. Now it was bringing them back again. It did not bode well for Spanish politics. The military was no longer just the "sword-arm" of the parties — now it was "saviour of the nation." By the time of the Restoration, liberalism in the army had shrivelled to insignificance. Most officers accepted the *moderado* coalition of monarchy, church and landowners as the natural order. That was the real significance of Alfonso's return. The new soldier-king showed signs of becoming a good ruler (working long hours on state affairs), and the future looked relatively bright. The Carlists were soon crushed, having missed their golden opportunity.

The Constitution of 1876 was a solid document that recognized the joint rule of king and parliament. It became the first great "liberal" success in erecting a stable political system. Key player in the new system was Antonio Cánovas del Castillo, a squint-eyed schoolmaster from Málaga who looked like an unmade bed. His opponents called him "the monster," but he was a hard worker and electrifying speaker. His goal was to bring stability to the political scene by injecting common sense instead of ideology. He explained: "The constitution should be formed on principles as liberal as the condition of the country will allow."

Common sense for Cánovas meant excluding groups on the fringe, such as republicans, Carlists and regionalists. His system also put an end to military meddling, now that the army was a reliable pillar of the system. Crucial to maintaining the new order was the concept of the *turno*, a periodic rotation of power between the two accepted political groupings, the conservatives (*mode–*

*rados* ) and liberals, represented by Cánovas and Sagasta. After decades of mock battles little of substance separated the two parties, and the system was a cynical perversion of true parliamentary democracy. But it worked.

The orderly "changing of the guard" depended on a corrupt electoral process. Election-fraud started at the top and filtered down to the smallest village, where political bosses called *caciques* (from an Indian word for chieftain) controlled voting and handed out patronage. The average person was politically indifferent in any case and couldn't care less about what happened in faraway Madrid.

The rigging of elections became a fine art. Lists of voters were drawn up locally, and on one occasion the occupants of an entire cemetery, 700 names in all, was called on to vote. During the 1886 general election which brought Sagasta to power, the results appeared in an official newspaper the day before voting took place. This corrupt system increasingly came to rest on the backward regions of Andalucia and Galicia, where the votes of an illiterate, apathetic electorate could be easily falsified.

The Cánovas system worked because the king, unlike his mercurial mother, let it work. Alfonso attended to routine matters and rarely meddled in real politics.

After his first wife died, he married Maria Cristina, daughter of an Austrian duke. She was fated to rule Spain for 17 years. In 1885, severe earthquakes in eastern Andalucia destroyed thousands of buildings and left hundreds dead, then a cholera outbreak killed 100,000 throughout Spain. Alfonso, whose health was never strong, insisted on visiting the stricken areas and died a few weeks later of a lung infection. He was not yet 28.

MARIA CRISTINA BECAME Regent of Spain, just like another foreign consort of the same name who ended in exile. But this time it would be different, and the Regency ushered in an optimistic era. When Alfonso died the queen was pregnant, and the nation yearned for an heir to head off another dynastic crisis. According to tradition, the royal artillery in Madrid would launch a 21-gun salute if a boy were born, but fire only 15 times for a baby girl. On May 17, 1886, normal life ground to a halt in the capital as crowds gathered outside the royal palace to await news. Suddenly the cannons started to thunder, and on the sixteenth salvo the city went wild. There would be a new king, after all.

The 1890s were good years for Spain as they were for most of Europe and America. On the surface everything looked fine: Cánovas hobnobbed with the aristocracy and handed out thousands of new titles. Queen Victoria even managed a visit during the fading glow of the "liberal century" (she found the tea undrinkable). Underneath, social and political tensions in the working class and regions were beginning to boil. In the next decade — the next century — they would erupt like steam from a kettle.

The best way to gain a feeling for the life and times of late 19th-century Spain is by reading the novels of Benito Perez Galdós (1843-1920). In the opinion of many critics, he was on a par with Zola, Balzac, Dickens and Tolstoi with books such as *Doña Perfecta* and *Fortunata y Jacinta*. Perez Galdós wrote of indolent bureaucrats and decayed aristocrats, and of small Castilian towns that embodied the stagnant, fanatical side of Spain. He championed the new literary theory of "realism" and captured the attention of critics on both sides of the Atlantic.

So long as the two elder statesmen lived, the illusion of Spain's stability and strength could continue. Then, in 1897, Cánovas was assassinated by an Italian anarchist. Sagasta died of natural causes a few years later. The "powerful ones" had built a house of cards that was about to come crashing down. Spaniards would discover how corrupt and inept their leaders had become, how far Spain had fallen behind, with the disaster of 1898 — the Spanish-American War.

Spain had been fighting a simmering revolt in Cuba for many years without much success, and tens of thousands of Spaniards had perished in Cuba, mostly from disease. The Spanish had repeatedly refused to reform the corrupt colonial administration or allow more autonomy, choosing instead to send in a get-tough general named Weyler to turn things around. His use of concentration camps and other harsh measures, although exaggerated by the American press, earned him the name "Butcher Weyler" and the hatred of Cubans. When Spain offered limited autonomy in 1897 it was too late.

Key to Cuban independence was the posture of the United States, where Congress passed a resolution demanding Spain's withdrawal. American newspapers, led by W. R. Hearst's *New York Journal*, unleashed blistering attacks on Spanish rule: "Weyler the brute, the devastator of *haciendas*, the destroyer of families and the outrager of women."

In order to "protect American life and property," the battleship *Maine* was dispatched to Havana harbour. Here, on the night of February 15, 1898, an explosion ripped open the ship's hull and killed 260 men. The Americans blamed the disaster on a mine, but Spaniards denied any involvement. Hearst offered a $50,000 reward for the "culprits" and banner headlines called for war. Future U.S. President Theodore "Teddy" Roosevelt bellowed: "The Maine was sunk by an act of dirty treachery on the part of Spain." In this atmosphere, it was not surprising that war was soon declared to the cry of "Remember the Maine!" (In 1976, the U.S. Navy admitted that "spontaneous combustion of coal in the fuel hold, followed by an explosion of ammunition" actually sank the ship.)

In 1898, Spain's military forces accounted for about half the national budget: of the 50,000 men on active duty, 500 were generals and 24,000 lower officers. The navy was a shore-based bureaucracy rather than a fighting force, with over a hundred admirals and few sea-worthy ships. The Pacific Squadron based in the Philippines existed mostly on paper, but it was here that action commenced in May. In a one-hour battle, the American navy led by Dewey blasted the Spanish ships out of Manila Bay as if they were practice targets.

The Spanish-American War lasted just three months. At a naval encounter at Santiago de Cuba, the entire Spanish squadron was destroyed with just one American casualty, completing the matched pair of modern history's two worst naval disasters. An expeditionary force including Roosevelt's "Rough Riders" landed in Cuba and stormed up San Juan Hill to victory. "It was a splendid little war," exclaimed Teddy.

By July peace negotiations were underway, and the Treaty of Paris was signed by year's end. Spain was forced to abandon the last crumbs of its once vast overseas possessions: Cuba, Puerto Rico, the Philippines and Guam. The historical cycle that started one October day in 1492 had finally ended. The Spanish Empire was no more.

## SIGHTS & SITES

**Alicante***: The Castle of San Fernando, constructed during the War of Independence, is now a park with a good view of the town.*
**Barcelona***: Liceo Theatre (1848) is one of Europe's biggest opera houses.*
**Bilbao** *(Vizcaya): Town Hall built in 1892 on the site of a monastery.*
**Cadiz***: Church of San Felipe Neri, site of the historic Cortes and Constitution of 1812; seafront promenades such as Parque Genovés reflect 19th-century styles.*
**Irún** *(Guipuzcoa): The San Marcial Hermitage lies on the site of a great Spanish victory over the French in 1813; excellent panorama of the province.*
**Madrid***: The Prado Museum's Goya rooms contain his "Disasters of War" series and the huge oils "May 2nd" and "May 3rd."; the Casón del Buen Retiro features a major section of lesser-known 19th-century Spanish artists; the Romantic Museum contains period furniture and paintings left by the Marquis of Vega-Inclan; the massive neo-classical Palace of the Cortes, inaugurated in 1850 by Isabel II, is a monument to the moderado order; the Plaza de Oriente next to the royal palace dates from the time of Joseph Bonaparte and is adorned with statues of Spanish kings; the Military Museum was founded in 1803 by Godoy.*
**Mallorca** *(Balearic Islands): At the Valldemosa Carthusian Monastery, George Sand and Frederick Chopin passed a few months in 1838-39; Sand wrote her book* A Winter In Majorca *from the experience.*
**Montserrat** *(Barcelona): The original monastery was sacked by the French in 1812, and existing buildings date mostly from the 19th century.*
**Nerja** *(Málaga): While on his tour of earthquake-ravaged Andalucia, Alfonso XII strolled out on the promenade and dubbed it El Balcón de Europa.*
**San Sebastian** *(Guipuzcoa): Interesting neo-classical buildings include the Town Hall and Diputacion; Miramar Palace was the summer residence of the royal family, dating from the era of Maria Cristina.*
**Villanueva y Geltru** *(Barcelona): The Casa Papiol house presents a perfect picture of bourgeois life in the early 1800s.*
**Vitoria** *(Alava): Plaza de la Virgen Blanca contains a massive monument to Wellington's crucial 1813 victory.*

## CHAPTER 9

# BEST OF TIMES, WORST OF TIMES

Antonio Gaudi's *Sagrada Familia* Church is to Barcelona what the Eiffel Tower is to Paris. Standing in front of this unfinished architectural treasure, visitors to Spain's "second city" encounter one man's transcendent vision cast in stone and mortar. Gaudi worked nine years on the swirling chaos of the Nativity façade, imbedding statues, sculpted stone and leering gargoyles into the fluffy surface. On the portal he carved trees, shells, animals, and the mountains and seascapes of his beloved Catalonia. Here too is a strange dragon-demon handing a bomb to an anarchist, an appropriate touch for turn-of-the-century Barcelona. The architect's later years were spent on four amazing towers that look like stone-and-mortar spaceships with nose cones of coloured glass-and-tile mosaics. There is an almost reptilian quality about these 90-metre spires, huge stones coating them like protective scales. You can climb one tower and look out on Gaudi's Barcelona, with its buildings that look as if they were molded from lumps of clay.

Born at Reus in 1852, Antonio Gaudi Cornet was a founding father of *art nouveau*, a highly decorative style that fused medieval and modern elements and used exotic — sometimes erotic — symbols for its ornamentation. (Salvador Dali called the *Sagrada Familia* "a gigantic erogenous zone.") But Gaudi cannot be pigeon-holed as part of a movement. His cosmic creations are highly personal, his unique church a religious poem written in "living" stone.

Gaudi's talents were not overlooked in the vibrant, freewheeling Barcelona of 1900, and he became the favoured architect of several wealthy patrons. Among his commissions were the Pedrera apartment building, a fantasy of wave-like facades, astounding chimneys and twisted wrought-iron balconies. The Casa Mila has an undulating roof and chimneys like huge corkscrews. Güell Park features fairyland buildings, strange towers and remarkably comfortable benches (Gaudi had workmen sit naked on wet plaster and used their impressions to form the seats).

Gaudi was just one figure in a head-spinning cultural revival in Spain, especially Catalonia, during the first years of the new century. In the very year 1900 a young, unknown painter named Pablo Ruiz Picasso held his first exhibition at a small Barcelona café called "The Four Cats." Born in Málaga in 1881, Picasso moved to the throbbing Catalan capital at the age of 14. Here he attended art school and spent several formative years before moving to Paris. His *Les Demoiselles d'Avignon* (1907), depicting a group of Barcelona whores, is cited as the first important Cubist painting, a major milestone for modern art. Picasso, of course, went on to become the century's most famous artist, a citizen of the world, but always a Spaniard.

Another crucial Spanish figure in modern art was Juan Gris, co-founder of Cubism. After studying in Madrid, he also moved to Paris, but his austere still-lifes hark back to the pure colour and line of Zurbaran. Other great Spanish artists of the era include Valencian Joaquin Sorolla, who painted dramatic landscapes splashed in colour and sunlight, and Ignacio Zuloaga, with his vivid renderings of bullfighters and Basque peasants.

There was a parallel explosion in music, particularly in Barcelona under the influence of master Felipe Pedrell. Enrique Granados is remembered for his piano works, *Spanish Dances* and *Goyescas*. The music of Isaac Albeniz, especially *Iberia*, combined Spanish folk material with brilliant pianistic idiom. Better known is Manuel de Falla, whose music is rooted in Andalusian folk songs (he was a Catalan born in Cádiz). Among his many masterpieces is *Nights in the Gardens of Spain* (1916). Yet another Catalan was Pablo Casals, a prodigy who began his concert career in 1891 and became the greatest cello virtuoso of modern times. Indeed, there is much truth to the adage that if you pinch a Catalan he or she will always cry out in perfect pitch.

After the turn of the century, Spanish literary figures were also breaking down cultural barriers. Jose Echegaray became the first Spaniard to win the Nobel prize (1904) for his skilful, if dated, melodramas, and Vicente Blasco Ibañez gained worldwide fame for his superb novels of simple life in Valencia. He and other Spanish realists were championed by North American literary critics, and Hollywood later discovered Blasco's potboilers *Blood and Sand* and *The Four Horsemen of the Apocalypse*. In 1904, the Hispanic Society of America was founded in New York; Spain's cultural revival was crossing the Atlantic as well as the Pyrenees.

The most important phenomenon of all was a loose-knit collection of writers who came of age around the time of the Spanish-American War and continued producing through the early 1930s. Although sharing no common creed or interests except Spain itself, they came to be called "The Generation of '98." Confronted with national humiliation and Spain's failure to keep pace with Western Europe, writers of widely varying talent and point of view took to dissecting their country. Their fundamental question: Where had Spain gone wrong?

Forerunner of the movement was Francisco Giner de los Rios, who founded the Free Institute for Education in 1875. Seeing a kind of intellectual malaise around him — few people read books, and science inched forward under a cloud of suspicion — Giner tried to create a school where Spain's future leaders could receive the type of modern education they would need to guide the nation into the next century. The school's point of view was liberal, secular and European — all the things that traditional Spain was not.

"There is a generation or two of intelligent people," Giner wrote. "Then comes a political catastrophe, and we have to begin all over again. We are so deeply divided between Catholics and liberals, right wing and left, that one-half can never profit by the knowledge and achievements of the other."

Just prior to the debacle of 1898, Angel Ganivet wrote an essay on the nature of "Spanishness" and Spain's place in the world, stressing the positive side of the national character. This search for "the soul of Spain" continued with Joaquin Costa, who urged Spaniards to mend their ways and become more European, that is, more "modern." It would not be easy for a nation that has always looked to the rest of Europe with admiration, but also with a fear of losing its own personality.

The main themes of this national soul-searching were just coming into focus when the military disaster in America hit like a Yankee broadside. To the pessimists, the entire 19th century seemed a dismal spiral of dwindling empire and decreasing national prestige. Preoccupied with religion and political intrigue, Spain lagged in scientific thought and invention, while most of its people lived in a kind of intellectual fog. As the poet Antonio Machado wrote:

> Wretched Castile, yesterday the ruler
> wrapped in rags and scorning all it does not know.

The empire was gone and good riddance, said most of the "Generation." It was high time to "lock the sepulchre of El Cid," to swap glory for progress and battleships for schools. Spain did not need heroes and martyrs but intelligence, restraint and enough food on the table.

"In Spain, there is a good deal to see but not much to eat," observed Jose Ortega y Gasset, one of the giants of the movement. This philosopher-writer studied in Germany and sought to bring Spain closer to Europe. In *Invertebrate Spain* he wrote, "Spain today, rather than a nation, is a cloud of dust remaining after a great people have galloped down the highway of history." Another key figure was Basque writer Miguel de Unamuno, a solitary and arrogant figure best known for his book *The Tragic Sense of Life*. Unamuno saw Spain's salvation in its own unique qualities. He held that the words "Spanish" and "European" were incompatible and disliked all schemes for the "regeneration" of his country, an attitude Ortega called "Africanism."

"Our defects, or what others call our defects, are usually the root of our excellencies," wrote Unamuno. "The qualities that are censured as our vices are the foundation of our virtues." He was far from being a reactionary, but he wanted the world to know that if Africa did not begin at the Pyrenees, Spain certainly did.

The first quarter of the 20th century witnessed the highest cultural level in Spain since the 1600s. Among many other writers normally included in the Generation of '98 were the Sevillian Machado, Nobel-prize winner Juan Ramon Jimenez (*Platero y Yo* ) and Pio Baroja (*The Tree of Knowledge*), whom Hemingway idolized. One writer of notable success (a Nobel prize, 1922), but *not* part of the group, was Jacinto Benavente, who rescued Spanish theatre from its overwrought melodramatic style.

Besides providing fodder for intellectuals, the Spanish-American War took a heavy toll on the political system of the Restoration, and on the facile optimism and national pride of an essentially corrupt government. In the soul-searching aftermath inept politicians rather than the military were blamed for Spain's disastrous performance against the upstart "nation of sausage eaters." And Spaniards wanted change.

SPAIN'S POLITICAL HISTORY from 1898 to 1923 was a prolonged attempt — in the face of regionalism, violent labour strife, assassinations — to redeem the dying parliamentary system of Cánovas. For two decades it tottered on the brink, hopelessly out of step with the changing times. In simpler days, the radical and conservative factions had represented most of the country's economic interests. But the Spain of 1900 was changing, and many new voices strained to be heard among the old elitist chorus. A fistful of new problems would break down the old Restoration consensus.

For a start, Spain's economic growth was very uneven. On one hand, the first two decades of the new century witnessed sudden vitality in industry, commerce, mining, banking and transportation. Spain made progress in light industries like cement and chemicals, producing such marvels as a concrete boat and the highest cement chimney in Europe. For the first time there were more industrial workers than artisans.

On the other hand, virtually all the economic strides occurred in Catalonia and the Basque provinces, followed later by Madrid. (By 1920 Catalonia was using half the national power output.) Spain as a whole was still a rural country with half its workers employed in agriculture, the highest percentage in Western Europe. And its farms were the least productive, with millions of hectares lying fallow while much of the nation went hungry. Part of the problem was Spain's harsh climate and poor soil, but it was also a question of attitudes. In 1907, some Catalan peasants destroyed the local meteorological station and killed its director because they believed it caused drought.

Modern Spanish cities took shape with the new economic realities, bursting out of their almost medieval confinements. Squares were opened up and wide streets — such as Madrid's Gran Via and Barcelona's Via Layetana — built through congested areas. Opulent neo-classical banks testified to the power and wealth of the new business class. Madrid in 1900 was Spain's administrative and educational capital, and over the next three decades would also become a city of bankers, businessmen, and factory workers. The last group formed 70% of Madrid's population by 1930, and the capital could no longer be considered merely a paradise for bureaucratic parasites.

With its sumptuous buildings and middle-class trappings, Barcelona seemed respectable and prosperous. The city was staging modern plays, producing architects like Gaudi, and attracting a lively bohemian world to its old Gothic quarter. But all this was on the surface. Underneath lay another dimension, a seething world of wild-eyed anarchists and common hoodlums. Occasionally it boiled over, as in the 1893 bombing of the Liceo theatre. There was indeed another Barcelona, described by the Czech writer Karel Capek: a city with a dirty, noisy harbour, a murky red-light district (the *barrio chino*), and a famous street called Las Ramblas, "designed to ogle the girls and to start a revolution." For Capek, working-class districts were full of "men with clenched fists in their pockets and rabid, defiant eyes."

Industrialization in Spain meant the same things Britain experienced half-a-century earlier: large-scale peasant migration from country to city to escape rural poverty, only to find that in the city their poverty was no longer picturesque. Barcelona in particular gained ill-repute for its squalid slums of workers' shacks, occupied by poor Catalans and starving peasants from Murcia and Almeria provinces, the social pariahs of Spain. These desperate men would form the armies of working-class agitators that seemed so out of place in bourgeois Barcelona.

Between 1900 and 1913, 1.5 million Spaniards (from a population of 18.6 million) moved to cities or emigrated to Latin America. Many more yearned to go, including all 300 inhabitants of the village of Boado, who offered their services in a letter to the president of Argentina (he declined). Emigration abroad was an important safety-valve, especially in poor regions like Galicia and Andalucia, and it peaked in the years prior to the First World War.

Amid these profound changes, the Catholic Church remained Spain's most important social institution. Since the Restoration of 1875 it had regained much of the power, prestige, and wealth lost during its struggles with the liberals. For the most part, the Spanish church abandoned its historic role as a positive force for the common man and embraced the wealthy and reactionary classes. The Jesuits in particular succeeded in joining the elite — by 1912 they controlled an estimated one-third of Spain's capital wealth. They also had an iron-grip on secondary education. ("The Jesuits do not educate, they domesticate," it was said.)

Aligned with the forces of reaction, the church took up a rabidly anti-liberal posture. Clericalism in Spain was not just a matter of religion. The church's insidious presence was felt in every realm of thought and action. Students were taught that if they associated with liberals or Freemasons they would go to hell. A Catholic catechism (1927) featured a series of questions and answers for young pupils: "Q: What kind of sin is Liberalism? A: It is a most grievous sin against faith. Q: What sin is committed by him who votes for a liberal candidate? A:

Generally a mortal sin."

And yet by 1900 many Spaniards had lost their faith and, as former believers tend to be, many ex-Catholics were strongly anti-clerical. Less than 5% of the men of New Castilla and Andalucia attended Mass, although the figures were much higher in the north, especially among the staunchly Catholic Basques. The most significant trend was the largescale rejection of religion by the new urban working class, who viewed it as one more pillar of a system that oppressed them. There were also strong feelings about religion among the middle class; for example, an anti-clerical play, Perez Galdós's *Electra* (1901), sold 10,000 copies in two days.

In fairness, not all church leaders were knee-jerk reactionaries. A Catholic reformist wing, gathering round the teachings of Pope Leo XIII, tried with some success to create workingmen's associations and promote social justice. But there were other new creeds, preached by more persuasive "miracle workers," which vied for workers' allegiance: anarchism and Marxian socialism.

The astounding growth of anarchism is modern Spain's most distinctive political feature. In no other European country did it have such an impact. Anarchism as a political philosophy was created by the Russian Mikhail Bakunin, who broke with Marxists and called for the end to all government. ("The new world will be won only after the last king has been strangled in the guts of the last priest.") It first entered Spain in 1868, and within five years there were an estimated 50,000 Spanish anarchists.

Part and parcel of the creed was the mystique it attached to revolutionary violence, "propaganda by deed." In 1883, a conspiracy called The Black Hand, which supposedly planned to murder the entire upper class of Andalucia, was uncovered and 14 anarchists were garrotted in Cádiz. A few years later, thousands of peasants armed with sickles marched into Jerez de la Frontera and attacked anyone wearing good clothes. Political bombings began in the 1890s and included the famous attack on the Liceo which killed dozens. In the next few years, anarchists killed three prime ministers and wounded another and made two nearly successful attacks on the king.

Anarchism may have appealed to the Spaniard's famed independent spirit, the natural inclination to imagine himself an "absolute monarch" of his own destiny. But there was more to the story. In the south anarchism was more a state of mind than an organized movement and fit nicely with the village mentality of complete self-reliance and distrust of outsiders. In a region of grating poverty and huge, unworked estates, it became almost a religion with its promises of "salvation" through the distribution of land — the mystical *reparto* that would usher in a utopian society called "libertarian communism." Every *pueblo* had its village anarchist, often austere preachers of vegetarianism, sexual abstinence and atheism as well as hatred of government. "Converted" workers suddenly gave up smoking, drinking, gambling and whoring. They never married, but lived openly with a *compañera* and refused to baptize any children that might arrive.

There was something strikingly backward about the rural anarchists' vision, as if they were trying to recover a lost medieval bliss, when there were common lands and every man enjoyed equality and dignity. In their resistance to modern economic conditions, anarchists shared much with Carlists. Hence, the new "political religion" also appealed in rural Catalonia and Aragón, once Carlist strongholds.

Anarchism also took root in Barcelona, usually known for its *seny* (Catalan common sense), but with a tense new working class to deal with. Here developed the anarcho-syndicalist strain that appealed to factory workers by using trade-union tactics (the CNT). The general strike was the ultimate weapon to bring down the system, and with it would come one final outburst of violence "to end all violence." Many of these true believers were puritanical teetotallers and vegetarians, as interested in closing *barrio chino* brothels as in economic progress.

Spanish socialists (the PSOE, founded in 1879) despised the sentimental brand of revolution preached by these "left-wing Carlists." The UGT was the socialist party's moderate and disciplined trade union, Marxist in theory but cast in the European social-democratic mould and led by the son of a poor washerwoman. Its numbers rose sharply: from 115 branches in 1906 to twice as many four years later. The UGT was strongest in Madrid and Bilbao and came to represent Castilian centralism as opposed to the separatism of Barcelona. Yet party membership lagged behind the anarchists; a miraculous *reparto* was more appealing than tedious Marxist doctrines about slow economic transformation.

Growing regionalism further complicated the Spanish political landscape around 1900, dominated by the "Catalan Question." Catalans disliked centralizing Madrid, but Catalanism was more a product of new economic realities than traditional rivalry with Castilla. Catalanism always had its radical-left side, which often overlapped with anarchism, but around 1900 conservatives took charge. Catalan businessmen had enjoyed a virtual monopoly of Cuban trade and the disaster of 1898 hit hard. Over the next two decades, the main goal of the *Lliga Regionalista* party became trade tariffs and other protection for industry. Later, Catalans would demand much more.

The Basque movement was quite different, springing from a kind of primitive peasant nationalism based on fuzzy conceptions of the "Basque race" that advocated isolation to preserve "racial purity." Make no mistake, Basques *are* different (they have been called the Scots of Spain) and their language is unique. But unlike Catalans, Basques lacked a truly distinctive culture other than their quaint folk festivals of wood-chopping, stone-lifting and other "manly sports." Basque writers like Baroja and Unamuno invariably wrote in Castilian.

Basque nationalism became a force in the 1890s through the ideas of Luis and Sabino Arana, who realized that Carlism was a hopeless cause but shared the movement's archaic values. They considered Basques superior to other Spaniards and invented the term *Euskadi* to describe the seven provinces (four in Spain, three in France) which should comprise a new Basque nation. Sabino also designed a Basque flag, worked to produce a standardized language, called *euskera*, and founded the Basque Nationalist Party (PNV).

Basques have always been Spain's most fervid Catholics (remember St. Ignatius) and there was a large degree of ultra-conservative Catholicism in their philosophy. Extremists muttered about lost *fueros* and isolating the Basque lands from the outside world in order to recover the old pre-liberal way of life. Indeed, all that liberalism seemed to bring were higher taxes and military conscription. *Euskadi* would be a theocratic state which excluded non-Catholics.

In addition to its rural roots, Basque nationalism also sprang from very real social-economic changes after 1900. The population of Vizcaya province, for example, had doubled since 1850, largely from the massive immigration of Castilian workers to Bilbao and other industrial centres (hence the panic about losing Basque identity). Moreover, Basque businessmen — among Spain's most successful — had their own commercial needs which often clashed with policy from Madrid. They too became "nationalists."

SPAIN'S NEW KING, Alfonso XIII, found out how much things were changing on his wedding day in 1906. A crazed anarchist hurled a bomb at the royal carriage, killing 24 and barely missing the king and his bride. Alfonso had come of age four years earlier, assuming power from his doting mother, the regent. He was taller than average, robustly healthy, affable and fairly good looking. He was also the king of Spain. In short, Alfonso was Europe's most eligible bachelor.

While a guest of Edward VII in London, he fell madly in love with Victoria Eugenia, the king's niece and grandchild of Queen Victoria. (Her father was Prince Henry of Battenberg, great-grandfather of England's Prince Philip.) Once back in Spain, Alfonso bombarded "Ena" with affectionate postcards, and the couple were married in Madrid's San Jerónimo church a year later. And so the British and Spanish royal families became inextricably linked.

Alfonso seemed a decent fellow at first: he was self-confident but with a good sense of humour, even at his own expense. He practiced a methodical routine, rising precisely at seven to begin his day, and lived in spartan surroundings. (You can see his bedroom exactly as it was in Madrid's Royal Palace.) Most important, the king swore to observe the constitution.

There were troubling signs, however, that Alfonso did not intend to reign in the detached style of a constitutional monarch. With his constant meddling in the government, he became merely one more politician, and many ministers resigned angrily or were sacked. Sixty-six (including eight prime ministers) came and went during the first four years of Alfonso's reign, and there would be 33 different governments in all from 1902 to 1923, the year he turned to a dictator to save the monarchy.

Like his brother-in-law, Kaiser Wilhelm II, Alfonso adored military parades and uniforms, and he changed clothes four or five times a day. Since boyhood his closest contacts were military attachés, and the army came to represent all that was manly and admirable for him — his "right arm" emotionally if not yet politically. Whenever parliament became critical of military blundering, the crown stood behind "its" officers.

Even after its pasting in 1898, the army proved remarkably resilient. The military budget, for example, was considered something beyond question, even though it ate up half the government's revenue. Most of the money went to salaries of the swollen officer corps (one for every ten men, compared with one for twenty in France; when reformers tried to deal with this problem, a panel of generals suggested ending the imbalance by calling up more men!)

In truth an army of bureaucrats more than soldiers, the military became a state within the state. The war minister was a general, and there were no civilian watchdogs to stem corruption or waste. The army's main concern became "defending its honour against insults," that is, against press criticism and objectionable newspaper cartoons. In 1905, it won a major victory by gaining the power to try civilian critics in military courts.

After the loss of America, the army's main interest shifted to Morocco. Many Spaniards brought up on Reconquest lore held a vague belief in their historic destiny to control North Africa, and Spain already boasted two tiny colonies on the Mediterranean coast — Melilla and Ceuta. In the 1880s the desolate Rio de Oro outpost on the Atlantic side was added. Then, at the Algeciras Conference (1906) France and Spain were entrusted with the "supervision" of Morocco. Eventually Spain's protectorate would include the entire north-coastal strip excluding Tangier. (French Morocco was much larger.)

Spain received poor compensation for accepting the French land-grab. Its zone was poor, nearly without roads, and filled with restless Berber tribes that not even the sultan could control. Anyone who dared enter the mountainous interior was either castrated or murdered and sent back lashed to a donkey. In 1909 a handful of natives wiped out a Spanish column, which led to a serious crisis when the government tried to call up reserves in Catalonia to serve in Morocco.

The "Tragic Week" in Barcelona began with a general strike and became much more. Street barricades were thrown up, bombs tossed, some fifty churches and convents destroyed or damaged, nuns "liberated" from their virtue, tombs desecrated. The general frenzy led to some macabre scenes — drunken workers dancing in the streets with corpses of disinterred nuns and other shocking outrages.

The Tragic Week also saw the emergence of a new political force with an interesting future — the Radical Republicans of Alejandro Lerroux, a strange group even in the weird world of Barcelona politics. Lerroux was a young journalist with an outrageous streak who relished his role as "Emperor of the Paralelo," referring to a vice-ridden slum quarter where he drew support. His inflammatory speeches and articles became legendary: "Young barbarians of today, enter and sack the decadent civilization of this unhappy country; destroy its temples; finish off its gods; tear the veil from its [religious] novices and raise them up to be mothers to propagate the species." Many of Lerroux's "young barbarians" manned the barricades during the revolt and vied with anarchists for worker loyalty.

Government reaction to the violence was swift and merciless: 175 workers were shot in the streets and many more executed in the aftermath. In some cases, simultaneous hanging and shooting satisfied both civil and military justice.

Naturally, all this led workers and police alike to swear more oaths of hatred and revenge for "the next time." There would be many next times.

The troubles in Catalonia ruined the conservative coalition of Prime Minister Maura. The liberal party was hardly in better shape, with its promising leader, Jose Canalejas, killed by an anarchist's bullet in 1912. By the time of the World War (1914-18) the parliamentary system was in its final throes, but the economy of neutral Spain boomed and helped delay the imminent wake. Public opinion split over the war, and the king carefully walked the tightrope of neutrality: his mother was Austrian and his wife English, enough to seal the lips of any man.

As in most of Europe, the post-war years brought more troubled times for Spain, a deadly cocktail of working-class strife, regionalism, wild price fluctuations, revolving-door government ministries (about one every six months) and a new twist — a labour union of some army officers, the *juntas de defensa*.

In 1917, various unhappy elements converged on the government to demand "renovation." Trouble started in the spring with the army unions, when the champions of law-and-order turned against the state with the very power it had entrusted to them. However, when labour organized a general strike that summer, the army returned to the fold and ruthlessly crushed unrest. It had "saved" the nation once again.

These were heady times for revolutionaries, who could reflect on recent events in Russia which had toppled an old order in some ways so similar to Spain's. (One anarchist changed his name from Cordon to Cordoniev.) The anarchist union (CNT) surged from 14,000 members in 1914 to *700,000* five years later. The socialists — who regarded anarchists as gun-toting cranks — also gained ground.

In the following years political violence grew worse, especially in Barcelona, which became a refuge for every type of sordid character — spies, gangsters, hired gunmen called *pistoleros*, professional agitators — all offering their services to police, employers, and unions alike. Virtual gang-warfare broke out between the CNT and the owner-backed Free Syndicates. In five years about a thousand people were gunned down in Barcelona; in January 1921 alone there were 21 assassinations in 36 hours. After the government responded with force, Prime Minister Eduardo Dato met with a hail of bullets from a passing car as he walked across Madrid's Plaza de Independencia.

SPAIN'S CONSTITUTIONAL MONARCHY was deeply wounded by 1920. What finished it off, however, was not revolutionary violence but the war in Morocco. Local tribes under the leadership of the charismatic Abd-el-Krim were stirring up trouble, and an impatient Alfonso ignored the head of the war office (whom he called "an imbecile") and decided to direct the campaign himself. The king's choice as commander was the brash and daring General Silvestre, who proceeded to lead his men into the greatest military blunder since the "charge of the light brigade." In July 1921, at a place called Anual, a small force of Berbers ambushed a meandering Spanish column and slaughtered about 10,000 men (Silvestre promptly killed himself).

The news of the Anual disaster staggered a nation just starting to forget the army's previous failures. It arrived only two days before Alfonso planned to announce a great Moroccan victory during a speech at the grave of El Cid in Burgos, on the feast day of Santiago, St. James the Moor Slayer. Needless to say, the event was spoiled. Even more serious, everyone blamed the king personally for the defeat and parliament called for an investigation. In addition to Alfonso's meddling, there were other troubling questions, such as why there was not a single armoured vehicle in Melilla when half the national budget went to the military.

After two years, on September 17, 1923, the report was finally scheduled to be presented to parliament. But on September 13 General Primo de Rivera led an army uprising and offered his services to the king. It was the first *pronunciamiento* in almost 50 years and the final nail in the coffin of parliamentary Spain. Primo commanded the important Barcelona garrison, but few of his colleagues around Spain rallied to his *grito* before hearing the king's reaction. According to one story, when the general called in the middle of the night, Alfonso muttered, "Am I awake? Am I dreaming? Am I mad?" Others claimed he had prior knowledge of the coup. In any case, the king did nothing to stop it.

The next day Alfonso's ministers resigned en masse, and he asked Primo to form a government. Many never forgave the king for naming an upstart general as prime minister while the coup's fate was still in doubt. Even worse was his refusal to abide by the constitution and reconvene parliament within three months. The supposedly provisional government lasted six years. When Alfonso broke his oath, he undermined the foundations of the Bourbon Restoration. If the constitution was dead, the king too must go.

Miguel Primo de Rivera y Orbaneja, the Marquis of Estella, was born at Jerez de la Frontera in 1870. He came from an old Andalusian family of landowners with a taste for military service (his uncle was also a general). Primo was in many ways a prototype of the old-style Andalusian aristocrat: hard-drinking, horse-loving, skirt-chasing, garrulous and outspoken, hugely generous and disarmingly sincere. Primo thought he represented a new order, but he belonged more to the same breed of 19th-century conspirators as Riego and Pavia.

Primo de Rivera believed he was saving the country from ruin, that he was the "iron surgeon" writer Joaquin Costa had prayed for. But cynics called this misguided knight-errant a kind of glorified café politician, with a vague dream of righting all wrongs by making himself ruler. The great historian Salvador de Madariaga wrote that this was in fact the ambition of every Spanish general, if not every Spaniard.

Primo's coup was welcomed with a wave of popular approval and good will. The masses could see themselves in this sincere Andalusian squire, and Primo played on the paternalistic image by speaking frankly to his fellow citizens on a new contraption called the radio. To the politically naive, Primo seemed the kind of benevolent dictator who could produce the miracles Spain needed, the way a winning lottery ticket can create a rich man in an instant.

During a visit to Rome, Alfonso introduced Primo to the Italian king with the words "This is my Mussolini." But Primo was no Mussolini. Although sometimes ruthless, he was too easy-going and optimistic about his fellow man to be a good modern dictator. Censorship was rigid, but he never executed a single political opponent — remarkable for Spain.

The virtue of military rule, said Primo, was that it saved on salaries by replacing civilians with soldiers. It was this kind of irrefutable illogic that gained mass support and caused others to tear out their hair. He had a genius for doing the unexpected. Once, when he learned that the budget deficit had vanished, he announced that the government would redeem all the mattresses the poor had pawned. He loved sitting up till the wee hours discussing politics over a brandy in some dingy café, then he'd weave home to pen a decree that would be issued the next day, only to be cancelled the following. Worn out from these late nights and hard work, he took the old-fashioned *siesta*, donning nightcap and night-dress before retiring for several hours. There was always the Primo touch: one night at the theatre he lit a cigar but was told that smoking was prohibited. Spain's ruler jumped up and announced, "Tonight everyone may smoke."

Primo was respectful to the king, but never let him have much to do with government. Alfonso seemed content to live the life of a royal playboy, dominating the social pages with his "horsey" wife and flitting between Madrid and aristocratic gathering spots like San Sebastian and Biarritz. The 1920s were a relatively prosperous, carefree decade, and Alfonso enjoyed the sporting life — he was a crack shot — and the frivolity of social affairs. The spirit seemed contagious among Spain's swollen aristocracy. Even Don Jaime, the Carlist pretender, was more interested in nightclubs than in pressing his claims.

Despite his eccentricities, Primo de Rivera brought Spain more than belly laughs. While everyone had their own plan for "regeneration," Primo put his faith in industrialization and public works: roads, harbours, dams, electric power plants. He left Spain with a good road system and encouraged tourism by establishing the network of government hotels called *paradores*. Some claim he even made the trains run on time. In other words, he brought all those things benevolent dictators are supposed to.

Primo's problem was that his dreams were far too grandiose for Spain to pay for. Lacking all but a superficial understanding of a situation, he would issue wildly optimistic proclamations, then discover there was no money in the treasury. Economic planning was bogged down in committees which frittered away time and resources on half-baked projects. Moreover, his creation of state monopolies, such as the CAMPSA petroleum company, outraged foreign investors. Unamuno said of Primo: "Spain needed an iron surgeon and got a quack dentist instead."

Primo nonetheless achieved many of his goals. Like all Spanish generals he was anti-regional and especially disliked the Catalan movement. He even forbade innocuous cultural aspects such as the *sardana* folk dance. Catalanism had grown more demanding by the early 1920s, moving from autonomy to the outright separatism preached by the nationalist party *Estat Catalá*. When the socially conservative *Lliga* supported Primo, Catalanism split in two and the radical wing slowly gained the upper hand.

Primo also drove a wedge between socialists and anarchists by embracing the UGT. The union's president was Francisco Largo Caballero, a plasterer who learned to read at age 24 and favoured cooperation with Primo's paternalistic notions. (Largo would become a crucial figure in the politics of the next decade.) Driven underground by Primo, the anarchist union grew more revolutionary, creating a terrorist wing called the FAI. One of the leaders was Buenaventura Durruti, who shot the bishop of Zaragoza in revenge for the killing of a CNT official.

The dictator's greatest success came in Morocco. Here, the Berber tribes of the Rif Mountains had unified under Krim and an aristocratic cattle-thief named El Raisuli, whose capital was the holy city of Chechaouen. Primo's decision to negotiate a treaty of withdrawal was bitterly opposed by the "warrior party" in the army (the *africanistas*). Especially indignant were the crusty leaders of the new Foreign Legion — generals Sanjurjo and Millan Astray and a young major named Francisco Franco.

Just when things were becoming tense within the military itself (General Weyler of Cuban fame was caught plotting a conspiracy at the ripe old age of 86), the over-confident Moroccans attacked French territory. The two colonial armies crushed the revolt; the campaign was crowned by Sanjurjo's victory at Alhucemas Bay (1927). The army had redeemed itself and created a legend.

As might be expected, Primo had trouble with Spanish intellectuals and students. His mildly authoritarian state gave new ammunition to writers of the Generation of '98 such as Unamuno, who called Primo "a coward, a robber, a felon." It had to be admitted by the disillusioned prophets of renovation that parliamentary institutions did not seem to take root in Spain.

Nevertheless, a new generation of Spaniards, reaching maturity in the 1920s, gave new impetus to the positive trends in Spanish life. A trio of gifted *enfants terribles* — Federico Garcia Lorca, Luis Buñuel, and Salvador Dali — met as students in Madrid and blazed new cultural trails over the next few years. Born near Granada in 1898, Lorca is undoubtedly the best-known writer of 20th-century Spain. His many masterpieces of drama and verse explore the themes of death, violence, and sex in a hostile world.

The "mad Catalan" Dali eventually became a self-promoting showman, but his best work — from his surrealist period of the 20s and 30s — remains essential to the history of modern art. Paintings such as "The Great Masturbator" and "Sodomy of a Skull with a Piano" assaulted conventional taboos with an almost anarchistic contempt for bourgeois values. Buñuel was a brilliant filmmaker who collaborated with Dali in surrealist projects (*An Andalusian Dog*).

A more solitary genius was Catalan Joan Miró, who studied in Barcelona and moved to Paris (1919), where he encountered Surrealism and Cubism. Here he explored the role of the subconscious in art and developed a remarkably personal style of pure, brilliant colour and the playful juxtaposition of lines and abstract shapes. Miró later returned to Spain and spent many years creating astonishing masterpieces at his retreat on Mallorca.

IT HAS BEEN SAID that nowhere else are heroes so quickly built up and torn down as in Spain. No one can survive long in a country where half the population sits for hours in cafés criticizing the government. So it was with Primo de Rivera, whose own inabilities helped in the demolition process. The dictator's swansong came in 1929 with magnificent international expositions in Sevilla and Barcelona. Then came the crash on Wall Street and a disastrous fall in the peseta's value which shattered Spain's temporary prosperity. The end was near.

Although Primo had many enemies, his downfall came after he crossed swords with the army's artillery corps over the subject of promotions. This broke rule number one in Spain: do not disturb the harmony of the "military family." A conspiracy was soon uncovered and its leaders rounded up, but when an army court declared them innocent the message was clear: Primo had lost the support of the one institution that kept him in power.

True to his unpredictable form, Primo conducted his own popularity poll among army brass and learned the truth. This breach of royal prerogative was enough grounds for Alfonso to dismiss the old warhorse in 1930. Primo moved to Paris, where he divided his time between the local church and brothel, and died within a few months. The king believed that by sacking the dictator he could somehow erase his part in the coup of '23, that his questionable actions would not come back to haunt him. But he was wrong.

With Primo gone, public attention focused on the king himself, who had alienated just about everyone. Calmly assuming that things would soon return to normal, he appointed General Berenguer to head the government until elections could be held.

Proponents of a republic were weak in 1930. There was Lerroux and his Radical Republicans, but though the "Emperor of the Paralelo" had toned down his shrill rhetoric somewhat his brand of verbally violent republicanism failed to gain middle-class support. Many liberal monarchists, socialists, and Catalans leaned towards a republic, but there was no concerted plan to that end. Then, in August 1930, the leaders of various anti-Alfonso factions created the Pact of San Sebastian, the "birth certificate" of Spain's Second Republic. Everyone agreed they were against the monarchy, but there were few positive ideas yet. Significantly, they felt that elections would be rigged by the monarchists and that a coup was therefore a legitimate means to achieve power.

A revolt was planned for December 15, spearheaded by republican army officers. But, as sometimes happens with Spanish coups, plans went haywire and a certain Captain Galán rose up three days early at Jaca (Aragón). In Madrid, republican leaders were unable to rally support for the premature uprising, except for the playing of "The Marseillaise" in a few bars. On December 16, Major Ramon Franco (an aviation hero and Francisco Franco's brother) flew over the capital scattering leaflets which threatened to bomb Madrid if the garrison did not rise. (Alfonso watched the performance from the roof of his palace.) Nevertheless, within a few days all the rebels were captured and Galán executed. The republicans had botched the rising but they had their first martyr.

Alfonso finally called for municipal elections for April 12, 1931. The results were startling: 46 of 50 provincial capitals went republican. It was said that even conservative Madrid police, worn out by strikes and student riots, voted republican to get a good night's sleep. Although suspect votes from the corrupt rural areas in the end gave a majority to the monarchists, the popular will was clear. As Alfonso himself remarked, "I had the impression of calling on an old friend and finding him dead."

Events followed rapidly: a republic was declared in Catalonia; in Madrid unruly crowds gathered to demand the king's abdication; Sanjurjo, by then commander of the civil guard, informed Alfonso that he could not guarantee the loyalty of his men; most important, the army did nothing — a kind of negative *pronunciamiento*. Outside the royal palace the hooting, cursing crowd grew larger, and the king's chief minister, Count Romanones, advised him to leave for his own safety. On the evening of April 14 Alfonso declared, "Sunday's elections have shown me that I no longer enjoy the love of my people." With that he scurried off to Cartagena and boarded a ship bound for France — and exile. The great Bourbon dynasty — after 231 years — had succumbed with but a whimper.

THERE ARE MANY myths and misconceptions about the Second Republic. Many believe it brought five years of uninterrupted progress toward a democratic Spain, which was then smashed by a military uprising in 1936. In fact, the republican experiment can be divided into three periods: roughly two years of radical social change under the left-centre; another two years controlled by the right-centre during which much of the previous legislation was overturned; and finally, about six months of Popular Front rule before the civil war. Each of the three periods had to contend with a serious armed rebellion.

Another myth is that a progressive government was destroyed *solely* by a reactionary right. In reality, the moderate-centre parties that launched the great experiment were assaulted mercilessly by both political extremes. Because of the need for coalition governments, the centre was never really stable. In the end there was no middle ground, and no one remained to support the Republic. The course of moderation and compromise, pragmatic politics in other words, was totally abandoned.

Supporters called the Second Republic *la niña bonita*, the pretty girl. It was the last great hope for the "regeneration" of Spain and began with a wave of optimism. Left-wing republicans wanted to finish the aborted liberal revolution of the 19th century, and the masses of "have-nots" were wildly enthusiastic that a great social revolution had arrived to end their misery. Meanwhile, conservatives watched warily. The key to the Republic's success hinged on the attitude of the middle class, relatively small by European standards but still a pivotal force.

Soon after the king's departure, a provisional government was formed from the same coalition that made the Pact of San Sebastian: left-republicans, right-republicans, socialists and regionalists. Much of what was to come was due to the gradual disintegration of this coalition. A moderate Andalusian lawyer named Niceto Alcalá Zamora was elected prime minister to reassure the middle class, already nervous about recent events.

The Republic's honeymoon lasted about a month. During this time the royal flag of red and gold was replaced by the tricolour banner, the royalist national anthem changed to "The Hymn of Riego," and streets and squares around Spain renamed. But by the end of April, the Carlist pretender Don Jaime had already called on anti-republicans to rally round his cause, and peasants in Navarra started oiling their rifles.

By May a wave of church-burnings and looting around the country (mostly the work of anarchists) had shattered the wild optimism of April. The all-pervasive religious problem was raising its head again, ready to divide Spanish society down the middle. One story tells it all: upon hearing of the monarchy's fall, the mayor of one town telegraphed the new government to ask "We have declared for the Republic. What shall we do with the priest?"

In the June elections the socialists emerged from a pack of 26 others as the leading party, followed by the radicals and the Republican Action party. The first *cortes* (parliament) opened on July 14, Bastille Day in France, and boasted 123 lawyers, 41 doctors, 65 professors, and 24 working men. The socialists were led by Largo Caballero and Prieto, the Republican Action party by newcomer Manuel Azaña, and the radicals by Lerroux, a rather misplaced (and often shady) cynic among all the idealists.

The most intriguing figure was Azaña, fat and ugly but a strong-willed intellectual who had been president of Madrid's Ateneo, a literary-political club closed down by Primo for its republican sympathies. The chain-smoking Azaña was consciously modern and a believer in the "European solution" of the Generation of '98. He was a writer of some merit, if not success, leading Unamuno to write: "Beware of Azaña. He is an author without readers. He would be capable of starting a revolution in order to be read."

Azaña was named minister of war and promptly embarked on a daring policy of trimming back the military behemoth. He disbanded ten divisions and offered retirement to all officers *with full pay*. Nearly half accepted the plan, but many of them would soon join the ranks of café politicians, each with his own plan for saving the nation. Azaña made still more enemies by closing down the new military academy at Zaragoza, eliciting a bitter speech from its director, General Franco.

Conspicuous by their absence from the republican coalition were the powerful anarchists of the CNT. Philosophically, they rejected the very idea of government, hence a "workers' state" was as evil as a bourgeois one. Organization was considered a socialist vice; with over a million members in 1936 the CNT had only one paid secretary. Their idea of politics involved strikes and random violence, anything to weaken the government and bring on the revolution. In response to this threat, the new Republic created its own police force, not called "peace officers" or "constables," but *guardias de asalto* — the assault guard.

The Republic's first order of business was a new constitution, and its drafting created serious rifts from the outset. Rather than a broad statement of principles, it became a controversial political document, full of emotive language and threatening statutes. Spain was defined, with certain illogic, as "a republic of workers of all classes." It would have a president with carefully limited powers and a one-house parliament chosen in free elections.

The democratic consensus unravelled abruptly, however, with the infamous Article 26 dealing with religion. Rather than merely ending the cozy arrangement between church and state and establishing religious freedom, anti-clericals like Azaña seemed eager to grind the clergy into the mud. Spain, he declared, had ceased to be a Catholic country as of April 12, 1931, and he intended to prove it. Curiously, most members of parliament had received their education at Catholic schools. Azaña himself lost his faith while a student at the Augustinian college of the Escorial, and much has been made of his own personal motives — rebelling against his education by denying that Spain was Catholic.

Article 26 removed Catholicism as the official religion, barred religious orders from teaching, abolished clerical salaries, legalized divorce, and paved the way to disbanding the Jesuits. Later laws banned Catholic burials unless requested in the deceased's will and prohibited such things as religious processions and ringing church bells. Many provisions were wildly unrealistic; for example, the state lacked the means to replace the church's secondary schools, where most Spanish youths were educated. (Ironically, since the Jesuits in theory no longer existed, many continued to teach as laymen.) Many Catholics in parliament vigorously protested Article 26, and Prime Minister Alcalá resigned. It was happening again — half of Spain was beating up on the other half.

Part of the problem was Azaña himself, a lonely and arrogant man with an acid tongue who refused to admit mistakes and took every opportunity to pour scorn on opponents. Politics as "the art of the possible" was not Azaña's style; he equated intransigence with integrity and compromise with weakness. (There is no word in Spanish that really translates as the English "to compromise.")

The Republic's anti-clerical legislation threw down the gauntlet to Catholic Spain, still a formidable force. In the 1930s the church had thousands of religious communities with more than 50,000 priests, monks and nuns. While it is true that two-thirds of Spaniards did not practice their faith, many resented the slap at their collective heritage — something essentially Spanish since the Reconquest. As Unamuno said, "Here in Spain we are all Catholics, even the atheists."

Even so, there was a strong anti-clerical current supporting the legislation. Catholic workers' federations claimed hundreds of thousands of members, mostly in the country, but the church had come to represent the entrenched ruling class to most working men. Anarchists in particular equated the church with everything evil and attacked it with their own peculiarly "religious" passion.

The new constitution also promised a Catalan autonomy statute, agrarian reform and other measures. Among the most important was granting the franchise to women, who could be expected to vote more conservatively than men. After much wrangling, the document became law in December of 1931; in a spirit of consensus Alcala agreed to become president and then named Azaña as prime minister. The preliminary stage was over; now it was time to get down to business.

However, it soon became clear that the "new Spain" created by the constitution was *too* new for half of the country and not new *enough* for the other half. Attempts at land reform were typical of republican laws in being threatening in principle but weak in practice. The constitution included a vague clause which made property of all kinds "the object of expropriation for social utility." This and later laws affected not only the large landowners but also middling farmers. Hence, aside from the pitiful landless class of Andalucia, the countryside never really supported the Republic.

Agrarian reform was probably the most serious issue facing the new government. Spain in the 1930s remained a predominately rural country. Farm owners tended to have either very large estates or tiny plots; the middle sector was small. In Andalucia, 1% of the owners controlled 42% of the land, much of which was not worked. For example, near Jerez de los Caballeros, 56,000 acres served as a shooting estate. Agricultural methods were backward and produced poor harvests on large estates and *minifundia* alike. The landless workers of the south (*los braceros*) formed Spain's most wretched class. Well over half were illiterate and chronically unemployed or under-employed. They worked part of the year on the wheat or olive harvest, then subsisted in idleness and semi-starvation in their white-washed *pueblos* (not yet considered picturesque) until the next work came along.

These workers were soon flooding the ranks of the socialist union or were confirmed anarchists awaiting the revolution. Their sworn enemies were the hated civil guard, often men of their own class who ruthlessly protected the property owners. Organized as part of the army and led by a general, the *guardias* — with their green uniforms, tri-cornered hats and Mauser rifles — numbered about 30,000 at the time.

Reformers pointed to statistics and advocated land re-distribution, but they were torn between handing out small parcels or creating large, more efficient collective farms. What was most needed — investment in irrigation and other measures to improve production — was given short shrift. The only real solution to the agrarian problem — reducing the rural population by encouraging industry — was a long-term project. And hungry workers did not think in the long term.

Agrarian reform was therefore a disappointing muddle. Any un-worked farm over 56 acres could be confiscated at its appraised value, and in two years about 12,000 families received land. But the total area under cultivation had actually dropped by 750,000 acres. Largo Caballero called the reforms "an aspirin to cure an appendicitis."

Catalonia's autonomy statute gave the region a powerful government called the *Generalitat* with its own president, parliament, tax system and flag, but it stopped short of outright independence. Catalan autonomy was attacked by both socialists and the right wing as a threat to national unity, but it made Catalonia a stronghold of the Republic. Legislators began working on another statute for the Basques, eager — as all Spaniards — for local rule.

With all the changes right-wing reaction was sure to come eventually, and it cropped up first with an ineptly planned coup in the summer of 1932 led by General Sanjurjo, a brave, hard-drinking philanderer. This haphazard plot was discussed in Madrid cafés for weeks (one of the conspirators kept up with the constantly changing dates through his concierge) and the government learned details through a chatty prostitute. When Sanjurjo finally "pronounced" in Sevilla it was a fiasco and he was arrested.

The bungled coup was merely the comical side of a host of threats to the Republic. Opposition to reforms — from both left *and* right — grew steadily stronger during those first two years, while few seemed satisfied. Azaña's religious policy had virtually forced every practicing Catholic to oppose the Republic, splitting the middle class. The working class too was wary. The success or failure of the republican experiment depended on its ability to please the workers without triggering violent reaction. But was this possible? The anarchists had dismissed the Republic as a bourgeois façade and sponsored ceaseless strikes and disruption. The extremist wing in particular (the FAI) wanted to get on with the real business of class revolution.

The southern anarchists — angry with the slow pace of *reparto* — were likewise becoming more restive. Villages were striking at will. In January 1932, four civil guards were murdered during a riot in the town of Castilblanco (Extremadura). Their bodies were hacked to pieces while village women danced around them in glee.

Another less dramatic but no less deadly enemy of the Second Republic was the sluggish Spanish economy, just starting to feel the effects of the Great Depression. By mid-decade exports were about one-quarter the 1930 level, and the ranks of the unemployed swelled to 600,000 by the end of 1933. And men without jobs are usually unhappy with whomever is in power. Although Spain did not suffer the same collapse as more industrialized nations, it was not an auspicious time to initiate a political experiment.

The powers of high finance and big business also detested the egalitarian Republic. Among them was a swashbuckling capitalist named Juan March, whose life became the stuff of legend. March was a farmer's son from Mallorca who became Spain's richest man by intelligence, daring and ruthlessness in equal portions. In 1916, he founded the Transmediterranea shipping company, controlling maritime traffic between mainland Spain and the islands. Later he snared the tobacco monopoly in Spanish Morocco and created a thriving smuggling empire.

After being elected to the republican parliament by admiring Mallorcans, March was charged with fraud and hauled off to jail. He escaped, and then proceeded to sabotage the Spanish currency from abroad.

The republicans themselves helped undermine the "beautiful girl." Of the three major parties, the socialists and the misnamed radicals (really quite conservative) were bitterly opposed, leaving Azaña's weak left-republicans holding the balance of power. In that role, the party's coldly detached leader succumbed to petty squabbles and personality conflicts with Lerroux and others. He therefore allied with the fickle socialists, who were ready to abandon the Republic at the slightest provocation.

As the two extremes loomed menacingly in the wings, the centre grew steadily weaker. Spain needed statesmen or, at the very least, pragmatists to solve problems, not ideologues passing quixotic resolutions. It seemed that Azaña had read but not digested the message of the Generation of '98: bring reason to Spanish society or perish.

Contrary to conservative claims, however, the Azaña government was far from weak toward social upheaval. There were more police in uniform than under Primo, and large numbers of suspects were held in prison without trial or were deported, as in the case of one Azaña opponent sent to a remote village and forced to live in a stable.

A SERIOUS BLOW to the Republic's prestige was the affair of Casas Viejas, a poor village in Cádiz province which proclaimed itself independent under *comunismo libertario* in January of 1933. When the *guardia civil* and assault guards besieged a group of ringleaders about 20 people died under questionable circumstances. Outrage among the left ensued when the commander swore that Azaña had ordered a take-no-prisoners policy, adding "Shoot them in the belly!" (The prime minister vehemently denied the charge.)

A swing to the right began with the elections of 1933, in which six million women voted for the first time. Chief beneficiary was a union of conservative Catholic factions called CEDA, under the leadership of Jose Maria Gil Robles. This loose coalition included monarchists, Carlists and anyone else appalled by Azaña's religious policies, and by anti-clericalism generally (in the Republic's five years about 200 clerics were killed and 500 churches damaged or destroyed). Gil Robles had been a attorney for the Jesuits and the Sanjurjo conspirators and was rather slippery in his politics, refusing to confirm or deny his support of the Republic.

One reason for the rightward turn was that left-republicans and socialists had refused to cooperate in the elections. Nevertheless, they were outraged by the prospects of a CEDA government, and President Alcalá named Lerroux as a compromise prime minister. Naturally, the new centre cabinet was inherently unstable.

Thus opened a period dubbed *el bienio negro*, the two black years, in which much of the previous legislation was overturned or ignored. Particularly galling was the release of Sanjurjo and his cohorts, a virtual green-light for future military meddlers. Soon the left began to look at new options, and socialist labour-leader Largo Caballero declared that revolution was the "workers' only hope." When one clerical newspaper called for "peace and harmony" amid the growing tension, *El Socialista* replied: "Harmony? No! Class war! Hatred to the death for the criminal bourgeoisie!"

The anarchists in turn were outraged by Largo's attempt to steal their revolutionary thunder and stepped up their own agitation. Meanwhile, another force had emerged on the left: the Spanish Communist Party (PCE). Since splitting with the socialists over the course of the Russian Revolution, the communists had been the odd-man-out in Spanish politics, with only about a thousand party members in 1930. But three years later they numbered 25,000 and received 400,000 votes. The first communist was sitting in Spain's parliament.

Another newcomer to the *cortes* was the leader of the Falange, a fascist group not unlike others sprouting up across Europe. And like the Italian fascists, German nazis and Belgian rexists, it forged an odd blend of working-class sentiment, blatant nationalism (in this case calls for a new Spanish empire) and plain hooliganism. The group's name, which meant "phalanx," was taken from the Macedonian army unit that overthrew the republic of Athens in the 4th century BC.

The Falange's leader was the charismatic Jose Antonio Primo de Rivera, 30-year-old son of the fallen dictator, whose tarnished honour he swore to defend. Jose Antonio was a complex figure, born to the life of a *señorito* (a wealthy Andalusian playboy) but in reality much more — charming, daring, and passionately concerned with the fate of Spain and the average Spaniard.

Falangism as a political creed owed much to the soul-searching of the Generation of '98, especially the elitism  of  Ortega y Gasset, and Jose Antonio mesmerized throngs with brilliant oratory about the "new Spain." He called for land reform and socialization of the banks and railways, which angered conservatives. Even so, conservatives knew how to use someone like Jose Antonio.

Despite its lip-service to the working class, the core of Falangists were students, disgruntled anarchists, and offbeat intellectuals. Besides Madrid, Spanish fascism drew support in the Sevilla-Cádiz area, precisely where the communists were most active. In 1933, Jose Antonio merged his band with kindred spirits, and they adopted fascist trappings such as blue shirts and the raised-arm salute. For their flag they chose the same colours as the anarchists — red and black. Their symbol was the yoke and arrows of Fernando and Isabel, and the maudlin tune "Face to the Sun" became their anthem. All this sentimentality could not disguise their use of hard-core street violence to achieve their goals. This disruption — and the reaction it caused — proved to be their chief political influence.

Alongside the Falange, the red-bereted Carlists seemed positively antiquated, but their ranks grew steadily with ultra-conservatives, especially in Catholic Navarra. In splitting with the Basques, Carlists had chosen the monarchy and nation over the old issue of local rights. And they now had an efficient organization under Fal Conde, a pretender in Alfonso Carlos, and hidden stockpiles of arms in remote corners of  Navarra. There were also reports of 400 Carlist officers, disguised as Peruvians, training in Italy.

The Republic had banished Alfonso XIII for "high treason," and he lived out his life in Italian exile, occasionally travelling as the Count of Covadonga. Monarchists grouped around the *Renovacion Española* of Jose Calvo Sotelo, former finance minister under Primo. They gained 44 seats in the November 1933 elections.

As the year 1934 began, therefore, the Spanish political scene was splitting into two hostile camps. Each side became convinced that the other was on the verge of seizing power and planned the appropriate counter-measures. That summer in Madrid a young falangist was beaten to death at the Casa del Campo by a group of socialist thugs; his eyes were gouged out and a girl in the mob urinated into the empty sockets. When news of the outrage spread, a falangist posse drove to a working-class district and began shooting randomly at suspected socialists. Somehow they managed to kill the girl who had squatted so eloquently for her principles.

It was but one incident of hundreds in a spiralling cycle of violence. In the purely political sphere, it was growing evident that the exclusion of CEDA from the cabinet could not continue. When parliament adjourned in July, everyone assumed that October would bring a crisis. It came on schedule with the inclusion of three CEDA members in the Lerroux cabinet, which sparked a full-scale socialist revolt against the "fascist conquest of the Republic." (The far left was convinced that Gil Robles was a secret fascist.)

The UGT called for a general strike, and from the balcony of the Generalitat, Luis Companys proclaimed an independent Catalan state *within* a federal republic. But the trouble soon died out or was crushed throughout Spain — everywhere except in Asturias. This rugged mining region in the north had strong communist unions and a reckless tradition of direct labour confrontation. One local communist heroine was Dolores Ibarruri, dubbed *La Pasionaria* (the Passion Flower), who always wore black and was regarded as a kind of revolutionary saint. The right spread rumours that she had once cut a priest's throat with her teeth.

Upon learning of the general strike, rebels in isolated mining towns south of Oviedo rose up and attacked police and army posts by hurling sticks of dynamite "liberated" from the mines. For about a week workers' committees controlled Asturias without opposition as the government waited, fearing that regular troops might not fire on the miners if a showdown came. Finally, as reports of murdered priests and other atrocities spread, Madrid decided to send in the Legion. With them were mercenaries called *regulares*, actually Moroccans under Spanish command. The irony was biting — Muslims being called in by Catholic Spain to crush the one region never conquered by the Moors.

BASED ON THE FRENCH model, the Spanish Foreign Legion was created in the twenties as a crack unit to fight Moroccan mountain tribes. The legionnaires, mostly Spaniards, were a tough, harshly disciplined force trained to cry "Long live death!" as they rushed into battle. They were led by one-eyed, one-armed General Millan Astray and an eager understudy who had designed the legion's uniform: Francisco Franco.

Franco's army of legionnaires and Moroccans moved through Asturias with bloody precision, village by village, house by house. There were many reports of murder, torture, rape, and other crimes against the population, especially by the Moors. When the smoke cleared about 2,000 were dead and thousands more wounded or in jail. The split between right and left widened into a gaping chasm: no one could sit on the political fence after Asturias.

About 30,000 Spaniards were in jail, among them opposition leaders Azaña and Largo Caballero. The aging socialist remained behind bars more than a year, giving him the chance to read Marx for the first time and ponder the coming revolution he felt destined to lead. (*Pravda* deemed him "the Spanish Lenin," and Largo was intoxicated with the image.) The revolt had failed, but there could be another — and still another if necessary.

In the months of right-coalition government that followed October 1934, the Catalan Statute was suspended and much of the agrarian reform repealed. The country remained in an official "state of alarm," but the right, significantly, did not try to take over, even when the appointment of Gil Robles as prime minister became long overdue. The reason, perhaps, is that reactionaries did not yet have the full support of the ultimate arbiter of Spanish politics — the army.

In the years following Sanjurjo's failed coup, a hidden but heated debate simmered within the ranks. An officer's first duty was loyalty, said some, whether to a monarchy or republic. Yes, replied others, but what if obedience conflicted with "dignity"? In 1933, a secret society of disgruntled junior officers (the UME) formed and began plotting. Everyone in the army continued to watch and wait, among them the tight-lipped Franco, named chief-of-staff in May 1935.

While the political world seethed, there was a final radiant glow from the fire of Spanish culture lit earlier in the century. Garcia Lorca published three new plays in 1935, and the poets Alberti, Aleixandre, and Guillen contributed to the ongoing literary flowering. The same year, Buñuel produced his documentary masterpiece *Land Without Bread* about the squalid Las Hurdes area in Ex-tremadura. And in Barcelona, Pablo Casals created a symphony orchestra and choral society. This exuberant cultural scene stood in stark contrast with the political disintegration all around.

Corruption finally brought down the Lerroux government, the twenty-eighth cabinet in five years, and Alcalá decided to call elections for February, believing that the nation was ready to elect a moderate government. He could not have been more wrong. Remembering the last electoral debacle, leftist parties merged into the Popular Front, a communist-inspired tactic (the Popular Front per se was not communist) already used in France to defeat "fascism." Previously aloof (they called socialists "social fascists" and anarchists "petit-bourgeois pseudo-revolutionaries") the communists now championed the spirit of working-class cooperation.

In response, conservative groups united in the so-called National Front, lumping together parties from conservative republicans to fascists and appealing to the Catholic middle class and peasants of northern Spain. The centre was growing smaller, but could count on the Basque nationalists, still going their own myopic way.

Fierce campaign rhetoric swirled around the issue of the October 1934 revolt. Leaders of the major parties all stated publicly that they would only respect the election results if they won, *never* if they lost. Largo declared that if the right won, he would "proceed to declare civil war," and Calvo Sotelo told Spaniards that "a red flag would fly over Spain" if they did not vote for the National Front.

Voting took place on February 16, 1936, Carnival Sunday just before Lent, and about 70 per cent of the electorate went to the polls. Although the popular vote was extremely close — 4.6 million (PF) and 4.5 million (NF) — Popular Front candidates won 263 seats in parliament to the right's 133. The centre captured only Vizcaya, Guipuzcoa and Soria provinces, but held a good deal of power with 77 seats. Conservative Spain was shocked at the results, and General Franco offered support if the interim prime minister chose to declare a "state of war" rather than hand over power. But he declined.

Thus Spain's last elected government for forty years was born amid general panic — the left fearing an army coup and the right a social revolution. Azaña (having been freed earlier) was named prime minister of the Popular Front government, and he moved quickly to grant amnesty to political prisoners, restore Catalan autonomy and move generals of questionable loyalty to remote posts. Franco was sent to the Canary Islands. Jose Antonio of the Falange was arrested in March on a weapons charge and languished in an Alicante jail.

The new government was doomed to failure from the outset, however, by Largo's refusal to cooperate. Socialist post-election victory marches featured huge portraits of Stalin and Lenin, as thousands of slogan-chanting workers with clenched fists carried banners reading "Long live the red army." All the while an increasingly horrified middle class looked on. With the socialists' refusal to join the government, Spain began its final dance of disintegration.

That spring the countryside was on the verge of social revolution. Early one morning in March, 60,000 peasants in Extremadura occupied unworked farms, cried "Viva la República," and started to plough. In just over two months there were 196 peasant strikes in Andalucia alone.

Things were indeed getting out of hand. In Madrid, vendors of the communist journal fought pitched battles with newsboys hawking conservative papers. Cars full of falangists, armed with machine guns, cruised the main avenues looking for "lefties" to mow down. Often the resulting funeral turned into a political rally that ended with a pitched battle between rival factions right in the cemetery.

In this violent atmosphere, enrollment in extremist factions swelled. The moderate right began to abandon Gil Robles' CEDA for the more inflammatory Calvo Sotelo, who openly longed for the nation's missing "spinal column." The army itself was divided; a pro-republican group (the UMRA) was picking up support and began trading random assassinations with the UME. Despite it all, Azaña scoffed that rumours of army coups were "as plentiful as the acacia trees on the Castellana."

In mid-June, Gil Robles stood up in parliament and indicted the government for its failure to maintain order. In four months, he said, there had been 269 murders and 1,287 injuries in political attacks, 341 strikes and almost 400 churches had been destroyed or damaged. He went on: "A country can live under a monarchy or a republic, with a parliamentary or a presidential system, under communism or fascism. But it cannot live in anarchy."

Gil's figures were exaggerated, but the point was clear nonetheless. On July 11, Calvo Sotelo delivered another bitter attack on the government. When he sat down, Ibarruri (*La Pasionaria*) reportedly shouted, "That is your last speech." (Some sources dispute this incident.)

Four days later, an officer in the assault guard (and UMRA member) was cut down by falangist gunmen. Vowing revenge, several of his comrades, led by a communist civil-guard captain, went to the home of Calvo Sotelo early the next morning. The politician was suspicious, but he agreed to accompany them to an undisclosed destination. He left home promising to telephone his family soon, "unless these gentlemen are going to blow out my brains." A few hours later, his battered body — with a bullet in the back of the neck — was dumped at the gates of the local cemetery.

The murder of Calvo Sotelo by a squad of off-duty police sent a shudder throughout Spain. Many believed the government was responsible, proving that the Republic was unfit to rule and that Spain itself was out of control. On Friday, July 17, 1936 the army garrison at Melilla revolted, and the next day other commanders around Spain rose up against the Republic. The Spanish Civil War had begun.

## SIGHTS & SITES

**Algeciras** *(Cádiz): Hotel Reina Cristina, named for the queen regent, welcomed diplomats and spies alike; the Casa Consistorial (town hall) was scene of the 1906 conference that led to Spanish Morocco.*
**Astorga** *(Leon): Episcopal Palace by Gaudi blends Gothic, Moorish and Art Nouveau.*
**Barcelona**: *Spanish Village (Pueblo Español), erected for Primo's 1929 exhibition in Montjuich Park, re-creates nation's architectural heritage; Joan Miró Foundation contains a vast selection of the artist's work; Pedralbes Palace, erected for Alfonso XIII in Italian Renaissance style; Gaudi's Barcelona includes Sagrada Familia Church, Güell Park, Casa Mila, and the Pedrera building; Picasso Museum contains excellent collection of early works, including blue and rose periods; the Art-Nouveau Palacio de la Musica was designed by Domenech i Montaner; Museum of Modern Art features Dali, Miró and Tapies; Four Cats Café still exists in Barrio Gótico.*
**Madrid**: *Royal Palace features the private apartments of last occupants, Alfonso XIII and Queen Victoria Eugenia; main post office on the Plaza de Cibeles designed by Palacios; Sorolla Museum was formerly artist's studio; Banco de España facing the Paseo del Prado built at turn of century by new commercial wealth.*
**Málaga**: *Museum of Bellas Artes includes very early work by Picasso; artist's birthplace is marked on Plaza de la Merced.*
**Sevilla**: *Maria Luisa Park was re-designed in 1929 for the Ibero-American Exhibition; several buildings remain, including many used in the filming of Lawrence of Arabia.*
**Vich** *(Barcelona): Paintings by Catalan artist Jose Maria Sert cover walls of cathedral.*

*Antonio Gaudi's Sagrada Familia Church in Barcelona. (PHOTO BY AGE FOTO-STOCK, BARCELONA)*

*Right, King Alfonso XIII pictured with his bride-to-be, the English princess Victoria Eugenia. Above, the bombing of Guernica by German planes during the Spanish Civil War inspired Picasso's famous painting (PHOTOGRAPHY BY AGE FOTOSTOCK, BARCELONA)*

The ruins of
Belchite, a town
in Zaragoza
bombed during
the 1937 Ebro
offensive, were
left unrestored as
a reminder of the
ravages of war

*Above, US President
Eisenhower's 1959 visit
to Franco's Spain
signalled the end of the
country's isolation.
Right, two days after
General Franco's death
in 1975, Prince Juan
Carlos rides in the old
dictator's car for the
ceremony of his
proclamation as king.
(TOP: ABC/AGE
FOTOSTOCK,
BARCELONA; RIGHT:
ROBERT ROYAL)*

## CHAPTER 10

# THE SPANISH WAR

W hat is quite possibly the most famous painting of this century hangs behind bullet-proof glass in Madrid's Reina Sofía museum, across the street from the Prado. In addition to its aesthetic qualities, Picasso's masterpiece "Guernica" has a remarkable history behind it.

In January 1937, the Republic invited the artist to paint a mural for the Spanish Pavilion at the Paris World's Fair in June. Picasso began doing preliminary drawings, but the project had not really come into focus. Then, on April 26, a swarm of German planes bombed and strafed a defenceless Basque village. Guernica was not just any village, but the traditional home of Basque liberty, which Spanish kings swore to honour beneath a famous oak tree. Guernica was nearly levelled and hundreds of civilians were killed during a three-hour rain of explosives and incendiary bombs. On hearing the news, Picasso decided to make the brutal attack the subject of his painting.

More than fifty studies on display at the Reina Sofía preview the kind of powerful images — a mother gripping her dead child, a screaming horse, a soldier's fingers clutching a broken sword — that the artist would employ in "Guernica." Many were motifs from earlier works such as the "Minotauromachy". The huge painting itself (3.5 by 7.8 metres) does not convey its message by using blood and gore, or even the passionate colours of Goya's "Third of May". It is surprisingly cool in tone, its baffling images rendered in black, white, shades of grey and a faint, rinsed-out blue.

Even so, the painting's distorted, agonized human and animal figures perfectly transmit the brute force and sheer terror unleashed at Guernica. Whereas Goya's masterpiece did not quite escape from the "history genre" of painting, Picasso soared above it, using one small incident in a much larger conflict to give the world something truly universal: a profound protest against war and violence.

Unwanted in Francoist Spain, Picasso's masterpiece lived an exile's life for 44 years, residing most of the time at New York's Museum of Modern Art until "coming home" in 1981. For two generations of Spaniards "Guernica" was much more than a painting, and smuggled prints were snapped up and hung in quiet, secret defiance. The work became a symbol of all the shattered dreams and mindless brutality of the Spanish Civil War.

CALVO SOTELO'S MURDER did not cause the military revolt of 1936 — there had been plotting for months — but it may have been the last straw for one reluctant rebel who would rise to supreme power in Spain. Serious planning had started soon after the February elections and the decision to transfer grumblers like Franco to distant posts. The conspiracy's nominal head was old General Sanjurjo, exiled in Portugal, but the real leaders early on were generals Goded and Mola. Franco straddled the fence, doubting the chances for success and fearing a rupture within the army.

In March, several high-ranking officers met at the home of a Madrid financier. They agreed to support a *golpe* (military rising) if Largo was named prime minister, if the civil guard was disbanded, or if anarchy overwhelmed the country.

By a stroke of luck, Mola was deemed trustworthy by the government and transferred from Morocco to Pamplona, heart of Carlist country. General Emilio Mola, a stone-faced puritanical type who wore spectacles and looked like a stern schoolmaster, soon took over planning in earnest.

By late spring everyone, including the government, knew something was up. Calvo Sotelo and Jose Antonio were not made privy to details, but pledged their support. Mola's plan called for a classic rising of army garrisons around Spain to form a national government under military command. But the sympathies of regional commanders were by no means clear, and Mola was eager for the highly respected Franco to commit himself. Continuing to hesitate he was dubbed "Miss Canary Islands 1936" by some cynics.

The reticent general even wrote to the prime minister in June and warned — in carefully vague terms — of the dangers of anarchy and its effect on "the discipline of the army." The letter fell somewhere between an ultimatum and a final attempt at conciliation. Ill at the time, the prime minister did not respond, and sometime shortly after Franco joined the plot. Another recent convert was a flamboyant loudmouth named Queipo de Llano, a republican who switched sides after the sacking of President Alcalá (Queipo's son was married to Alcalá's daughter).

By July 1 it was only a question of fixing a date. Plans calling for the revolt to start during San Fermines(the running of the bulls) at Pamplona were scrapped when word leaked out. Finally, Mola sent out telegrams reading "On the 15th last, at 4 a.m., Helen gave birth to a beautiful child." This meant that the revolt would start in Morocco on July 18 at 5 a.m. followed by garrisons throughout Spain. Plotters hoped that their *pronunciamiento* would come off, as so many others, quickly and with relatively little bloodshed. But this time it would be different.

Due to a last minute change, the Melilla garrison rose up a day early, and a certain colonel Segui arrested and shot the loyal commander, General Rome-rales, and others who resisted. Martial law was declared in the city. The in-surgents had lists of all members of suspect groups — trade unions, left-wing parties, masonic lodges — and quickly made arrests and some executions. It was a pattern soon to follow throughout Spain.

After hearing of events in Morocco, Franco proclaimed the reasons for the coup in his Manifesto of Las Palmas, which ended on an incredible note by appeal-ing to "Fraternity, Liberty, and Equality." In slightly different order, these were the ideals of the French Revolution, everything Franco professed to despise.

On July 11, the *Dragon Rapide*, an aircraft chartered by Mallorcan Juan March, had left Croydon Airport near London on a circuitous route destined for the Canary Islands and the eagerly waiting Franco. On the 19th he boarded the aircraft bound for Tetuan and his expectant legionnaires, a trip that would culminate in supreme power over Spain for four decades.

Who was this remarkable creature? Forty-three at the time, Franco had a distinguished army career behind him, but only a psychic would have predicted his breathtaking rise. Francisco Franco Bahamonde (both his surnames have possible Jewish origins) was born in 1892 at the naval base of El Ferrol in rainy Galicia, whose residents are known for their thriftiness and unnerving patience. Franco came from a family of navy men (his philandering father was a paymaster) and yearned to enroll in the naval cadet school. And yet, in one more reverberation from the disaster of 1898, enrollment was cut back and Francisco was forced to enlist instead at the infantry academy at Toledo. He was to be a soldier instead of a sailor, and Franco always blamed politicians who had "lost the war" for his fate.

Francisco was a tender 15 years when he entered the academy, and his small stature and high-pitched voice made him the butt of pranks. His academic performance was mediocre (ranking 251st out of 312 graduates), hardly indicative of a career that would make him the youngest general in Europe since Napo-leon. After graduation he volunteered for Moroccan service and rose rapidly, winning 13 medals and other honours for leadership, discipline, and bravery. The Moroccans claimed he had *baraka*, a phenomenal luck, and entering a battle on his white charger he incarnated the ideal of a dashing commander. With the regular army and later with the Legion, he became (in succession) the young-est captain, major, colonel and general — the latter at 33.

Franco was army to the marrow. Unlike most officers, he did not smoke, drink, or hang out in seedy Moroccan brothels, preferring to spend evenings poring over maps or supply lists. Shy around women, he apparently remained aloof from worldly temptation prior to his marriage to Carmen Polo in 1923. But though he wore the armour of self-righteousness, he was not especially religious until later, when the influence of his pious wife began to seep in. His values were military ones: patriotism; belief in the unity of Spain; hostility to politicians; and exaggerated concepts of honour, integrity, order and discipline. Above all discipline.

Franco was known as the scourge of slackers, especially Catalans. One time while he was inspecting the troops, a legionnaire unhappy with the quality of the food threw the contents of his mess kit into Franco's face. He betrayed no emotion, calmly wiped his face and continued the review. After dismissing the men, he had the offending soldier arrested and shot.

Then he gave orders that the food be improved.

THE SPANISH CIVIL WAR (1936-39) is the second-most-written- about military conflict in history, trailing only the Second World War. For many observers, the Spanish war was the dress rehearsal for the European conflict to come (it ended just five months before Hitler — and Stalin — invaded Poland). It was "the good fight," the battle to stop fascism, a death struggle between the forces of light and darkness. Wrote George Orwell: "The question is very simple. Shall the common man be pushed back in the mud, or shall he not? That was the real issue of the Spanish war..."

Nevertheless, though the war did have its universal qualities, it was essentially a Spanish struggle, springing from the army's peculiar political role since the last century.

When news of the rising first came, many people shrugged it off, especially after hearing that Sanjurjo was involved. Madrid radio announced "No one, absolutely no one on the Spanish mainland has taken part in this absurd plot."

After Spaniards called in foreign aid (which they grew to detest), the struggle took on its much discussed European implications. But Franco was not the "fascist" of enemy propaganda, nor was he doing battle with "reds" (at least in the beginning) as his supporters claimed. It was a Spanish affair, a rebellion that started off no better or worse than scores of others since 1820, but which grew into something incredibly ugly and frightful. It was almost as if the old anarchist dream of one final outburst of violence "to end all violence" had arrived — but in a way no anarchist imagined.

It was a struggle on many levels: between classes (peasants vs. landlords, workers vs. factory owners, anti-clericals vs. the clergy), between ideologies (at least a dozen political parties and two monarchist factions as well as fascists and communists) and between regions (roughly western vs. eastern Spain, a division which some claim dates from the days of Celts and Iberians). And yet for all its myriad aspects, the war itself transformed complex issues and tensions into one simple choice — to attack the Republic or defend it.

Nevertheless a man's loyalty sometimes depended on where he happened to be at the time of the rising. The rebels quickly captured Spanish Morocco, the Canaries, Galicia, Navarra, and most of Old Castilla and Aragón. In Sevilla,

Queipo de Llano bluffed the entire city into surrender with just 150 men. First he rounded up all the loyal officers and shouted at the top of his lungs "You are all my prisoners!" (They meekly complied.) Next he captured the radio station and bombarded the city with news that a huge army from Africa was advancing, and that anyone resisting would be "shot like dogs." His handful of men darkened their faces with walnut juice (to look more like the dreaded Moors), jumped into lorries and drove round the city repeatedly to create the impression of overwhelming strength. The ruse worked and Sevilla fell with hardly a shot fired.

Wherever the populace and security forces supported the government, or where the military was divided or hesitant, the rising failed. In Madrid rebel General Fanjul dallied too long, and a crowd stormed the Montana Barracks and overwhelmed the insurgents, killing many. In Barcelona, armed workers and loyal *guardias* and *asaltos* took to the streets and defeated the rising even before its leader, General Goded, had arrived from Mallorca. Goded was soon shot, and Sanjurjo died in Portugal when his plane crashed on takeoff (he had insisted on bringing two heavy trunks loaded with dress uniforms). That left Franco, Mola and Queipo in charge, each acting as a kind of independent warlord.

The revolt had not failed, but it had not succeeded either, which meant only one thing: civil war. A week after the rising, the rebels' situation looked hopeless: they had failed in five of Spain's six largest cities and held less than a third of the mainland. The Republic also controlled about 75% of Spain's industry and commerce. Contrary to myth, at least *half* of the army and security forces remained loyal to the Republic. This included most of the generals (many recently appointed) and half the lower officers. Both Mola's and Queipo's forces were weak, so Franco's Army of Africa seemed to be the decisive factor. But it was stuck in Morocco; most of the navy and air force had remained loyal, dashing rebel plans for transporting troops to Spain, something essential to any hope of success.

From the outset, the Republican cause enjoyed a wave of popular support. In Madrid, a delegation of drivers offered 3,000 taxis "to fight fascism," and there were other similar gestures. But Azaña's government seemed to slip into paralysis by refusing to hand out arms to the workers. Weak leadership in Madrid in these early days meant that soon there were not just two Spains but two hundred, each acting in a vacuum. Local power fell to the strongest political party or union; in Catalonia the mantle was shared between the Generalitat and the CNT. The Basque provinces were bitterly divided over the rising, but Vizcaya and Guipuzcoa went with the Republic upon being promised an autonomy statute. From that point the Basques governed as an almost independent state.

The first weeks after July 18 unleashed a fury of popular violence seldom seen or imagined before this century. Wild stories circulated among the panic-stricken middle class and foreign community, like the one about reds crushing naked nuns with steamrollers in the streets of Málaga. But each case of hyperbole was matched with cold fact. Barcelona's bourgeoisie virtually vanished as a class overnight, many killed and the rest suddenly converted into workers. To wear a coat and tie or carry a briefcase was to invite physical attack. In the town of Ronda (Málaga), about 500 members of the middle class were herded to the Tajo gorge and hurled 150 metres to their deaths. (Hemingway adapted the scene for his novel *For Whom The Bell Tolls*.)

The clergy stood out as the most-hated symbol for the "uncontrollables" of the so-called Red Terror. About 7,000 priests, monks and nuns (as well as 12 bishops) perished in the bloodbath. In one case, rosary beads were forced into a monk's ears until the drums were perforated; another monk was thrown into a ring of fighting bulls and gored into a bloody pulp. In Barcelona, a crowd set fire to the Carmelite church and machine-gunned priests as they ran out. Hundreds of churches were destroyed during the summer outburst, but much valuable petrol was wasted trying to burn Gaudi's Sagrada Familia, made of stone and mortar.

Estimates of political murders behind republican lines vary widely, from 20,000 to over 50,000, with most coming during the first three months. Body counts on the Nationalist side — as the insurgents came to be called — were even higher, and the executions lasted far longer. Having little popular support in most areas, the desperate rebels knew they must terrorize residents into submission. This was especially true in regions which had voted for the Popular Front like Andalucia. From Sevilla Queipo conducted wicked nightly radio broadcasts, threatening the terrified populace with brutal murder and the legendary sexual appetite of Franco's Moroccan soldiers.

Sure candidates for nationalist death-lists were loyal officers, labour union or party leaders, Popular Front deputies and anyone else suspected of belonging to "anti-Spain." Sometimes there were summary trials lasting a few minutes; others were executed without pretense. Among them was Spain's literary genius Garcia Lorca, shot gangland-style near Granada, a town in precarious rebel control. (In a seldom remembered counter-crime, Loyalists killed right-wing intellectual Ramiro de Maetzu, a member of the Generation of '98.)

As in most civil wars, family loyalties came second to political ones as brother fought brother and father battled son. Even Franco had his own cousin shot when he arrived at Tetuan. At least 50,000 died at the hands of nationalist death-squads during the first six months, perhaps twice that number before the war ended. Most were shot or hanged, although there were more imaginative techniques: some prisoners were beaten to death with crucifixes (a tradition from the Carlist wars) or buried alive with mocking final eulogies about agrarian reform. ("Here is your piece of ground, you son of a whore!") Captured loyalist militiamen were often shot en masse, there being little exchange of prisoners. When approached with an offer for such an exchange a startled General Mola replied, "How can you expect us to exchange a Spanish gentleman for a red dog?"

THE REVOLT'S SUCCESS hinged almost entirely on Franco's getting his crack troops — about 30,000 strong, chiefly legionnaires and Moroccan mercenaries — across the straits and into Spain. He decided to seek foreign help, and by July 25 his agents were in Rome negotiating with Mussolini for planes. Things were speeded along by the presence in Italy of Juan March, who arranged credit, and a call from a foreign resident of note, Alfonso XIII. About the same time, Hitler also agreed to send aircraft: twenty JU-52 transport planes and six Heinkel-51 fighters to support them.

In the first major airlift of troops in history, thousands of men crossed over to Algeciras on several hundred flights during August and September. (Said Hitler: "Franco ought to erect a monument to the glory of the Junkers-52.") More men were ferried across later, after two German battleships in Spanish waters prompted the loyalist navy to retire to port. Franco himself flew to Sevilla on August 6 to direct the Nationalist campaign.

This was not to be a fumbled coup d'etat, after all, and Loyalists immediately had to think about creating a fighting force to meet the threat. The Republic still had thousands of loyal officers, but they were regarded with suspicion by some and hence not used effectively. Instead, militia units began forming under control of the anarchist or socialist parties and often acted independently of the war ministry. One of the first republican counterattacks involved militia from Barcelona (led by the famous terrorist Durruti) which tried to retake Zaragoza without any artillery or battle plan.

The quality of the militias started to improve after Largo Caballero was named prime minister in September to rally worker support. Even the CNT abandoned anarchist principles of non-involvement and joined the coalition.

Generally speaking, it was a "pauper's war" for both sides, with a shocking lack of modern weapons and equipment. When the war started the army did not have a single tank or modern airplane. Even the Legion had to use old machine-guns with defective firing pins. On the other hand, the war was the first to make effective use of inventions like the radio and telephone and, with the arrival of foreign weaponry, such military innovations as rapid tank deployment and aerial bombing of cities.

Lacking the proper means to fight a war, both sides immediately turned to other nations, whose response did much to decide the final outcome. French president Blum at first seemed enthusiastic about the Republic's appeals, but a trip to London made him aware of Britain's cool attitude. Foreign secretary Eden warned that if French involvement south of the Pyrenees (in what he called "the war of the Spanish obsession") led to conflict with Germany, Britain would step aside.

By July 31, Britain introduced a unilateral ban on arms shipments, and Blum followed suit and closed the French border in August. Thus the Republic was denied the internationally accepted right of a government to purchase arms to defend itself from rebellion. But then, this was the age of non-intervention and appeasement. Two years later, the infamous Munich Pact would extinguish the Republic's last faint hope of receiving help from the western democracies.

Nevertheless, France unofficially provided more aid than is generally recognized. About 25,000 of its citizens fought in Spain, and the Nationalists brought down more than a hundred French aircraft. Far more important was military assistance from the Soviet Union, especially critical during the first few months.

This included planes, tanks and artillery, as well as hundreds of trained advisers. These "commissars" would later help whip the chaotic militias into a real army.

In one of the war's most-debated incidents, Largo and his finance minister, Negrin, decided to move most of Spain's huge gold supply (the world's fourth largest) to Russia. Their reasons were twofold: fear that it might fall into rebel hands and the need to pay for arms purchases. In October 7,800 boxes of gold bars, valued at about half-a-billion U.S. dollars, were loaded onto four Soviet steamers bound for Odessa. (After the war it took Spain 20 years to accumulate the same amount in dollar reserves.) There is a story that when the shipment arrived, Stalin held a banquet and announced: "The Spanish will never see their gold again, just as one cannot see one's own ears." (When Spain tried to reclaim the gold in 1956, the Russians said there was none left and claimed an additional $50 million owed by the Republic.)

Although Russian aid was substantial, it already began to dry up by mid-1937. More important in tipping the scale for the Nationalists was aid from Germany and Italy. Like the Soviet Union, they had accepted a non-intervention pact, but all blatantly ignored it, offering only feeble excuses. Mussolini claimed that the 70,000 Italian troops in Spain were "volunteers" without government sanction and tried to deny that Mallorca was virtually an Italian base throughout the war. (Palma's main street was renamed Via Roma.)

The Germans were eager to test new equipment and strategy in the field. Spain also provided "a convenient sideshow" (as Hitler put it) to distract Britain and France from Germany's skullduggery in central Europe. Although their numbers were far fewer than the Italians (about 5,000 maximum), the Germans provided technical advisers and the best air unit in Spain, the renowned Condor Legion. Consisting of about one hundred planes and pilots and commanded by a General Von Sperrle, the legion helped transform Salamanca into "a German military camp," according to the American ambassador at the time.

Speaking of the Americans, President Roosevelt and his government, despite some sympathies for the Republic, toed the non-intervention line. The policy was nearly reversed in 1938, but a last-ditch effort by Joseph Kennedy, American ambassador at the Court of St. James (and father of the famous Kennedy brothers), convinced Roosevelt to back down. There were just too many Catholic voters in America.

BY AUGUST THE NATIONALISTS held most of south-western Andalucia, as well as Córdoba and Granada, and the bulk of north-western Spain, except for the Asturian and Basque coast. Franco decided to push north through Extremadura and link up with Mola's army, then attack Madrid to end the war quickly. In the first such raids in history, German bombers were already softening up the capital. Staying close to the Portuguese frontier, the African Army sliced through resistance and soon reached the border-town of Badajoz in Extremadura.

Here transpired one of the war's most disgusting spectacles, which shocked world opinion and gained much sympathy for the Republic. Legionnaires singing "I am the fiancé of death" and Moroccan *regulares* entered the town and vicious hand-to-hand fighting soon degenerated into a bloodbath. Among the dead were two defenders slain on the steps of the cathedral's high altar and about 2,000 republicans rounded up and shot in the bullring. As was Moroccan custom, corpses were castrated and strewn throughout Badajoz that night.

The next objective was Madrid, but first another drama waited to be played out in Toledo. Here the revolt had fizzled, and about 1,300 conspirators and 700 non-combatants retreated to the old Alcázar fortress under the command of a Colonel Moscardó. The Loyalists tried every means to dislodge them, including tunneling under and dynamiting one tower, but the defenders held out like true Iberians.

One day early on, someone phoned Moscardó and announced that he had ten minutes to surrender or his son would be shot. When the captive son came on the line, the colonel (much like Guzman El Bueno centuries earlier) responded: "My son, commend your soul to God, shout *Viva España!* and die like a hero." This incident was recalled *ad nauseam* by nationalist cheerleaders for the next forty years. (The son *was* shot, but not until a month later.)

Franco saw the Alcázar's propaganda value and decided to divert his attack from Madrid to relieve the defenders from the two-month siege. The nationalist army under Varela reached Toledo on September 27, captured the historic town, and began a reign of bloody reprisals. Realizing their fate, a group of 40 anarchists got roaring drunk on anisette and set fire to the building they were holding. All perished in the flames.

The war saw many such incidents. A lesser-known last stand took place near Jaen at Santa Maria de la Cabeza, where about 350 insurgents and their families held out for nine months before being overwhelmed. During the siege supplies, including delicate medical instruments and bottles of wine, were air-dropped by a most ingenious form of parachute: live turkeys, which landed gently after a largely vertical flight.

There was also the ultimate statement made during the war's first month at Gijon, where a group of 180 desperate rebels faced certain defeat. Finally, a message was sent to a nationalist ship lying offshore: "Defence is impossible. The barracks are burning and the enemy are starting to enter. Fire on us!" The request was honoured and all were killed.

The crucial delay when Nationalist troops were diverted to Toledo gave *madrileños* time to shore up defences, a task made more difficult by the widespread refusal to dig trenches — a tactic viewed as cowardly. Four nationalist columns were marching on the city, and Mola coined a phrase now used in every language by stating that a "fifth column" of Nationalist sympathisers was already in Madrid. He remembered that almost half the residents had voted for the National Front a few months before.

The city was surrounded, but Franco left a wide corridor open to the southeast, believing (as Madariaga wrote) in the Spanish saying that "a fleeing enemy should have a bridge of silver." Indeed, Largo and his government soon moved to Valencia, and defence planning fell to General Miaja and Colonel Rojo, the Republic's finest military mind.

The ten-day battle of Madrid became the civil war's central epic, as the world's attention suddenly riveted on Spain. Women and children threw up barricades and shouted *No pasarán!* (They shall not pass!) and "Madrid will be the tomb of fascism!" La Pasionaria toured the streets with a loudspeaker, urging wives to prepare boiling oil for the invaders. And just as the attack began, another heroic element was added with the dramatic arrival of the first men of the famed International Brigades.

Although the initial group of 1,900 were mostly French and German, delirious crowds greeted them with cries of "*Viva Rusia!*" This was because — despite the presence of many idealists and adventurers — the International Brigades were conceived, organized and manned by communists. The whole concept sprang from a Comintern meeting a few days after July 18; even Largo viewed the brigades as a potential tool of Stalin. (They were also disliked by the anarchists.)

Recruiting of these "armed tourists" remained in communist hands, and no one of questionable political background was supposed to be admitted. Of the 30,000 or so who came to Spain, most were from working-class backgrounds and were either party members or sympathizers. The British Battalion contained mostly unemployed industrial workers — plus 174 Welsh miners experienced at fighting police. The American Abraham Lincoln Battalion, on the other hand, consisted mainly of students and sailors and was not as politically motivated as the others. Many were bitterly disillusioned upon realizing they were pawns in a planned communist takeover. Casualties were also extremely high among the brigades, as much as half in some units.

Nevertheless, the brigades' presence at the battle of Madrid was not only inspirational, but decisive in holding back the assault. Fighting took place west of the city in the Casa del Campo and university campus (the pride of Alfonso XIII). This is where the Nationalists were to attack, but the defenders had captured a battle plan the day before and were ready. After fierce fighting the lines were drawn. They would not move more than 50 metres in either direction for the next two-and-a-half years. One final note on the battle of Madrid: for some reason the attackers never thought of cutting off the city's water supply, which would have ended the siege in short order.

After the "victory" of November 1936, Madrid took on the appearance of a communist city, with red flags and pictures of Lenin everywhere. Cinemas played films about the Russian Revolution instead of more popular MGM musicals. Workers with clenched fists roared around in lorries shouting "*No pasarán!*" and La Pasionaria's "Better to die on your feet than to live on your knees." Communist party membership in Spain rose dramatically to a million by mid-1937. It seemed as if Franco's wild rhetoric about fighting "the reds" had become a self-fulfilling prophecy.

THE CIVIL WAR unleashed a spontaneous yet profound social revolution in much of Spain during the second half of 1936. Seventy per cent of Catalan factories were seized outright by the unions, the CNT controlled all public services, and in the country farms were collectivized or parceled out and property records destroyed. Debts and even money were abolished with the stroke of a pen, and luxury hotels and private residences were converted into schools or hospitals.

George Orwell arrived in December to join a trotskyist militia unit (*not* the International Brigades) and later described Barcelona in his classic account *Homage To Catalonia*: "Even the bootblacks had been collectivized and their boxes painted [anarchist] red and black. Waiters and shop-walkers looked you in the face and treated you as an equal..."

Barcelona became much more proletarian than Madrid, with a passion for equality. Everyone said *tu*(you) rather than the more formal *usted*, and *Salud* replaced *Adios* in this classless, godless world. Women in particular experienced tremendous liberation under anarchist "rule" by taking jobs and responsibilities previously denied them. Righteous reformers opened "anti-brothels" where repentant prostitutes could learn to cook and sew. Bars were closed, and coffee and alcohol outlawed. There were no private cars or well-dressed people any more; even judges and doctors wore blue overalls, and a Russian diplomat was denounced for wearing a hat. The obsession with rejecting the "class tyranny" of clothing reached comic extremes with the Mangada Column of militia, organized by the eccentric vegetarian and nudist, Colonel Mangada. Lorries filled with his half-naked male and female followers could be seen roaring around Barcelona in troop lorries with no apparent destination.

The policy of the well-disciplined communists was to create a strong central government and army and to concentrate on winning the war. However, the anarchists of Barcelona and Valencia had other ideas — to launch the long-awaited social revolution that would smash the old order. To extremists, the Republic was "not worth a single drop of worker blood." Many anarchists joined Catalan nationalists in calling for a complete break with Madrid and washing their hands of Spain once and for all. After Luis Companys declared himself "president of Catalonia", a power struggle was sure to come.

The splintering of the Republic must have bemused General Franco, who had successfully consolidated his own power — and that of the Nationalists — at Salamanca in October. With the sullen consent of Mola and Queipo, the insurgent officers agreed to a single command under Franco, the *generalisimo* (highest of all generals). Soon after, he also claimed to be head of state and began using the title *caudillo* (an awkward translation of *duce* or *führer*). Much like Julius Caesar two millennia before, Franco was making himself dictator. Some protested, but when colonel Yagüe, "the hyena of Asturias" and one of Franco's strongest supporters, threatened a coup within a coup, the muttering abruptly ceased. But no one among them could have imagined the duration of the regime they had created. In August, Franco had stated that Spain would remain a republic, but one based on law and order, and the bombastic Queipo ended his broadcasts with *"Viva la república!"* Suddenly such references vanished, and nationalist posters read "One state, one country, one chief."

The insurgents won the war because they united more quickly to create a more efficient, better-trained and equipped military force than the republicans. From their new headquarters at Burgos, nationalist generals began to build a huge army around a nucleus of veterans. Middle-class youths became temporary second lieutenants, but casualty rates were so high that a popular saying soon went: "temporary second lieutenant, permanent corpse." The rank-and-file came from the tradition-bound peasantry of northern and central Spain, pious and city-hating.

Somewhere along the line the Nationalists began to view their struggle as a holy crusade, like the ones that had expelled the Moors and baptized millions of native Americans. Said one new crusader: "We fight for love and honour, for the paintings of Velazquez, the plays of Lope de Vega, for Don Quixote and the Escorial." The previously indifferent Franco began attending Mass regularly, and the clergy thundered from their pulpits about a war of extermination.

AFTER A WINTER LULL, fighting resumed in the spring of 1937. Black-shirted Italian troops spearheaded the ignominious defeat of Málaga, which was followed by gruesome nationalist reprisals and pillage. Among the booty was the reputed hand of St. Teresa, a treasured relic that Franco kept at his bedside for the rest of his life. The battle of Jarama near Madrid, at which the Lincoln Battalion saw its first action, ended in a stalemate. But near Guadalajara, the republican army gained a rare victory by routing a largely Italian force, the first of many mishaps for *Il Duce*'s "volunteers." At one point Mussolini declared that no Italians could return home until they won another victory.

Later that spring, the action shifted north to the isolated coastal strip still under loyalist control. From the war's outset the Catholic Basques had been going their own way, deeply suspicious of the revolutionary, anti-clerical bent of their "allies" elsewhere. Generally, Basque units refused to fight outside *Euskadi*, and when they did would often withdraw from battle at critical moments.

Perhaps the war's best-known event occurred during the nationalists' big push north. Monday, April 26, was market day in the quiet town of Guernica, historic home of Basque liberties but with no strategic value. Suddenly and without warning, a swarm of German aircraft descended on the town with wave after wave of bombs and machine-gun fire. Flying with the Condor Legion that day was a Colonel Von Richthofen, cousin of the legendary Red Baron.

Most of the town was levelled and about a thousand civilians killed during the three-hour nightmare, and Guernica became a worldwide symbol of fascist terror and the horrors of modern warfare. Reacting to the international outcry, nationalist leaders claimed they had no prior knowledge of the attack and revised the death count to twelve. Later they explained that it never occurred, but that Guernica was destroyed by retreating Basques. But there were too many witnesses who knew better.

Summer brought more bad news for the Republic, with the fall of Bilbao, Santander and Asturias, the last collapsing "like meringue dipped in water."

The short-lived Basque republic was soon just a memory, and firing squads were kept busy dealing with Catholic "traitors," among them many priests. Franco's Catholic supporters worldwide suddenly became very confused about the Crusade.

The capture of Basque iron ore and industry was vital for the nationalist effort. Their "alternate" economy was in good shape, with enough food, a steady supply of armaments, and the backing of most Spanish and European financiers. The ubiquitous Juan March alone chipped in 15 million pounds sterling. By 1937, the nationalist peseta had a higher rate of exchange than republican money.

Another important event of the northern campaign was the death of General Mola, Franco's only serious rival, in a plane crash. All evidence points to an accident, but for years after a man in Valladolid kept two loaded pistols with him at all times, ready for the man who killed his son, the pilot. Said Hitler: "The real tragedy for Spain was the death of Mola; there was the real brain, the real leader..."

Loyalist counterattacks near Madrid (Brunete) and on the Aragón front failed to halt Franco's war machine. Adding to the Republic's woes was an internal crisis that had been simmering for months. The multi-headed revolutionary hydra was about to devour itself. The Spanish communist party, by then taking direct orders from Moscow, was determined to seize control of the war effort by crushing troublesome anarchists and a new player, an anti-Stalinist (trotskyist) group of marxists called the POUM. The communists were also determined to dump the dour and incompetent Largo, who had outlived his usefulness.

The crisis came in May over control of Barcelona's *Telefónica*, the main telephone exchange, held by the CNT and POUM. On May 2, an operator interrupted a conversation between presidents Azaña and Companys, stating that the lines should be used for more important things. It was just one of many incidents that prompted the government to take control, and some unidentified gunfire coming from the building unleashed a furious battle that spread through the city. About five-hundred people were killed. Largo was bitterly discredited by this shadow civil war and resigned after refusing to punish the POUM for its role in the outburst. The Revolution was over, and the communists had won.

Looking around for a new puppet, the party of Stalin found Dr. Juan Negrin and managed to convince Azaña — by then a mere whisper of his former self — to name him prime minister. Negrin was a respected scientist with many admirable qualities. But his earlier decision to export half of Spain's assets left him tied to Moscow with a "golden chain," as he would soon find out.

Negrin inherited a disastrous state of military affairs and vowed to put all effort into winning the war, the not unreasonable communist policy. With the help of Russian advisers, the ragtag loyalist army began to shape up. But something seemed to go out of the Republic after the events of May. Workers' collectives were disbanded and Catalan dreams of independence shoved aside in favour of unity. The last flicker of Catalan separatism was snuffed out when Negrin moved his government from Valencia to Barcelona.

A darker side of the Negrin regime soon emerged. These were precisely the months of Stalin's infamous show-trials in Moscow, at which political opponents confessed to being "fascist spies" and to other crimes. Stalin's paranoia spilled over into Spain through his agent Colonel Orlov and a dreaded new security force intent on rooting out trotskyists and other rivals. This particular reign of terror climaxed with the brutal murder of POUM head Andres Nin, who just happened to have been the secretary of Stalin's arch-foe, Leon Trotsky. Nin was tortured mercilessly in a secret communist prison near Madrid, but refused to "confess" and was killed. Negrin did nothing to stop or condemn the outrage and lost his last shred of respectability. Wrote a bitterly disillusioned Orwell: "This war, in which I played so ineffectual a part, has left me with memories that are mostly evil."

Meanwhile Franco grew stronger. One possible rival had been Jose Antonio, but the falangist leader was executed by the Republicans in November 1936. (Largo's son was shot in revenge.) The young fascist had actually despised Franco as an unreformed "reactionary," but agreed to support the rising nonetheless. The Falange's "socialist" wing — which hated capitalism as much as international communism — survived with the "old shirts" of Manuel Hedilla. But a phenomenal increase in "new shirts" (a million by 1937) threatened to swamp the Falange's original ideals.

Inevitably, power struggles and anti-Franco plots began to brew in Falange circles, and the *generalisimo* used one violent incident as an excuse to arrest Hedilla. He spent the next four years in solitary confinement. At the insistence of his brother-in-law, Serrano Suñer, Franco used the trouble as an excuse to cement his position as Spain's once-and-future *caudillo*. In yet another "coup," he created a single political umbrella called the *Falange Española Tradicionalist* (FET) which embraced *all* groups on the right and neutralized their often contradictory philosophies.

The original Falange, for example, was socially revolutionary, anti-monarchist and merely tolerant of religion. Carlists and Alfonsists each had a would-be king and were intensely Catholic. Franco needed to rein them in if he was to survive as dictator after the war. His decision to retain the name *Falange* for the movement, along with important symbols like blue shirts and the fascist salute, did much to foster the myth that he himself was a fascist. But Franco was never more nor less than one thing — a Francoist. His tactic of unite-and-conquer toward the feuding nationalist factions laid the foundation of his forty years in power. And the base was rock solid — all army officers were obliged to join FET.

The new coalition (later called "the Movement") issued 26 points defining the future state, mostly lifted from the Falange. Spain would be totalitarian, unitary, anti-capitalist, anti-marxist and fervidly Catholic. There was one important omission: no mention of the monarchy. This obvious slight upset supporters of Alfonso, who had settled into a life of polo and bridge in Rome, and of his heir Don Juan. But the army had not lifted a finger to save Alfonso in 1931 and was not about to have him back; and when Juan showed up in Spain during the war, Mola had sent him packing.

Meanwhile, Don Carlos, the Carlist pretender and last of the original line, had died, leaving a distant relative named Francis Xavier as heir to the great lost cause. Aside from their red berets (now worn with falangist blue shirts) as part of the Movement's uniform, very little of Carlism survived in the FET. And despite all the fascist claptrap, members of the old Falange had to settle for mostly ceremonial rewards, like the officially sanctioned cult of Jose Antonio, henceforth called "the absent one" at all party functions. His name was emblazoned on the walls of most Spanish churches, and only now is fading away.

Franco's power-play really marked the victory of ultra-conservative Spain, its principles more akin to Fernando and Isabel than to anything in this century. (In one of the regime's more curious propaganda feats, one ideologue of the Movement tried to claim that the Spain of the Catholic Monarchs was "fascist," the genuine precursor of Mussolini's Italy). Franco and his ilk yearned for the days of Spain's glory and tried to root out foreign influences of the past two centuries. Much of the attitude was dangerous (calls for a new empire) and much merely silly (the banning of Russian salad and French omelettes). But the Movement now had its own myths to fight for — the glories of a Spain long gone — which seemed as powerful as any modern "ism."

IN DECEMBER 1937, the Republicans tried to derail the nationalist juggernaut with a bold offensive at Teruel. Caught off guard, Franco dropped his own plans and managed a successful counterattack by February, and another loyalist defeat. Not a tactician of great imagination, Franco was actually held in contempt by his German advisers as a hopelessly hesitant plodder. Gaining ground and holding it seemed Franco's style, rather than the Third Reich's swift mechanized warfare, which went for the throat. Franco's approach — in military strategy as well as politics — was to wait cautiously for the right moment to attack, to wear down the enemy by attrition, above all to *endure* longer than his opponents.

In the spring of 1938, Franco's army — 100,000 men, 1,000 planes, 150 tanks — broke through the Aragón front and swept east to the Mediterranean, cutting the republican zone in two. Confounding his advisers again, Franco then turned south toward Valencia rather than marching on Barcelona. The Catalan capital was weak, having recently suffered heavy bombardment by the Mallorca-based Italians, which drew more international protest. Mussolini boasted, "I am delighted to see Italians horrifying the world for a change instead of charming it with their guitar-playing skills."

But Franco stubbornly turned south, and soon his army was bogged down along the coast. Using this turn of events, the loyalist army enjoyed its last hurrah by launching a daring offensive in July along the Ebro River aimed at Franco's rear. Wedged between the Pyrenees and Iberian ranges, the Ebro Valley is one of Spain's two great depressions (the Guadalquivir Valley is the other) and summer temperatures are brutal. Here the two armies massed for a bloody artillery duel and war of attrition that cost more than 50,000 casualties, including

20,000 dead. In its last action of the war, the British Battalion suffered staggering losses, with more than half killed. After three months, nationalist air superiority decided the battle, and the republican army collapsed. "You could break our front with bicycles," observed Negrin.

Even before the battle's conclusion, the International Brigades were being disbanded and sent home, their ranks decimated and their propaganda value nil. Even the Lincoln Battalion had a majority of Spaniards by 1938. Yet their farewell parade in Barcelona equalled their inspiring entrance into Madrid. All stood while La Pasionaria gave her famous speech. "You gave us everything: your youth or your maturity; your science or your experience; your blood or your lives; your hopes and aspirations. You are history. You are part of our land. When the olive trees blossom again, come back." (In 1988 about 300 original members did return to Barcelona on the 50th anniversary of their departure.)

In late December Franco finally attacked Catalonia, and a month later nationalist troops, led by Carlist *requetes* and Moroccans, poured into Barcelona unopposed — a victory parade rather than a battle. In early February, Azaña, Negrin and other leaders crossed the French border on foot, two days ahead of nationalist troops. Hundreds of thousands of refugees were herded into France and told not to return. Many never did.

On February 27, Britain and France recognized the Franco government, and Azaña resigned as president the next day. Negrin, who remained as prime minister, pinned defeat on the western democracies for failing to help the Republic. Among the exiles, ideological feuds continued to flourish, old scores were settled (one security officer was buried alive) and everyone argued about who was to blame for the disaster.

The Loyalists still had half-a-million men under arms and held Madrid and Valencia. But the war was effectively over, and only Negrin and the communists wanted to fight on. The prime minister, who had returned to Spain, wanted to gain time to bargain with Franco over surrender terms. Others were taking the "Numantian posture," vowing to fight to the last man in the manner of the ancient Iberians.

This was the stage-setting for the war's bizarre finale in Madrid. While nationalist forces gathered on the outskirts and waited, republicans conducted their own mini-civil war to decide how to end the larger war. It began when a Colonel Casado staged a coup against the communist-run government, hoping to stop the fighting and elicit better terms from Franco. Claiming that the legitimate government and popular will were represented by *the army*, not by politicians like Negrin, he "pronounced" in the name of the so-called National Council. To complete the irony, Casado claimed to be saving Spain from communism.

Six days of fighting broke out, leaving about 250 dead, but the communists were broken. After Franco's promise of pardon for "all who are not criminals," the loyalist army seemed to melt away. On March 28, 1939, nationalist troops entered Madrid through the rubble of University City, where they had been thrown back two years — and half a million lifetimes — before. Crowds of nationalist sympathizers, many sheet-white from years of hiding, gave the fascist salute and shouted *"Han pasado!"* (They have passed!). On April 1 Franco announced that the war was over.

Supporters of the Republic around the world were stunned. Wrote the French philosopher Camus: "It was in Spain that men learned that we can be right and yet be beaten, that force can vanquish spirit, that there are times when courage is not its own reward. It is this, doubtless, which explains why so many men, the world over, regarded the Spanish drama as a personal tragedy."

The Spanish Civil War was Spain's share of the general breakdown of Europe — and most of the world — during the 1930's and 40's. Yet it was distinctly Spanish. Rather than a return to the 16th-century empire as Francoist propaganda would pretend, the victory of "traditional" Spain brought back the old *moderado* order. With greater power than ever before, the unholy trinity of church, army, and landowners made one final, desperate attempt to halt the forces of liberalism and modernization unleashed in the 19th century. And for another three decades they succeeded, largely through the efforts of one man and the state he created.

## SIGHTS & SITES

**Belchite** *(Zaragoza): Nearly razed during civil war, the town was left intact as a monument to nationalist dead.*
**Guernica** *(Vizcaya): Town that came to symbolize the horrors of civil war after being bombed by Germans; famous oak tree remains a symbol of Basque liberty.*
**Madrid**: *Picasso's masterpiece "Guernica" hangs in the Reina Sofía museum; the Casa del Campo and University City were sites of fierce fighting during civil war, now completely rebuilt but still evocative.*
**Mount Teide** *(Santa Cruz de Tenerife): This superb vantage point has an obelisk marking the start of Franco's rising, called Las Raices. (It's worth a trip for the view.)*
**Pamplona** *(Navarra): Monumento de los Muertos is a memorial church dedicated to civil-war dead.*
**Toledo**: *The Alcázar, destroyed and rebuilt many times since 13th century; in 1936 it withheld eight-week republican siege in epic fashion; today it's a military museum.*

# SPAIN IN THE FIRST MONTHS OF CIVIL WAR

# CHAPTER 11

# THE AGE OF FRANCO

A few kilometres north of Felipe II's El Escorial lies another man's grandiose statement on his life and times. Inaugurated on the twentieth anniversary of the end of the Spanish Civil War, the colossal Valley of the Fallen monument took many years to complete and involved thousands of men toiling as virtual slaves. Most workers were war prisoners, although in theory the monument honoured the dead of both sides.

Like Felipe, Franco supervised the plans and often visited the site. The design reflected the overblown style favoured by all totalitarian governments, in this case "victorious" Spain's pretensions of a holy crusade and an imperial past. Since 1975 it has served as the tomb of Francisco Franco, and of an entire era as well. In its sheer pomposity, the Valley of the Fallen also expresses the ultimate folly of the Spanish Civil War and, indeed, of all wars.

This neo-Valhalla was carved and blasted from the innards of a huge granite mountain in the Sierra de Guadarrama. The first thing visitors see is a gigantic stone cross, 150-metres high and weighing thousands of tons, clutching the rock like some freak bird-of-prey. You enter the monument via a long, cavelike tunnel lined with chapels whose walls conceal the tombs of thousands of civil-war dead. At the far end is a massive basilica — 275 metres long and boasting a 60-metre-high dome — with marble floors, priceless tapestries, and intricate mosaics of Christ and the saints. Like Franco's Spain, the scene is the perfect blending of religion and military pomp.

For the grand opening in 1959, the remains of Jose Antonio Primo de Rivera were transferred here from the Escorial (where he had been buried many years earlier). Blue-shirted members of the Falange were out in force that day to hear Franco proclaim: "The struggle between good and evil never ends no matter how great the victory. Anti-Spain was routed, but it is not dead." This sentiment dominated nearly forty years of Spanish history.

The figure of "a million dead" in the civil war has been refuted, but the eminent authority Hugh Thomas considers half that number a reasonable estimate. This includes about 200,000 killed in combat, some 150,000 murdered or executed behind the lines by both sides, and at least another 100,000 executed or dying in prison in the years immediately after the war. Another 300,000 fled their country, never to return, pushing the figure of "lost" Spaniards close to 800,000. This does not count the injured and maimed. Post-war Spain swarmed with armless, legless or otherwise crippled soldiers in search of work. Only the lucky ones got jobs selling lottery tickets.

Without any doubt, the war's crowning tragedy and Francisco Franco's greatest failing was his utter lack of mercy and compassion toward the defeated, millions of his fellow Spaniards. For Franco the vanquished represented "anti-Spain," and those not slaughtered on the battlefield should be exterminated or severely punished. There was no programme of national recovery and reconciliation to bind the nation's wounds, as President Lincoln proposed "with malice toward none" at the end of the American Civil War. But then Franco was no Lincoln.

In fact, the diminutive dictator never admitted that a *civil* war between Spaniards had been fought — instead Truth had triumphed over international Evil. The ultimate irony came when courts of rebel army-officers sentenced Loyalists to death for the crime of "rebellion." The Law of Political Responsibilities (1939) condemned nearly everyone connected with Popular Front parties or government as guilty of something and about a quarter of a million arrests were made in the first months (well over a million by 1942).

The summer of 1939 was an orgy of informing, private vendettas and sanctioned executions. Tens of thousands died in the mass bloodletting; Mussolini's son-in-law reported 250 executions a day in Madrid alone, mostly by firing squad. It got so bad that many of Franco's supporters protested the bloody reprisals. But they did not subside. (Franco gave orders that a maximum of one in five suspects could be acquitted.) When France fell to the Germans in 1940, many republican leaders were sent back to their death in Spain. Among them was Catalan President Luis Companys. Facing the firing squad, he took off his shoes and socks so that he could die touching the soil of Catalonia.

Another side of the tragic story was Spain's loss of virtually an entire generation of artists and intellectuals, either killed like Lorca or in exile. Machado died in France. Jimenez and many others went to live and write in Latin America. Other exiles were writers Américo Castro, Madariaga, Ramon Sender, Rafael Alberti, the cellist Casals and film-maker Buñuel. Spain did not begin to make cultural progress again for many, many years.

Wrote Hugh Thomas: "Upon the heaped skulls of all these ideals, in the dust of the memory of so much rhetoric, one more cold-hearted, dispassionate, duller and greyer man survived triumphant..."

The man named Franco who had risen to supreme power remained an enigma. "A less straightforward man I never met," said one American journalist. He was short, increasingly stout and had a shrill voice "like that of muezzin," according to one observer. Moreover, he had an ordinary manner and was a poor speaker — hardly the charismatic traits of a modern dictator — yet it was said that those in his presence grew frightened and submissive.

Franco had proved his military skills and personal bravery. Yet he had a nasty vindictive streak which said much about the man. One time he strongly reprimanded Yagüe, a fervid supporter, when he praised the bravery of republican troops. Thirty years after the war, when someone suggested that loyalist veterans receive pensions, Franco was outraged: "You can't combine a glorious army with the scum of the Spanish population."

Spain's conservative powers clearly dominated the post-war landscape. The army had proved it had the last word in Spanish politics and was showered with special privileges. Yet though cabinet members during the first twenty years were 39% military men, Franco's Spain was not literally "governed" by the army (generals nevertheless continued to loom in the background). With Franco in charge, the military slipped back to a state of political indifference, concerned more with promotions and getting new hardware. Many veterans joined the ranks of the beefed-up *guardia civil*.

In April 1939, Pope Pius XII congratulated those who "rose in defence of the ideals of faith and Christian civilization." The Catholic Church, in its new role as catalyst among all elements of the nationalist coalition, was another clear winner of the civil war. The loyal church would receive its rewards. Bishops sat in parliament and on the Council of the Realm, and laws had to conform to Catholic dogma. Once again classrooms had crucifixes and pictures of the Virgin Mary, along with that of the *caudillo*. The Jesuits were allowed back and given charge of most secondary schools, proving again the adage that "Night and the Jesuits always return."

The clergy also assumed the role of guardians against "moral lapses" such as holding hands in public, wearing sleeveless shirts, or being seen conversing with Protestants. In short, it was a hidebound brand of Catholicism going back to the age of the Inquisition. The church and military often linked arms in defending the new regime. One naval training handbook read: "Other nations struggle to gain more territory, more food, more petroleum. Spain has battled and will continue to do battle so that there are more Catholics and honourable men in the world."

Initially at odds, the church and Falange began to cozy up, and blue shirts and fascist salutes became common at Mass. Even bishops and nuns thrust out a raised arm at every opportunity. And the church had a new "saint" in Jose Antonio; the falangist founder's disinterred body was carried on the shoulders of falangists all the way from Alicante to the Escorial for reburial — a 500-

kilometre trip lasting ten days and nights. (His burial at the royal site stirred monarchist ire.)

Franco had crushed the Falange's radical wing, and post-war attempts to create a fascist state were thwarted by conservatives. One exception was the Spanish labour movement, awarded as a kind of booby-prize to the Falange, which created "vertical syndicates" combining both management and labour of each economic sector into individual unions. The idea was to replace class struggle with cooperation in a kind of a state-run paternalistic world. The Falange also controlled the press and government propaganda machine, the bark if not the bite of power.

The monarchists might also be considered winners in post-Republic Spain, but it was a hollow victory without the return of the king — or his heir. Alfonso XIII was reasonably content with life in exile, though he complained that with each passing year he was seated one row farther back at polo matches. He died in Rome in 1941, shortly after he renounced his rights to Don Juan, who began to drum up support and issue manifestos calling for a return to the monarchy. This merely served to annoy Franco, who had no intention of relinquishing *any* of his power. Noting the presence of anti-monarchists among his supporters, Franco claimed his rule was "that which divides us least."

Many of the more realistic political exiles came to realize that a constitutional monarchy was the only hope for a return to some semblance of liberty. It was a great irony indeed when these republicans looked to the Bourbon pretender to deliver them from Franco. On the subject of pretenders, after the war Francis Xavier pressed his claims; later the Carlist torch was passed to his son Hugo Carlos. (This odd bird made nonsense of the entire movement by becoming a socialist in the 1960s.)

JUST A FEW MONTHS after the surrender of Madrid, the Second World War broke out with the joint German-Soviet invasion of Poland, a cynical act of collusion that shocked Franco. Although indebted to the Axis powers, he decided to steer an evasive course that would keep Spain out of the war. Especially after Hitler's pact with Stalin, Franco had reason to suspect the Germans, who couldn't care less about Spain except for its vital importance as gateway to the Mediterranean.

After the fall of France, Spain became distinctly less neutral, and talk surfaced about inheriting French North Africa as part of the "New Order." In October Hitler and Franco had their famous meeting at Hendaye in France. After keeping the *führer* waiting an hour, the little Spaniard proceeded to drive Hitler to distraction with a masterly display of his strongest quality — the ability to promise everything but give nothing. Franco willingly agreed to become an ally, but would not commit to any timetable for Spain's entry into the war. Every request by the German was met with a counter-request in Spain's interest — material aid, sovereignty over Morocco, anything to stall a firm commitment. Finally Hitler gave up, later remarking "I would rather have three or four teeth pulled than meet that man again."

Through January of the next year, German diplomats continued to press for safe passage of troops through Spain for an attack on Gibraltar, in a campaign to be called Operation Felix. But Franco would not budge, and even stated that any attempt to cross the Spanish border would be resisted. At last Hitler wearied of the debate and turned his attentions to the invasion of Russia. The German failure to gain passage proved to be a major turning point. In October 1941, a great Anglo-American invasion force massed at Gibraltar for the crucial invasion of North Africa, the beginning of the end for the Axis. No less than Churchill praised Franco's role — however selfish — in turning the tide. (Franco also gained points by allowing many Jewish refugees — some of them Sephardics speaking antiquated Castilian — to seek haven in Spain.)

Still, Franco regained much of his pro-Fascist ardour with Hitler's invasion of Russia. Nearly 20,000 Spanish "volunteers," the famed Blue Division led by General Muñoz Grandes, set off for the eastern front to help fight communism. They saw some of the war's bitterest fighting, including the battle of Stalingrad, and suffered heavy losses. And in a 1942 speech Franco offered a million Spanish volunteers to defend Berlin.

By 1943 the war's outcome was uncertain, and Franco began to backtrack, recalling the Blue Division and affirming Spain's neutrality. Spanish pyrites and tungsten for munitions were sold to the highest bidder at unheard-of prices. After the Normandy invasion, the American ambassador noticed that the photos of Hitler and Mussolini in Franco's office — previously flanking another of the pope — had suddenly vanished. The defeat of Germany marked the end of Spain's so-called fascist period. Even the infamous raised-arm salute was banned. Franco was beginning to work on his image abroad.

With the defeat of the Axis, much of Europe — and all exiled Spaniards — expected Allied armies to cross the Pyrenees and oust the "last fascist dictator." But this was not to be, largely due to growing concern about the intentions of the Soviet Union. Nevertheless, in 1945 the new United Nations voted to formally exclude Spain from the same community of nations that included the likes of Stalinist Russia. The next year France closed its border, and most governments withdrew their recognition of Franco's regime. With consummate skill, Franco used this diplomatic isolation to rally Spanish patriotism and to consolidate his own power.

"Francoism" came to be, in the words of its wily architect, "a novel solution." After so many rigid ideologues, Franco was the supreme pragmatist, who sought to achieve a perpetual balance of power among the loyal but sometimes rival "clans" that formed his power base: church, army, Falange, monarchists, bankers, etc. To all he gave something, to each never enough. And no one was really sure how he would act or react. Most of the political history of his 36-year reign involved the ebb and flow of each "family member."

Franco's attitudes about government were simple: politicians were corrupt and should be eliminated; the press was biased and should be controlled. In politics as in war, procrastination was his main policy; he always preferred to delay action rather than act unsuccessfully. His alleged filing system: one folder for "problems solved with time" and another for "problems which time has solved."

The secret of Franco's power lay in his right to name and dismiss ministers at will. (Over almost four decades there were 19 major shakeups and 120 different ministers sitting on the council.) These officials ran the government under a fairly loose rein, but were replaced whenever squabbling grew too vocal or their power too great. Quite unlike a ranting Hitler or Mussolini, Franco would preside over council meetings with a detached serenity, rarely making a comment. Said one monarchist: "A lot of the time he didn't have anything to say. He was a sphinx without a secret."

The Spanish *cortes* was a rubber-stamp parliament of appointees. Of the thousands of laws passed during the Franco era, only two actually originated in parliament. The courts were likewise mouthpieces for official policy: all power resided in the executive branch and ultimately with Franco himself. One critic shrewdly observed that he was really "the supreme Spanish anarchist," answering to no law but his own.

In 1945, as part of his window-dressing campaign to improve Spain's image abroad, Franco gave the nation its Charter of Rights. But the new clothes were threadbare, denying such basic liberties as freedom of expression and political association. Many of the rights granted were routinely trampled on, and with the courts part of the monolith, the average citizen had no place to protest government or police abuse. The press was totally controlled, and the string of state-sponsored provincial dailies of abysmal quality. Reading them became an art in itself; if headlines pronounced "No Strike in Catalonia," it meant something big was happening.

Franco's social philosophy was likewise simple: "For the good of Spain, I should like there to be rather fewer rich people and rather fewer poor," he once remarked. Labour laws used a clever blend of carrot and stick to bring the traditionally unruly working class to heel. Reflecting falangist influence, both capitalism and socialism were rejected in favour of a "corporative state" of government paternalism. Workers gained a plethora of benefits like social security, numerous paid holidays and bonuses, and job security so sacred that only the most heinous offence warranted dismissal. On the other hand, strikes were considered acts of sedition punishable by long prison terms. The policies of long-time Labour Minister Jose Antonio Giron (1941-56) were very popular with workers and won much good will for Franco from the common man.

WHEN PEACE CAME to Spain the economy was in a shambles: fields lying fallow, factories smashed, cities bombed. Rebuilding would not be easy, especially when Franco maintained that things would "right themselves" in time. New labour laws defined Spain's economy as "totalitarian", designed — with its principles of self-sufficiency (the end of "exotic products"), government regulation and vertical syndicates — to complement the political system. This authoritarian version of economics was called "autarchy", which translated as inefficiency and corruption, a clumsy bureaucratic machine and thriving black markets to deal with people's real needs.

Spain's economy had numerous fundamental weaknesses. It was still based on a system of agriculture mired in backward techniques and the unresolved land problem (in Málaga province 1.8% of the landowners still controlled 55% of the land). Transportation was also backward; for example, until 1947 there was no railroad between Madrid and Valencia, Spain's third largest city. Goods to and from the provinces were forced to take the most roundabout routes, always via the capital. Additionally, worker productivity was low. In the 1950s, for example, is was estimated that a Spanish steel worker produced a third of what a French colleague produced.

In Franco's Spain, Madrid bureaucrats were free at last to carry out the centralization begun by Felipe V. Direct state investments into the economy were funneled through an unwieldy agency called the INI, whose name became a byword for ineptitude. Grandiose schemes were launched with little or no planning, then became bogged down in a sea of regulations, many self-imposed. The average businessman fought a losing battle against paperwork from Madrid.

The first decade after the war were the "years of hunger" for most of Spain, and economic life was primitive and often picturesque. Private cars practically disappeared due to a petrol shortage and strange contraptions burning charcoal or almond shells were seen rumbling through the potholed streets. Mechanical wizards kept the most dubious wrecks rolling. It was an utter contrast with a consumer society: toothbrushes were reconditioned rather than replaced and fountain pens sold on the installment plan. Electricity and water could be cut at any moment. Telephone service was sporadic at best.

State control left enormous loopholes for corruption, and favouritism and influence-peddling became part of the system. The only way to get things done — finding an apartment, getting a telephone, making a business deal — was through a friend or an *enchufe* (a contact, literally a "plug"). The idea of conflict-of-interest between government and business did not exist. Anyone who did not line their pockets given a chance was considered deranged.

Juan March was probably the ultimate product of the system; his smuggled cigarettes almost broke the government monopoly, and it was said he had 40,000 Spaniards on his payroll — from customs officials to ministers. When he died in 1962 (his Cadillac collided with another car) he was reputedly the world's seventh richest man.

Franco was personally honest, but turned a blind eye to those around him. His brother Nicolás, for example, got involved in many shady deals involving the Coca family. Economics was not Franco's strong suit, and there are indications that he never grasped how bad things really were in those first years. Like the Bourbon kings, he went shooting several times a week and, especially in the later years, spent little time on the nation's business.

PART OF FRANCOISM was a self-orchestrated personality cult that eventually reached the absurd with such titles as "minister of God" and "sword of the most high." Every Spanish town had its *plaza* or *avenida* named in his honour; his photo was in every office. Franco lived at El Pardo Palace outside Madrid, but played king in grandiose style at lavish receptions given at the *palacio real*. Imperial  touches included a personal bodyguard of turbaned Moroccans.

Franco was king in all but name and he might have considered taking that final title if he had sired a son (he and Carmen Polo had one daughter). One man who urged him to do so was his fanatically loyal aide, Admiral Luis Carrero Blanco. For thirty years he was the dictator's right arm, his alter-ego, and he came close to succeeding his mentor. Carrero was an interesting breed of arch-conservative; he detested the Falange, yet regularly made harangues about the usual liberal vices. Among them he counted Judaism, "the origin of all other evils from the Enlightenment to Marxism."

Over the years Franco's search for legitimacy and popular approval developed into a complex structure of institutions he hoped would outlive him. The Law of Succession (1947) defined Spain as a monarchy; Franco was regent with the right to name the successor to the throne. The new king had to meet specific criteria: he should be male, Spanish-born, Catholic, over 30, and must swear loyalty to the Movement's principles. A national plebiscite of questionable validity confirmed the law.

Don Juan, the legitimate heir, protested Franco's manipulations from his Portuguese exile. He correctly suspected that Franco the temporary guardian would become Franco the permanent dictator. The two rivals finally met in 1948 aboard a yacht off San Sebastian and disliked each other instantly. They agreed only that Juan's son, Juan Carlos, would be educated in Spain.

Under the stifling cloud of Francoism cultural achievements were meagre. One best-seller on the civil war theme was *The Cypresses Believe in God* by Jose Maria Gironella. Of more literary merit, perhaps, were works by Camilo Jose Cela, *The Family of Pascual Duarte* and *The Hive*, the latter about the miserable life in post-war Madrid. (Cela won the Nobel prize in 1989.) Another Nobel winner (1977) was Vicente Aleixandre, a surrealistic poet whose work spans the entire era.

Art made a tentative comeback in the late forties with Antoni Tapies, called "the black knight of modern painting." Miró continued to paint and to champion Catalan culture, "like a carob tree, deep-rooted and evergreen." Dali remained in Franco's Spain, opening a museum in his native Figueres that has been called a "temple of kitsch." Public architecture reverted to the "Escorial style" seen in massive buildings like the air ministry in Madrid and the ultimate travesty — the Valley of the Fallen. The year of its completion, Joaquin Rodrigo penned his brilliant musical masterpiece, the "Concierto de Aranjuez."

With Buñuel in exile and censorship severe, the promising Spanish cinema took a sharp nosedive. All film scripts had to be submitted for approval, and the dubbing of foreign films was compulsory. Audiences tried to fathom the mind-boggling plots created by the censor's scissors for, at the risk of implying incest, mistresses were converted into sisters, lovers into uncles.

One amusing Spanish film in 1952 was *Bienvenido, Mr. Marshall*, a comedy by Berlanga about the new connection between the wealthy, powerful United States and impoverished but proud Spain. With the start of the Cold War in the late forties, Franco could play his anti-communist card with the Americans, who did not fail to see Spain's strategic location. The ice was broken in 1950 with an American ambassador to Madrid and a modest loan. President Truman disliked Franco — especially after discovering that in Spain Protestants had to be buried at night — but his successor was a general and had fewer misgivings. In 1953, Eisenhower and Franco signed an agreement permitting four American bases on Spanish soil in return for substantial aid ($1.8 billion by 1965). "It was like water to the desert," said one minister.

The treaty helped launch Spain's economic recovery — hence indirectly its later political reform — but at the time its most important result was to legitimize the Franco regime. Upon signing the accord he remarked, "At last I have won the Spanish war." In 1955, Spain was admitted to the United Nations.

Franco also played his Catholic card by concluding a concordat with the Vatican (1954). Priests were put on the state payroll and in return Franco won the right to approve bishops. The Vatican even bestowed its highest honour on Franco: Knight of the Order of Christ. He became ever more pious, making a point of attending Mass and religious ceremonies. Spain's only other diplomatic successes were in fostering cultural and economic ties with Latin America, and in its friendship with several Arab nations. In the middle of his Arab overtures, Franco seemed caught off guard when France announced its withdrawal from Morocco (1956), but he too had to face the inevitable and Spain soon followed suit. Spain retained the ports of Ceuta and Melilla, and (until 1975) the phosphate-rich Spanish Sahara, but it marked the end of Franco's neo-colonial delusions.

In 1964, colourful posters began appearing all over Spain announcing the completion of 25 years of peace. The Francoist press claimed it was the longest period without domestic or foreign war since the Pax Romana, and many believed the time for reconciliation had come. By 1964, 43% of the population had been born since the war, and Franco was the only leader they had known. Unfortunately, the propaganda machine continued to dwell on the fear and hatred of the civil war and a film about the new Cid, called *This Man Franco*, played in theatres around Spain.

The old man had settled into a comfortable life of fishing and shooting. He also took up painting, favouring seascapes and dead game-animals, and even did a self-portrait in an admiral's uniform, the one denied him by his exclusion from the naval academy. He still dabbled in politics, especially if it involved sacking a minister who had grown too independent. His style spoke volumes: in 1966, Muñoz Grandes of the Blue Division, considered a possible successor, discovered he had been relieved as vice-president of the government when he read about it in the official gazette.

Franco registered in the Society of Spanish Authors under the pen-name Jaime de Andrade for his history of the Legion and a 1940 screenplay called *Raza* (Race). Using the pseudonym Jakim Boor, he also penned an astonishing treatise on Freemasonry called simply *Masoneria*. In it he claimed that all modern history resulted from a huge conspiracy to rule the world, and that all Spain's modern ills sprang from masonic intrigue. Order was the undeniable achievement of

Franco, but the price was high. By the 1960s Spain was still an authoritarian state with a rubber-stamp parliament, shackled press, and jails filled with political prisoners. Passing out pamphlets or "spreading false news" were considered acts of "military rebellion," and student pranksters could be tried by army courts.

Large garrisons were located just outside the major cities, and the civil guard had its fortress-like *cuarteles* in every small town, from which they patrolled the countryside in pairs. In the larger towns and cities a new force called the *policia armada* (nicknamed "the greys" for their uniforms) struck fear in potential criminals and dissidents alike. There was also a plain-clothes secret police based in the *gobernación* building on Madrid's Puerta del Sol.

A strong hand was often not necessary, however. Crime rates were low, and most of the populace had slipped into political apathy, a life of "bread and circuses." With rare exceptions — like Manolete (killed in the ring in 1947) and El Cordobés (a sixties mop-top) — soccer replaced bullfighting as the national passion. Franco himself was an avid fan. And the nation went berserk with its victories over England (1950) and the Soviet Union (1964).

Feeling a new prosperity along with the 25 years of peace, Spaniards of all classes began to appreciate the accomplishments of Francoism.Given a kick-start with foreign loans and freed from many government constraints, the economy was definitely improving. Facing ongoing disasters through the fifties, economic ministers from a new school had convinced Franco of the need for fundamental changes. His reluctant approval led to the Stabilization Plan (1959), the death knell of twenty years of state autarchy and its pitiful results. Price controls, import quotas, limits on foreign investment, and other economic dinosaurs were dropped in favour of a relatively free market.

Among the new ministerial voices were members of Opus Dei ("God's Work"), a lay-Christian group of hazy origins and purposes. Founded by an Aragonese priest in 1929, Opus Dei strives to increase Catholic influence in all realms of society, especially among the intellectual elite. Its handbook, *The Way*, reads like a Spanish version of the Protestant work ethic. And in the Sixties members' talent and effort (plus Carrero Blanco's support) propelled them into key positions in the government.

One vital element of the economic miracle was tourism. Numbers of foreign visitors rocketed from 4 million in 1960 to 14 million by 1965 and would go through the roof in the next decade. Tourism provided jobs and badly needed foreign exchange for purchasing imports like petroleum. More foreign currency poured in from Spanish workers abroad, more than half a million by 1970. With the influx of tourists, Spain seemed to go mad with building projects along its coast, and even old-shirt falangists like Giron made fortunes on the Costa del Sol and elsewhere.

Construction also boomed in the cities, where industries were suddenly humming like never before. During the decade Spain's overall growth rate was second only to Japan's, and in the 15 years after 1960, industry's share of exports rose from 21% to 78%. By 1965 Spain ranked sixth worldwide in shipbuilding, *ahead* of the United States. When the first SEAT factory was built in 1952, managers worried that the market could not absorb a hundred cars a month; by the 1970s SEAT employed 20,000 workers and Spanish automakers churned out 750,000 cars a year.

Manning these new factories involved a population shift from country to city. In 1960, agriculture still employed 42% of the labour force. This had shrunk to 25% a decade later. By 1970, 1.6 million Andalusians had left their region, and about half of those were living in Barcelona. Emigration from Extremadura and the bleak Castilian plain also reached tidal wave proportions. Except for the elderly who stayed behind, village after hopeless village was abandoned for the baubles of Bilbao or Barcelona. Said one admirer, "Francoism transformed a sandal-wearing Spain into one of the dozen most prosperous nations in the world."

In less than two decades Spain changed from a primarily rural, agricultural, industrially backward country to a leading industrial power. The old ways — pack animals lumbering along cobbled streets, plowing with mules, oil lamps and charcoal fires — were retreating to the remote *pueblos* for a last stand before finally succumbing to the onslaught of motorbikes and pinball machines. Sadly, for some at least, this century may be the last to witness the famed charm of Spain.

FRANCO'S SPEECHES during the 1960s dropped falangist rhetoric and hammered on the theme of prosperity. Naturally, he chose to ignore many problems like inflation and labour strife. Yet 1962 witnessed the most industrial unrest since the Republic, and there were also rumblings at the universities. The central drama of the Franco era was how to modernize the economy yet keep Spaniards content with the old social-political order. In the end it was not possible; changing realities made Franco-style rule obsolete. The ultimate irony for Francoism, therefore, was that the progress it spawned would come back to bring it down.

Consider the changes wrought by tourism. In the 1950s tourists were arrested for wearing bikinis or kissing in public. A Spanish cardinal stated, "Public bathing... constitutes a special danger for morality. Mixed bathing must be avoided because it almost always gives rise to sin and scandal."

By 1970 this world had completely changed as Spaniards were bombarded with foreign ideas like democracy, socialism and consumerism, not to mention comely *rubias* (blondes). In a survey of non-congenital mental illness in Málaga province, 90% of the afflicted were teenaged males who had gone to work on the coast and couldn't assimilate the new ways. One Málaga hospital even dubbed a section "the waiters' ward." And by 1975, more than 40 million tourists were coming to Spain every year, visitors outnumbering the Spanish population (which had grown from 30.1 million in 1960 to 35.6 million in 1975). Spain was also becoming a consumer society, less-interested in religion and political rhetoric than in "the good life." Television sets jumped from 50,000 in 1960 to 1.75 million by 1965, and there were over a million private cars by the same year.

Spain's economic miracle and its social effects were felt most strongly in the old regional bastions of Catalonia and the Basque lands. Here, the natives continued to regard themselves as more productive and culturally advanced, more "modern," than fellow Spaniards, especially the droves of uncouth immigrant workers flooding Barcelona and Bilbao. (By 1970, only 25% of the residents of the Basque provinces could speak the local language.)

Not surprisingly, regionalism began to raise its head again. The evolution of Basque nationalism defied all logic — from its ultra-conservative Carlist roots to reluctant support of the Republic, from crude racialism to an odd breed of revolutionary marxism. The now-infamous group called ETA was founded in 1959 by a few pseudo-intellectuals tired of the old Basque party; by 1967 extremists dedicated to violence had taken control. Of nine "states of emergency" called by the government from 1962 to 1975, six were in the Basque country. And when the police over-reacted, moderate Basques started to sympathize with ETA.

Faced with a host of new realities, the political world started to divide in the 1960s between those who wanted to "open up" Spain to modern influences and those who steadfastly resisted. The former included a new civil service based on a college-educated middle class, best represented by Manuel Fraga Iribarne, who became Minister of Information and Tourism in 1962. Opus Dei members favoured economic opening, but shied away from politics. The forces of reaction were called "the immobile ones" and later "The Bunker."

By the mid-1960s, the question on everyone's lips was *Después de Franco, ¿qué?* (What happens after Franco?) The aging dictator tried to head off an impending crisis by serving up the final course of political institutions, leaving things "tied up and well tied down" in his own words. The Organic Law of 1966 allowed the "contrast of opinions" but not political parties, and the election of one-fifth of parliament by "heads of families." These and other curious features comprised something called "organic democracy."

Many of the reforms were comical. According to the liberalized press law, there was no more "prior censorship," but copies of periodicals had to be in the government's hands half-an-hour before publication. If there was a problem, the issue was confiscated — often ripped from readers' hands right on the street. Thus the burden of complying with Francoist principles shifted from the censors to editors and reporters. One paper was fined for printing a critical article in which Franco was referred to as "De Gaulle." Another was closed for four months, then dynamited, after its editor criticized the regime in a *French* daily.

When the Organic Law was put to a vote in 1967, Spaniards said "yes" by a 95% majority. (A "no" vote meant leaving things as they were.) Franco had staged another triumph without granting more than a wisp of reform. The same year as the plebiscite, Carrero was named vice-president and heir-apparent. His views on reform were simple: "To offer change to a Spaniard was like offering a drink to a confirmed alcoholic."

Carrero was a strong supporter of Don Juan's son, Juan Carlos, to fill the vacant throne, and in 1969 Franco made the long-expected announcement. Little was known about the 31-year-old prince or his views, but nearly everyone was suspicious. He was born in Rome in 1938, baptized by the future pope, and brought to Spain for his education at the age of ten. This included stints at the three military academies and the University of Madrid and he was capable if not brilliant in school.

While still a student, Juan Carlos was invited by Queen Frederika to Greece, where he met Princess Sofia (sister of future-king Constantine). The attractive young couple were married in 1962 at a spectacular double-ceremony using both Roman Catholic and Orthodox rites. Their first-born son was Felipe (the future Prince of Asturias), and his baptism in Madrid was a veritable Bourbon reunion, with the exiled queen, Victoria Eugenia, making her first (and last) appearance in Spain since 1931.

Over the years it became evident that Franco had no intention of bringing back the legitimate heir, the feisty Don Juan. In 1962 he told Juan Carlos, "Your highness has a better chance of becoming king than your father." Two years later, Juan Carlos was asked to join Franco on the podium at the annual victory parade. By 1968, Juan Carlos had decided to "leapfrog" over his father to the throne, a decision which outraged many monarchists to whom the line of succession is sacred. Their displeasure grew after his investiture, at which he knelt and swore loyalty to Franco and the Movement. Thereafter Juan Carlos was usually present at all state affairs, stone-faced and, at six-foot-three, towering awkwardly over the lilliputian dictator 46 years his senior.

Supporters of Don Juan grumbled, but within the Movement only a few old falangists and Carlists opposed the choice of Juan Carlos. The Carlist pretenders Francis Xavier and Carlos Hugo had already been expelled from Spain and were not a threat; the latter became a favourite of the society pages after marrying princess Irene of the Netherlands. A more serious challenge was Alfonso, son of Don Jaime. (Jaime, Juan's elder brother, had renounced his rights in 1932, but tried to reclaim them in 1964.) Young Alfonso — actually Alfonso XIII and Eugenia's first grandchild — did not press his claims but tongues wagged furiously when, in 1972, he married one of Franco's granddaughters.

Juan Carlos was on notice not to deviate from his passive role. One time, after he was seen dining with a leading liberal, Franco remarked, "The choice is your highness's; you can either be a prince or a private individual."

FRANCOISM BEGAN to seriously unravel after 1969, with a major cabinet crisis, serious student unrest, wildcat strikes and ETA terrorism. At a *pelota* match attended by Franco, one zealous Basque doused himself with petrol, lit a match and jumped in front of the astonished crowd (he miraculously survived). There were even rumblings within two pillars of Francoism, the church and army. A group of young officers with democratic sympathies was discovered and punished.

Far more serious — and especially galling to Franco — were changes within the church during the 1960s. Basque and Catalan priests had traditionally supported more political and cultural freedom for their regions. Then, with the

223

winds of change blowing from the Vatican under liberal Pope John XXIII, the foot-dragging Spanish church began to loosen its grip. The younger clergy and even some bishops became more radical and supported worker and student groups.

One key figure in all this was Cardinal Enrique y Tarancón, archbishop of Madrid, who presided over the parting of the ways with full support from Rome. In 1971, an open letter from the Spanish bishops actually asked forgiveness of the church for taking sides in the civil war. Three years later, the Bishop of Bilbao was placed under house-arrest for writing a defence of the Basque language, and Tarancón warned Franco against interference in church matters. It was said that the pope even had a decree of excommunication for the general awaiting signature should the Basque bishop be expelled. Franco was livid; the circle had been squared.

In June 1973, Franco resigned as president of the government (retaining his other titles) and appointed Carrero, then 71 but the chief guarantor of Francoism after Franco. In December, a group of ETA commandos tunneled beneath the street where Carrero passed daily on his way to mass and deposited a cache of explosives. When it passed the spot the morning of the 20th, the president's special armour-plated Dodge was blown five stories into the air, over the top of the church, and into a courtyard on the other side. (Cynics dubbed the church Our Lady of the Ascension.) It was the first major assassination since the civil war.

The nation, and above all Franco, was severely shocked, and the hardcore right-wing began bracing for battle. At Carrero's funeral, Cardinal Tarancón was jostled and insulted by thugs, who yelled "to the firing squad!" Franco appointed a rigid conservative named Arias Navarro as president, indicating that he did not consider backing down. (Arias was called "the butcher of Málaga" for his role as state prosecutor in that city after the war.) But when Arias showed signs of "opening up," small groups of extremists like "The Warriors of Christ the King" began to make their presence felt, beating up "red" priests and slashing Picasso paintings.

The year 1975 was the most violent since the 1940s, with terrorist groups mushrooming on both extremes. ETA and new bands like FRAP continued a rampage of random violence in which many innocent people were slaughtered. Spain seemed to be lurching toward disintegration once again, and cynics began referring to the king-to-be as Juan Carlos, El Breve ("the Brief").

King Hassan of Morocco chose this, the worst of times, to launch his "Green March" of unarmed civilians against the phosphate-rich Spanish territory of Western Sahara, to press Morocco's claims of sovereignty over the region. (Spain tactfully withdrew, and Morocco inherited a colonial war against Western Sahara's independence movement.)

The nation's seeming decay was matched by that of Franco himself, suffering from half-a-dozen ailments in addition to old age. In September 1975, the trial and execution of several terrorists created an inexplicable international scene, with the temporary withdrawal of ambassadors and other measures. Soon after,

Franco had his last hurrah at a huge rally in Madrid's Plaza de Oriente. The old dictator, his hands shaking and his voice shrill, rallied the sea of supporters by blaming the uproar on a conspiracy of freemasons, communists, and other enemies of order. It was his final speech.

For the next five weeks all Spain — and half the world — watched Franco's inevitable decline. In a desperate effort to keep him alive, doctors (led by Franco's son-in-law) connected him to every life-support device imaginable, and he was heard to mutter "Why is it so difficult to die?" Like a true soldier, he bore the pain and endless operations with the famed Spanish stoicism, the mantle of the Virgin of Pilar and St. Teresa's hand by his bedside. Finally, the pattern of brain waves recorded on a bedside graph flickered and stopped. The age of Franco was history.

## SIGHTS & SITES

**Benidorm** (Alicante): *Classic example of the tourist boom that transformed Spain in the 1960s.*
**Cuenca**: *Museum of Abstract Art in one of famous hanging-houses includes work by Chillida, Tapies and Saura.*
**El Pardo** (Madrid): *Franco lived for 35 years at this palace, open to visitors; King Juan Carlos and his family reside five kilometres away at Zarzuela Palace.*
**Figueres** (Gerona): *Salvador Dali Museum in the town of artist's birth in 1904.*
**Madrid**: *The Reina Sofia Art Centre has more than 50 Dali paintings and much more; Spanish Museum of Contemporary Art has works by Fortuny, Rosales, Miró, and others; the Plaza de Oriente witnessed countless mass-rallies for the caudillo.*
**Torremolinos** (Málaga): *The good, bad and ugly of mass tourism in Spain.*
**Valle de los Caidos** (Madrid): *The Valley of the Fallen lies a few kilometres from the Escorial; gigantic cross and a basilica containing remains of Franco and Jose Antonio.*

# EPILOGUE

Thursday, November 20, 1975: the day began like any other for most Spaniards, until they turned on their radios to hear sombre requiem music on all channels broadcasting from Spain. Newspapers soon hit the streets with a headline long-since set in type: *Franco Ha Muerto*. After several false alarms in the past month, details were finalized for Franco's funeral, and for the investiture of Juan Carlos de Borbon y Borbon as king of Spain.

The *caudillo*'s body, dressed in a captain-general's uniform with a red sash, was first taken from La Paz Hospital in Madrid to El Pardo for a private service, attended by family members, ministers and a few old cronies. One of them was Jose Antonio Giron, who defiantly dressed in a falangist blue shirt rather than mourning clothes. Mass was celebrated by Franco's arch-enemy, the liberal Cardinal Enrique y Tarancón, who gave a restrained eulogy.

Before the public funeral and burial, Franco's body lay in state at the Palacio de Oriente and for two days hundreds of thousands of Spaniards passed before the open coffin. Many wept, prayed, or spoke aloud, like one crippled veteran who knelt and cried out, "*Adios*, my general... at your orders always!" Some mourners grew hysterical and had to be dragged away; others gave the fascist salute or silently clutched five red roses, a falangist symbol.

Held at the Plaza de Oriente, the state funeral service was attended by a handful of foreign dignitaries and half of Madrid. Afterwards, Franco's coffin was escorted by the red-bereted *guardia del generalisimo* to the Arch of Vic-

227

tory near the university. From there his body was transferred from a horse-drawn carriage to a hearse for the 46-kilometre drive north to the Valley of the Fallen. Later, as the body was lowered into the grave, artillery outside thundered a final 21-gun salute. But through these days of pomp and ceremony, the question on everyone's mind remained: after Franco, what?

When two days after Franco's death Cardinal Enrique y Tarancon called on Juan Carlos to become "king of all Spaniards," his meaning was clear. At the ceremony of investiture, the 37-year-old prince, dressed in the uniform of a Spanish general, stood up before parliament. On a nearby table were a golden crown and a jewel-encrusted sceptre, symbols of the monarchy absent from Spain for 44 years. Placing his hand on the bible, Juan Carlos swore an oath to uphold the laws of the state and the Movement.

At long last Spain had its king.

Everything seemed to hinge on Juan Carlos; would he be "king of all Spaniards" or merely a puppet for the old guard? He was still a political enigma. His statements had been vague and few people seemed to like or trust him. But at least the new monarchy was untainted by the civil war, giving Spain hope that at long last it could turn the page on that sad event. In the end Juan Carlos *did* play all the right cards; the "novel solution" did not outlive its inventor. There was no Francoism after Franco.

The achievements of Spain's young leaders — and the entire nation — during the decade after Franco were nothing short of remarkable, especially in the context of Spain's modern history. In the king's first decisive action, he replaced the vacillating Arias as president with a virtual unknown named Adolfo Suarez, a move that surprised and dismayed many. Both Juan Carlos, as Franco's wooden mannequin, and Suarez, a straight-laced official of the Movement, had poor credentials for leading a nation to reform. But the two statesmen managed to dismantle most of Francoism in several rapid, orderly stages. For his decisive role Juan Carlos — once "The Brief" — was dubbed "the motor of change."

In 1977, the Movement was abolished, and Spain had its first general elections in 41 years. The new parliament's task was to draft a constitution suitable for a monarchy, essentially a return to the system destroyed by Primo de Rivera's coup in 1923.

The same year saw the legalization of trade unions and the communist party, and the return of Dolores Ibarruri, "La Pasionaria" (after 38 years in Russia) and Josep Tarradellas, former president of Catalonia's *Generalitat*. The pace of change was breathtaking and army sabre-rattling noticeable only by its absence. The main reason everything went so smoothly was a genuine spirit of consensus and cooperation across the political spectrum. Republicans accepted the monarchy (and its flag), socialists abandoned marxism, communists disowned Moscow, strikes were infrequent, and through it all the steady hands of the king, Suarez and a newcomer named Felipe Gonzalez carefully guided the rhythm of reform. (In 1974 Gonzalez had been elected the PSOE's secretary general at the outlawed socialist party's conference near Paris; his codename in Franco's time was "Isidoro.")

The Constitution of 1978 established the basic political structures of the new Spain. The Catholic Church lost its dominant role as state religion, but otherwise the document did not attack the main forms of economic, social and military power. In other words, it was not a caulked-up version of the foundered constitution of 1931. Moreover, unlike the Republic's "manifesto," it had the passionate support of the large majority of Spaniards.

So much had changed since the 1930s that Spain was almost a different country. The old *moderado* order of large landowners, army and church had been based on a society of ignorant peasants who voted per *cacique* instructions. By 1975, most Spaniards lived in cities and had different expectations; if they never got their plot of land, at least they had an apartment with a bathroom and television set. The "two Spains" of city and country, which had produced so many clashes throughout history, had evolved almost beyond recognition.

If the landed class could no longer rely on the country folk, they had also lost much economic clout to a new élite — industrialists and bankers, financiers and businessmen. Moreover, there was a vastly larger middle class concerned with order and prosperity. The old-fashioned "Liberal revolution" had finally happened in Spain.

Other historic areas of tension had also subsided; the clergy no longer battled liberals, and working-class parties were not hotbeds of anarchism and revolutionary ferment. The socialists were an unthreatening Spanish version of the social-democratic parties found throughout Europe.

One historic trouble spot that had not vanished was regionalism, and the new government proposed autonomy statutes strikingly similar to those of the Second Republic. Everyone knew they must tread lightly, however, because any hint of outright separatism would be the one sure way to ruffle military feathers. The generals were already fidgeting; despite all the progress since 1975, the Basque provinces remained in turmoil from hundreds of ETA murders and strong police reaction. (During 1968-75 ETA killed 43; in 1976-83, 380 died.)

By 1980, the euphoria began to sour as people realized that "democracy" would not solve all Spain's problems overnight. Although Sancho Panza's two families — the haves and have-nots — might grow closer, they would always exist. And it was clear that the country's real bastions of power and wealth were not about to surrender their privileges.

Democracy also seemed to bring a plateful of social problems — crime, drugs, pornography — that did not exist or were swept under the rug before. Suddenly you could see and do things in Spain — from watching oral sex on stage to having lunch while topless at a beach-bar — that were forbidden in far-older, and relatively permissive "democracies." Spain was still managing to be "different."

Social change brought a profound improvement in the status of Spanish women. Divorce, contraception and limited abortion became legal, and women began working at jobs that would have been unthinkable 20 years earlier — even as civil guards and wardens of male prisons. Slowly, the infamous Spanish *machismo* seemed to be retreating in the face of women's rights. But there was a long way to go. Even in Spain, centuries of tradition are not erased overnight.

EARLY IN 1981, as consensus slowly eroded, there was a political impasse ending with the resignation of Suarez. Then, during the transition to a new government, the question "After Franco, what?" received a perverse response. On February 23, a band of gun-wielding civil guards, led by the mustachioed Colonel Tejero, invaded parliament and held the deputies hostage overnight at gunpoint. A handful of army brass, including a former Blue Division commander named Jaime Milans del Bosch, supported the attempted *golpe*. It was the boldest putsch since General Pavia rode his horse up the steps of the *cortes* building a century earlier. The army — albeit a tiny part of it — and "The Bunker" had finally spoken.

The plot failed, without bloodshed, after Juan Carlos rallied loyal generals and gave a stirring televised speech to the nation. But the message was clear: Do not let democracy become anarchy. Go ahead and change street names from "General Mola" to "Libertad", but don't rattle the powers-that-be.

Consensus returned, and the process of democratization was completed with the peaceful and resounding victory of Gonzalez's socialist party in 1982. Regional autonomy proceeded at a careful pace, and Tarradellas, who had signed the 1932 Catalan Statute, lived to put his name to the new one exactly fifty years later. Even with widespread autonomy, the army remained mute. (The PSOE was seen as a *national* party in opposition to regional ones.) And military men were pacified with a hefty budget and by Spain's 1982 entry into NATO, which increased the army's prestige and provided truckloads of new war-toys.

Foreign investment during the Franco era built Spain's economic miracle, which laid the foundations of post-Franco society. Along the same lines, Gonzalez (who would become the longest-ruling prime minister in Spanish history) believed that Spain's future success lay in its role as an integral part of a democratic, prosperous Europe. Sounding like one-half of the Generation of '98, he pointed to Spain's historic isolationism as the source of its political and economic catastrophes. Hence his fight for NATO membership against very heavy odds and his unflagging support for Spain's belated entry into the Common Market (EEC) in 1986.

It was a long road to Brussels, beginning with the community's refusal to consider Franco's Spain in 1962. But just a few years later, a trade agreement with the EEC (1970) was crucial to Spain's continued economic recovery. With Franco gone and Spain politically in step with Western Europe, economic integration was virtually assured.

Spain hoped that membership in NATO and the EEC might even provide a solution for the nagging (and historic) problem of Gibraltar, one issue on which 99% of Spaniards agree. Unfortunately, the same percentage of Gibraltarians wish to remain British. In 1969 Franco pulled a grandstand play by sealing the border between the Rock and Spain, and the green iron gates remained tightly locked for 16 years. But it made little sense to have a closed frontier between two otherwise friendly nations — and NATO allies — and the border was completely reopened in 1985.

WITH BREATHLESS OPTIMISM, Gonzalez liked to say that EEC membership, the final stamp of modernity, would produce such a leap forward that Spain will be unrecognizable by the year 2000. One must wonder, though, if Spain will ever be truly satisfied with being one small piece in the EEC's master plan, or content with things like "restructuring" and "improving productivity." For better or worse, Spaniards generally have never been as competitive in business or attached to money *for its own sake* the way, say, a Dutchman or Dane is. The Spanish have more than a little of Don Quixote in their collective psyche and love fighting for myths and ideals, whether Christianity, the Empire, a Workers' Paradise, or a National Crusade. But to live and die for pure materialism? Never! As Spain moves toward the 21st century, it is a nation searching for a new ideal in which to believe.

Spain has given much to European civilization and will continue to do so. But its contribution will not come from imitating other nations or by losing its own identity in the mad dash to "Europeanize."

Unamuno saw Spain as a bridge between two continents. But which two? Certainly not Africa any longer. Franco talked a lot about the virtues of *hispanidad* — increasing Spain's economic ties with Latin America by exploiting a common language, religion and culture. But the Francoist connection and a lingering belief in Spain's "Black Legend" by many Latin Americans have tarnished the ideal of *hispanidad*.

The year 1992 and its commemoration of the 500th anniversary of Columbus's voyage of discovery seemed the ideal occasion for Spain to become the natural bridge between Europe and Latin America. Spain's legacy in America has been a mixed blessing. What better opportunity for Spain to return to those lands and peoples it once knew so intimately, and to give them some of the things it may have botched or overlooked the first time? Now that Spain seems to have emerged from its long night, it has much to give to its former colonies.

ONE MIGHT FAIRLY ask if Spain really has changed as much as the optimists contend. What would happen if the monarchy produced another Carlos II or Fernando VII? Or if a political or economic crisis created another "saviour" clad in khaki brown? Recalling Santayana's words that "Those who cannot remember the past are condemned to repeat it," only time will tell if Spaniards have truly learned the lessons of their turbulent history. And if the Story of Spain will have a happy ending.

As one among them wrote: "Let Spaniards remember that each nation is a prey to its particular furies, and that they are different in each case. Spain's furies are the anarchical spirit, negative criticism, lack of solidarity between men, mutual enmity. Any political system which nurtures in its bosom the fostering of these defects, the setting loose of these familiar Spanish furies, will sooner or later wreak havoc on all material progress and all improvements in our citizens' lives."

The subject: Democracy. The author: Francisco Franco Bahamonde.

# Suggested Reading

GENERAL:

*The History of Spain*, by Louis Bertrand and Charles Petrie. Dawsons of Pall Mall, London (revised edition 1969)

*Spain: The Root and the Flower,* by J.A. Crow. University of California Press, Berkeley (3rd edition 1985)

*The Spaniards In Their History,* by R. Menendez-Pidal. W W Norton & Co, New York (1966)

*Tree of Hate*, by Philip Powell. Basic Books, New York (1971)


ANCIENT AND MEDIEVAL:

*Spain at the Dawn of History*, by Richard Harrison. Thames and Hudson Ltd. London (1988)

*The Making of Medieval Spain*, by Gabriel Jackson. Harcourt, Brace, Jovanovich Inc, New York (1972)

*A History of Islamic Spain,* by W. Watt and P. Cachia. Edinburgh at the University Press, Edinburgh (1965)


EARLY MODERN:

*The Golden Century of Spain, 1501-1621,* by R. Trevor-Davies. Harper & Row, New York (1965)

*Imperial Spain, 1469-1716,* by J.H. Elliot. St Martin's Press, New York (1964)

## MODERN:

*Spain,* by Richard Herr. Prentice Hall, Englewood Cliffs (1971)

*The Spanish Bourbons,* by John Bergamini. C P Putnam's Sons, New York (1974)

*Spain, 1808-1939,* by Raymond Carr. Oxford at the Clarendon Press (1966)

*The Spanish Labyrinth,* by Gerald Brenan. Cambridge University Press (1967)

*Spain, A Modern History,* by Salvador de Madariaga. Frederick A Praeger, New York (1958)

*Homage To Catalonia,* by George Orwell. Harcourt, Brace, Jovanovich Inc, New York (1969)

*The Spanish Republic and the Civil War,* by Gabriel Jackson. Princeton University Press, New Jersey (1967).

*The Spanish Civil War,* by Hugh Thomas. Harper & Row, New York (revised edition, 1977)

*Franco, A Biography,* by J.P. Fusi. Harper & Row, New York (1987)


## CONTEMPORARY:

*The Transformation of Spain,* by David Gilmour. Quartet Books, London (1985)

*Spain: Dictatorship To Democracy,* by R. Carr and J. P. Fusi. George Allen & Unwin, London (1979)

# Index

# More Great Books from Spain

## Inside Andalusia
*by David Baird. 240 pages (large format)*

A travel adventure through southern Spain. David Baird invites you to explore an Andalusia you never dreamt of, to meet its people, and discover fascinating fiestas. Illustrated with brilliant colour photographs.

## You and the Law in Spain
*by David Searl. 210 pages*

Thousands of readers have relied on the best-selling *You and the Law in Spain* to guide them through the Spanish legal jungle. Now, author David Searl brings you a new, completely revised edition with even more information on taxes, work permits, cars, banking in Spain, buying property, Spain and the European Community, and lots more. It's a book no foreigner in Spain can afford to be without.

## Spanish Property Owners' Community Handbook
*By David Searl. 100 pages*

Do you know your rights and obligations as a member of your community of property owners? Here, at last, are the answers, including full text in Spanish and English of the *Ley de la propiedad horizontal,* with comments by legal writer David Searl.

# Birds of Iberia

*by Clive Finlayson and David Tomlinson.  224 pages*
*(Hardback, large format)*

A journey throught the different regions of this fascinating peninsula which describes the main habitats and birds found there, migrations patterns and ornithological sites. Beatifully illustrated throughout with fine line drawings and more than 150 colour photographs, the book is an appreciation of the extraordinarily rich and varied birdlife of Iberia.

# Cooking in Spain

*by Janet Mendel. 400 pages*

The definitive guide to cooking in Spain, with more than 400 great Spanish recipes. Plus complete information on Spain's regional specialities and culinary history, how to buy the best at the market, a complete English-Spanish glossary with more than 500 culinary terms, handy conversion guide... all of it illustrated with colour photographs.

# Gardening in Spain

*by Marcelle Pitt. 176 pages*

Your most valuable tool for successful gardening in Spain, from the author of Lookout magazine's popular gardening column. How to plan your garden, what to plant, when and how to plant it, how to make the most of flowers, trees, shrubs, herbs. Illustrated with full-colour photographs.

# A Selection of Wildflowers
# of Southern Spain

*by Betty Molesworth Allen. 260 pages*

Southern Spain is host to a rich variety of wildflowers in widely diverse habitats, some species growing nowhere else. This book describes more than 200 common plants of the region, each illustrated in full colour with simple text for easy identification and enjoyment.

# Expand Your Spanish

*by Linda Hall de Gonzalez. 240 pages. Illustrated.*

Tackle the dreaded Spanish subjunctive and chuckle at the same time? You can with this book. The author keeps you smiling as she leads you through the minefield of Spanish grammar. Not a language book in the conventional sense, but it will help you over the obstacles that put many people off learning the language.

*On Sale in bookstores in Spain, or by post from Ediciones Santana, S.L. Apartado 422, 29640 Fuengirola (Málaga), Spain*